A 11299.   13th-century jug from London.
(Scale slightly over ¼.)   (See p. 213.)

LONDON MUSEUM

MEDIEVAL CATALOGUE

LONDON: HER MAJESTY'S STATIONERY OFFICE

1940

ISBN 0 11 290181 6*

PREFATORY NOTE

This catalogue is mainly the work of Mr. J. B. Ward Perkins, F.S.A., sometime Assistant in the London Museum, and later Professor of Archæology in the Royal University of Malta. It has involved not a little new research into the history or archæology of familiar but neglected antiquities of the Middle Ages, and may, it is hoped, serve as a summary text-book on the subjects with which it deals. Several sections of it were already in the printer's hands at the time of the outbreak of war in 1939, but other sections were still unfinished, and, as an officer of the Royal Artillery, its author was no longer at liberty to complete them. In particular, the finger-rings and the coins must await a post-war supplement, and the section on ironwork is inadequately illustrated. Nevertheless, in the uncertainty of the times it is thought advisable to publish the book as it stands, with such inter-mittent attention as its principal author is able to give it.

Comparative material for illustration has been selected as far as possible from London finds, and for this purpose the Guildhall Museum and the British Museum have responded with their usual generosity. Individual objects are illustrated also from the museums at Winchester, Avebury, Leicester, Hertford, Aylesbury, and Taunton, from the Ashmolean Museum at Oxford, the Pitt-Rivers Museum at Farnham, and from the collections of the Society of Antiquaries of London and of H.M. Office of Works ; also from the Swedish National Museum, Stockholm, and from the Musée de Cluny, Paris.

The sections on leatherwork and on later medieval spoons are the work of Miss Janet Russell, those on pottery and on schist hones of Mr. G. C. Dunning, that on seals of Mr. H. S. Kingsford. Mr. T. D. Kendrick and Mr. A. B. Tonnochy have given invaluable help at every stage, not least by reading the text in proof, and Mr. J. G. Mann very kindly read and criticized the section on swords. Thanks are due also to Dr. R. W. Murray, Mr. Basil Gray, Mr. E. C. Hohler, Mr. M. R. Holmes, Dr. P. Nelson, Mr. Q. Waddington, and Dr. G. R. Ward, and to all others, both in this country and abroad, who have put their knowledge at our disposal. Miss B. de Cardi and Miss M. Eates have helped greatly in the final preparation of text and plates.

R. E. M. WHEELER,
Keeper and Secretary.

The London Museum,
Lancaster House,
St. James's, S.W.1.
March, 1940.

CONTENTS

III. DOMESTIC AND AGRICULTURAL OBJECTS

6

ILLUSTRATIONS

PLATES

7

8

FIGURES IN THE TEXT

9

10

BIBLIOGRAPHICAL NOTE

The most valuable general work on medieval archæology is undoubtedly S. Grieg's *Middelalderske Byfund fra Bergen og Oslo* (Oslo, 1933). The relative abundance of stratigraphically datable material from these sites affords a valuable check upon the evidence of contemporary illustration. The Scandinavian results can, however, only be applied with caution to this country, particularly in the case of minor domestic articles. There is no comparable work on British medieval archæology as a whole. The material is for the most part scattered in the learned Journals. Wherever practicable a short bibliography of relevant articles has been appended to each section. Published references to effigies are quoted only where they illustrate in sufficient detail the point at issue. By far the most important published source is still C. A. Stothard's *Monumental Effigies* (1817). A complete bibliography of monumental brasses will be found in J. Mill Stephenson's *List of Monumental Brasses in the British Isles* (1926). Of the many facsimile reproductions of manuscripts two are of exceptional importance and are here referred to throughout in abbreviated form, as follows:

The Maciejowski Bible	S. Cockerell, *A book of Old Testament Illustrations from a French Manuscript in the Pierpont Morgan Library* (Roxburghe Club, 1927).
The Luttrell Psalter	E. Miller, *The Luttrell Psalter* (British Museum, 1932).

An excellent selection from all types of contemporary illustrations can be found in the series of semi-popular volumes by D. Hartley and M. Elliot, *The Life and Work of the People of England* (London, Batsford).

PLATE I.

To face p. 13.]

View of London, from the *Chronycle of Englonde*, printed by Wynkyn de
Worde at Westminster, 1497 (½).

INTRODUCTION

MEDIEVAL LONDON

> London, thou art of townes *A per se*.
>   Soveraign of cities, seemliest in sight,
> Of high renoun, riches and royaltie ;
>   Of lordis, barons, and many a goodly knyght ;
>   Of most delectable lusty ladies bright ;
> Of famous prelatis, in habitis clericall ;
>   Of merchauntis full of substaunce and of myght :
> London, thou art the flour of Cities all.
>   (William Dunbar, 1465–1520 (?), *In Honour of the City of London*)

Three centuries before these familiar lines were written
William fitz Stephen, the clerk and biographer of St. Thomas
of Canterbury, with equal fervour if perhaps with less poetry,
wrote his *Description of the Most Noble City of London* (*Historical
Association Leaflets*, Nos. 93–4, 1934, translated by Professor
H. E. Butler). " Among the noble cities of the world that
are celebrated by Fame, the City of London, seat of the
Monarchy of England, is one that spreads its fame wider,
sends its wealth and wares farther, and lifts its head higher
than all others. It is blest in the wholesomeness of its air,
in its reverence for the Christian faith, in the strength of its
bulwark, the nature of its situation, the honour of its citizens,
and the chastity of its matrons. It is likewise most merry in
its sports and fruitful of noble men." In the Middle Ages,
as indeed at all times, there was something about London
which stirred the minds of all men. It was easy then, as now,
to lavish superlatives on the city that was the first in England
and yet so different from any other town that medieval England
could show. Civic pride may have made some claims which
were hardly matched by fact ; nor can every aspect of life
in medieval London command from us now the same romantic-
ally inspired admiration as it could from our great grandparents.
Yet even when the mists of romanticism are dispelled, there
is something about the achievement of London and of its
citizens that must stir the most prosaic mind. The Londoner
was a citizen of a great city, and he knew it.

When William the Conqueror landed in this country,

13

London had four centuries of prosperous growth behind it since the obscurity and decay into which it had fallen after the collapse of Roman civilization. That prosperity was due ultimately to geographical facts. Here at the head of a great tidal estuary, at the lowest point where a bridge could be built to link firm ground on either bank, was the inevitable meeting-place of land- and sea-trade (see *Royal Commission on Ancient Monuments, London*, Vol. III, Introduction ; also *London in Roman Times* (*London Museum Catalogue*), Introduction). These were factors which lay outside the ebb and flow of politics and war. Trade was no doubt brisker in times of relative calm. But even before the Norman conquest there is abundant evidence for the presence of the foreign merchants—from Flanders, from Normandy, from Scandinavia —who were to become so conspicuous a feature of the later medieval economic life of London.

" To this city, from every nation that is under heaven, merchants rejoice to bring their trade in ships " (fitz Stephen).

Throughout the Middle Ages London was the natural port of entry for foreign goods ; and whenever comparative figures are available they reveal a pre-eminence of wealth and position only comparable with that of Roman London over the other cities of Roman Britain.

To its Roman predecessor medieval London owed three things : London Bridge, the City Walls, and the great system of roads that carried its traffic inland to all the towns of south-eastern and central England. Of the internal street plan of Roman London little, if any, remained. It had disappeared into the darkness of the 5th and 6th centuries. It had been, as far as we can tell, as orderly as its successor was incoherent. Yet it is the latter which has survived, a monument alike to the conservatism and to the vitality of the institutions which it represents. The extent of the city was predetermined by the line of the Roman walls. But if by the end of the Middle Ages London had already overflowed those bounds, it would be a mistake to think of Norman London as fully occupying the space within its walls. Considerable tracts immediately inside the walls and on either side of Walbrook were still open ; and the houses in the centre were crowded only by contemporary standards. In one of the open spaces, at the south-eastern corner of the city area, William the Conqueror planted his royal stronghold, the Tower of London. Its situation, well outside the inhabited centre of the city, was a mark no doubt of the healthy respect which he felt for its citizens. But for London, unlike so many contemporary towns, the controlling factor was not the fortress, the seat of power of its royal overlord, but London Bridge, which was the common heritage of every merchant citizen. In 1176 the citizens undertook to replace the old wooden bridge with one of stone. Begun a year before the equally famous Pont d'Avignon over the Rhône, it was the first stone bridge to be built in western Europe since the fall of the Roman Empire. No event could more fittingly summarize at once the position which medieval London occupied and the reasons for her greatness.

The importance of London was not solely economic. At least once during the Middle Ages, at the capture of Farringdon Castle, in 1145, an army of Londoners intervened with decisive effect in the military conflicts of the times. It was, however, rather through their wealth and corporate liberties that the citizens acquired a pre-eminence over other English towns. Even strong kings were glad to grant them rights and privileges in return for political and financial support. London never attained the legal status of a *commune*, such as existed in France and elsewhere on the continent. But throughout the 12th century, notably under Stephen, and again under Richard and John, its citizens were in fact acquiring an ever-increasing independence. In 1191 Henry fitz Ailwin was elected first Mayor of London. Four years later the citizens acquired the right to farm the taxes of London and Middlesex and to elect their own sheriffs. These and similar privileges might vary from one king to the next; nor were theory and practice always synonymous. Even so, it is clear that London entered the 13th century with rights and privileges far greater than those enjoyed by any other English town and, over and above all charters, with an effective prestige that had little need for formal grants.

In the economic sphere also the 12th century was marked

by the emergence of the organization which characterized the later Middle Ages. The first reference to a guild is to that of the Weavers in the Pipe Roll of 1130, and in 1156 a guild of bakers also is mentioned. These are isolated records, but they cannot in fact have been unique. In 1180 there appear no less than nineteen " adulterine " guilds, *i.e.* guilds that had received no official sanction, of which at least four, those of the pepperers, goldsmiths, butchers, and cloth-dressers, were associations of craftsmen. By the end of the century the communal organization of trade and industry was evidently a well-established practice.

These things belong to history. But they were also the background against which common men lived and died. Such were the people of whom Chaucer wrote, whom we see portrayed in the pages of manuscripts or wherever the medieval carver wrought his fancy. It was they who used the tools, the weapons and the ornaments which now form the collections in the Museum. These are not collector's pieces. They are a typical cross-section of medieval practice and craftsmanship, both rich and poor, from a city in which were gathered men of every nation and of every degree. They are with few exceptions the result of chance finds. Even where the precise details of their discovery are recorded these are rarely significant. In Moorfields extensive late medieval deposits can be correlated with the well-documented 15th- and early 16th-century reclamation-work undertaken by the citizens of London (between 1415 and 1511; see F. Lambert, " Some Recent Excavations in London," *Archæologia*, LXXI, 1920, 75–110); and in the filling of the City-ditch considerable late medieval deposits were recognized, together with others of the 16th and 17th centuries, all of which belong to the periods when the primary function of the ditch was that of a convenient rubbish-dump (*Archæologia*, LX, 1906, 169–250). Elsewhere, however, the upper soil of the city has been too often and too deeply disturbed to tell any coherent story. The age and purpose of the great majority of the objects found in London can only be determined by a study of the objects themselves.

MEDIEVAL ARCHÆOLOGY

The Middle Ages is a term justifiable by custom and convenience rather than by common sense. The four and a half centuries which followed the Norman Conquest were in reality only a part of the far longer period which intervened between the collapse of Roman rule in north-western Europe and that final, triumphant reinstatement of classical culture which we know as the Renaissance. Even the peculiar sanctity with which tradition has invested the date 1066 cannot disguise its insignificance relative to this larger canvas. The conquest of this country by Duke William of Normandy was indeed an important political event. But it was no more than the culmination of a long process of increasingly close relations, both political and cultural, between England and the continent. Moreover, while it undoubtedly involved the introduction of a great deal that was new, the basic conditions of life remained substantially unaltered. It would be easy to overstress the paradox. But no aspect of medieval archæology is more striking than the continuity of conditions throughout the 10th, 11th, and 12th centuries, a continuity sharply contrasted with the gulf that in so many ways divides the earlier from the later Middle Ages. The England of William the Conqueror was as remote from that of Henry VII as Tudor England was from that of Queen Victoria.

The close of the Middle Ages on the other hand does coincide with the close of an historical epoch. Of that there can be no doubt. The only possible ground for dispute is the date at which this change took place. On the 22nd of August, 1485, Richard III fell on Bosworth Field. This date is conventionally accepted as marking the close of the Middle Ages. But while the triumph of the House of Tudor undoubtedly set the stage for the changes that were to come, it was some time before their effect was really felt. In the field of art the arrival in this country of Pietro Torrigiani in 1512 may be said to mark the first serious impact of the new ideas ; and more than any other single event it was the Dissolution of the Monasteries, some twenty years later, that broke up the fabric of medievalism.

The extant remains of the medieval period mirror alike its

continuity with the preceding epoch and the separation from that which followed. Except in the major arts there is hardly any noticeable break corresponding to the Norman invasion. Viking types of weapons and tools continued to influence subsequent development well on into the 13th century ; and it may even be suggested that a large number of objects which are normally classified as " Viking " belong in fact to the later 11th and 12th centuries. At the close of the period there is little possibility of such confusion. A certain number of basically efficient types of tool and implement continued unchanged in use, as indeed in some cases they had done since Roman times. But in all the less indeterminate objects of daily use there is a marked break in the continuity of development, a break which marks a change of spirit as much as the introduction of new forms. It did not happen all at once. The armourer's craft, for example, was international (see Laking, *European Armour and Arms*, Introduction, pp. xliii–xlix, and especially p. xlix, a reference from Froissart to " armuriers en la cité de Londres moult ensoignés "). In consequence the new fashions in weapons and armour were already making themselves felt in this country in the closing years of the 15th century. Purses, on the other hand, were a product of purely domestic craftsmanship, and accordingly it was not until the middle of the 16th century that medieval forms finally died out. The end of the Middle Ages was not a finite moment of time. It was, however, the close of an epoch.

To the archæologist the Middle Ages present several problems that hardly arise in connection with the archæology of earlier periods. In the first place, with a few notable exceptions, such as Old Sarum, most medieval towns and villages are still inhabited and afford little opportunity for systematic excavation. Secondly, it must be admitted that the intrinsic quality of many of the remains of medieval craftsmanship has until very recently rather distracted attention from the systematic study of everyday objects, which is, of necessity, the essence of much pre-medieval archæology. And thirdly, the final triumph of Christianity, and with it the more or less effective suppression of the practice of burying grave-furniture with the dead, has robbed the excavator of one of his most valuable sources of evidence. To appreciate the importance of this last factor it is only necessary to compare our knowledge of the archæology of the pagan Viking epoch in Scandinavia with that of England in the same period.

To compensate for these difficulties, however, there is a wealth of comparative material in the form of contemporary illustrations. Manuscripts, wall-paintings, stained-glass windows, sculpture, woodwork, ivory carvings, all in varying degrees portray contemporary life. Not only do they supplement the evidence of surviving objects; they illustrate also perishable objects, such as clothing, of which actual specimens have only very exceptionally been preserved. Further, they show how and when such things were used. These are all features almost unknown to the pre-medieval archæology of this country; and, while they do not override the need for excavation and for typological study, they do supply an additional method of approach, which is of the first importance.

It does not follow that the evidence of contemporary representations is all of equal value. Manuscript illustrators were not always concerned with the minute accuracy of the scenes which they drew; and it was only an occasional draughtsman, such as Villard de Honnecourt (*Album de Villard de Honnecourt*, Paris, 1858), or the illustrator of the Maciejowski Bible (S. Cockerell, *A Book of Old Testament Illustrations in the Pierpont Morgan Library*), who combined artistic sense with a scrupulous observance of detail. Articles of dress, armour, and weapons appear, often in great detail, on monumental effigies and brasses. Even so, there is a danger, particularly in the later Middle Ages, that the detail may represent the convention of a particular workshop rather than actual contemporary practice. This type of evidence obviously cannot be used indiscriminately. It is, however, extremely valuable, and from its bulk alone it is bound to play a large, often a predominant, part.

The medieval collections of the London Museum are well suited to serve as the basis of a more general account of the various types of object which are likely to confront the archæologist. They constitute a cross-section of the things in everyday use in medieval England, sufficiently rich and varied to be fully representative but not so rich as to be divorced from common practice. Of the pages that follow, some pursue well-trodden paths, others are frankly exploratory. If justification be needed for the inclusion of the latter in a handbook such as this, it lies in the fact that in the present state of medieval archæology no other course is possible. The illustrations at least should prove convenient for reference, and the student may find his work the easier for the collection of some of the comparative material. In any case, there is nothing so stimulating to research as the discovery of ignorance. This catalogue will have served a purpose if it only shows how much still remains to be done in the field of medieval archæology.

PLATE II.

Medieval swords from London, 13th and 14th centuries.
1, B 306; 2, C 2251; 3, C 802; 4, A 24900; 5, A 25436.

PLATE III. [*To face p.* 21.

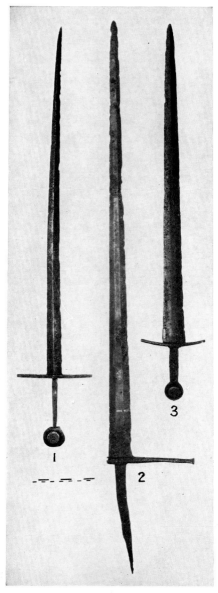

Medieval swords from London, 14th and 15th centuries.
1, C 2507; 2, A 2453; 3, C 2250.

I. WEAPONS

SWORDS

(i) 11th–13th Centuries

A striking feature of the early medieval sword in this country is the strong survival of Viking types. These seem to represent two distinct strains—the one derivative from the established British Viking forms (see *London and the Vikings* (*London Museum Catalogue*), pp. 29–37), the other from the types naturalized in Normandy. The latter have never been studied in detail, but certain general features are clear, notably the absence of the lobed pommel. Of the large series of Norman swords from the Loire in the museum at Nantes only one example has a lobed pommel of degenerate, probably 12th century, type; and it is not until the 13th century that it is found in French representations, *e.g.* a group of soldiers on Reims Cathedral (C. Enlart, *Manuel*, III, p. 411), or the Maciejowski Bible, ff. 12a and 38a. In Normandy two types of sword seem to have been current, the one with a softened version of the Norwegian " cocked-hat " pommel (Fig. 1, I; *cf. London and the Vikings*, Fig. 13, II) the other with a pommel shaped like a somewhat flattened hemisphere (Fig. 1, II). The latter bears a strong resemblance to a widely distributed Scandinavian and British type (J. Petersen, *De Norske Viking-sverd*, types W and X; *London and the Vikings*, type VII) and may in fact be connected with it. Outside Normandy, however, these pommels more often than not retain vestigial traces of the three-lobed division of earlier types; and of this there is no sign either at Nantes or at Rouen. The flattened hemispherical pommel in Normandy is probably, therefore, to be regarded as derivative from the " cocked-hat " form; and this is supported by the existence of intermediate examples. We are dependent solely upon internal evidence for the dating of these Norman swords, and it is therefore hardly possible to say more than that the pure " cocked-hat " form, Type I, was probably already obsolete at the time of the Norman Conquest.

The lobed pommel, Type VII, on medieval English swords

would seem therefore to be a survival from pre-Norman Viking types. It was remarkably persistent and occurs little changed as late as the 13th century. The most striking example is perhaps that on the posthumous effigy, *c.* 1290, of Robert, Duke of Normandy in Gloucester Cathedral

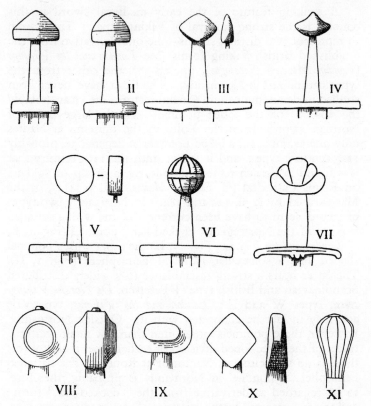

FIG. 1.—Types of medieval sword-pommel.

(Fig. 2, No. 5). Others may be seen on the effigy of a de L'Isle at Rampton, Cambs, *c.* 1225 (C. A. Stothard, *Monumental Effigies*, Pl. 20) ; in a developed form on an effigy at Sullington, Sussex (Fig. 2, No. 6) ; in the Carrow Psalter, *c.* 1235–50 (*Archæologia* LXXIX, 1929, Pl. XXI, 2) ; in Matthew Paris,

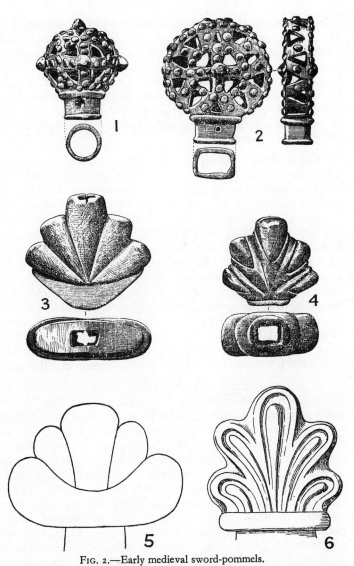

FIG. 2.—Early medieval sword-pommels.

1–4, bronze pommels in the British Museum (½); 5, on the effigy of Robert, Duke of Normandy, *c.* 1290, in Gloucester Cathedral; 6, on an effigy, 13th century, at Sullington, Sussex.

Historia Major, II, f. 147b, *c.* 1240–55 (*Walpole Society*, XIV, Pl. XV); and in several forms in the Maciejowski Bible. Its influence may perhaps be traced even later in the lobed forms current as late as the mid-14th century (see below, p. 26; for apparent Scottish survivals to a far later date, see O. Smith, *Zeitschrift für Historische Waffen-und Kostüm-künde*. 1937, pp. 25–31). The British Museum possesses two pommels of this type which can be ascribed to the 12th or 13th century (Fig. 2, Nos. 3 and 4).

The flattened hemispherical pommel (Type II), both as introduced by the Norman conquest and as already established by pre-Norman Viking settlers (*London and the Vikings* (*London Museum Catalogue*), pp. 32 and 36, Type VII), is less easily recognizable in representations. It can, however, be seen very clearly in the early 13th-century Psalter of Queen Ingeburga of Denmark at Chantilly (Musée Condé, MS. 1695, f. 18); and it is represented at its finest by the sword of St. Denis, now in the Louvre (G. Laking, *European Armour and Arms*, I, Figs. 112, 114–5). This sword can be assigned to the late 12th century on the strength of the ornament which it carries; and objections to this dating on the grounds of the form of the pommel (Conway, *Archæologia*, LXVI, 1915, 132) are hardly tenable in face of the large series of similar types, of unquestionably Norman date, which are preserved in the museums at Nantes and Rouen.

By the middle of the 13th century Type II seems to have given place to the derivative Types III and IV, the " brazil-nut " pommel. Swords of this type usually have long, straight quillons. Both forms are represented, *c.* 1250, in the Maciejowski Bible, ff. 3a, 29b, 33b, 36b, etc. Unfortunately in effigies of the 13th century the pommel is often gripped by the mailed hand, and only exceptionally is the type distinguishable. Neither Type III nor IV is, however, found on the series of brasses, and it may therefore be presumed that they were obsolete by the 14th century. There are extant British examples in Maidstone Museum (G. Laking, *op. cit.*, Fig. 106) and in the Ashmolean Museum, Oxford (from the Thames at Sandford Lock). *Cf.* also Laking, *op. cit.*, Figs. 101, 104, 108, and 119. A miniature sword, apparently a toy, with a pommel of this form is shown in Fig. 89, No. 2.

24

Contemporary with the swords of ultimately Viking derivation are a large series of swords with disc- or spherical pommels
(Types V and VI). Both forms were certainly in use in the
12th century. The evidence of contemporary representations
is inevitably somewhat confusing, and it is hardly possible to
say from these more than that circular pommels of some sort
are clearly represented on the enamel tablet of Geoffrey
Plantagenet, c. 1150–60, at Le Mans (C. A. Stothard, *Monumental Effigies*, Pl. 2) and in such precisely drawn 12th-century
manuscripts as B.M. Nero C. IV, c. 1125 (G. Laking, *European
Armour and Arms*, I, Fig. 14), and B.M. Harleian S. 102,
c. 1190–1200 (*Archæologia*, LXXIX, 1928, Pl. XXI, 1). There are,
however, a certain number of roughly datable examples extant.
The British Museum possesses two decorated bronze pommels
of Type V, probably of late 12th-century date (Fig. 2, No. 2 ;
for the other, see T. D. Kendrick, *Antiquaries Journal*, XVIII,
1938, 381, Pl. LXXIV, 5), and a third in bronze openwork of
Type VI (Fig. 2, No. 1). A 13th-century engraved copper-gilt
disc-pommel from Great Chesterford, now in the Ipswich
Museum, is published in *Antiquaries Journal*, XV, 1935, 476 ;
and there is in the museum at Bury St. Edmunds a fine iron
sword with disc-pommel (Type V) and inscribed, fullered
blade, which was found on the site of the battle of Fornham,
A.D. 1173.

In the 13th century, *e.g.* in the Maciejowski Bible, circular
pommels in some form or other are more common than any
other type. The majority of these are probably disc-pommels,
Type V. A certain number, however, *e.g.* the Maciejowski
Bible, f. 13a, are evidently of Type VI ; and this form survives
into the 14th century, where it is found on at least one early
brass, that of Sir John D'Abernon, junior, 1327, at Stoke
d'Abernon, Surrey (Fig. 3, No. 12). It is, however, from
Type V that the stock 14th-century wheel-pommel, Type
VIII, is derived.

Trefoil or multilobed circular pommels are fairly commonly
represented in 13th-century manuscripts. They are an obvious
development of the plain disc-pommel, perhaps under the
influence of lobed sub-Viking types. The Musée de Cluny,
Paris, possesses three pommels of this type, with enamelled

coats of arms, from Beyrouth and Saida, in Syria, evidently Crusader's weapons. They closely resemble the pommel of a sword illustrated in a drawing by Matthew Paris, *c.* 1250–60 (*Walpole Society*, XVI, Pl. XXVII). These lobed forms occur exceptionally as late as the mid-14th century, *e.g.* on an effigy, *c.* 1350, in Clehonger Church, Herefordshire (Fig. 3, No. 11).

Throughout the 12th and 13th centuries the quillons are normally straight, occasionally slightly curved, and of plain, stout build. The very short quillons of the Viking prototype gradually lengthen by the late 13th century into the proportions illustrated in Fig. 1, Types III and IV, Fig. 4, No. 1, but the process is not uniform. Throughout the period the blade is for the greater part of its length relatively wide ; and ordinarily it has a wide, fullered groove down the centre. The latter feature is sometimes omitted as early as the beginning of the 13th century, and possibly even earlier, *e.g.* on a number of French swords of Type II. On the other hand, it is not until well on into the 14th century that it is completely abandoned in favour of the tapering blade of diamond-section designed for thrusting as well as cutting. A late example with a strongly developed wheel-pommel (Type VIII) is the fine sword from the River Witham in the British Museum. This sword illustrates also another common feature of the early medieval series, an inscription inlaid down the fullering of the blade. Inscriptions of this sort are found as early as the Viking period ; and they are well illustrated on the 12th-century effigy of Roland on the porch of Verona Cathedral ; *cf.* the Maciejowski Bible, f. 34b.

(ii) *14th and 15th Centuries*

Throughout the 14th and 15th centuries the cruciform sword with a wheel-pommel and a straight double-edged blade was the basic type in common use. Monuments and paintings inevitably tend to reproduce the more elaborate forms, such as the hand-and-a-half sword of the second half of the 14th and early 15th century ; and on the whole the ornate specimens of these types have had a better survival value. They are, however, parallel to the main stream of

26

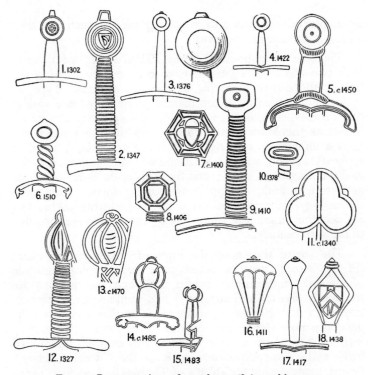

FIG. 3.—Representations of swords on effigies and brasses.

No. 1.   Brass of Sir Robert de Bures, d. 1302, at Acton, Suffolk.
No. 2.   Brass of Sir Hugh Hastings, d. 1347, at Elsing, Norfolk.
No. 3.   Effigy of the Black Prince, d. 1376, in Canterbury Cathedral.
No. 4.   Brass of William Wylde, d. 1422, at Dodford, Northants.
No. 5.   Brass of John Diggis, c. 1450, at Barham, Kent.
No. 6.   Brass of Henry Michell, d. 1510, at Floore, Northants.
No. 7.   Brass of a Dalison, c. 1400, at Laughton, Lincs.
No. 8.   Brass of Thomas de Beauchamp, Earl of Warwick, d. 1406, in St. Mary's church, Warwick.
No. 9.   Brass, 1410.
No. 10. Brass of Richard Charlis, d. 1378, at Addington, Kent.
No. 11. Effigy, c. 1350, at Clehonger, Herefordshire.
No. 12. Brass of Sir John D'Abernon, junior, d. 1327, at Stoke d'Abernon, Surrey.
No. 13. Brass of Ralph Cromwell, c. 1470, at Tattershall, Lincs.
No. 14. Brass, c. 1485, at Heacham, Norfolk.
No. 15. Brass of John Weston, d. 1483, at Ockham, Surrey.
No. 16. Brass of Thomas de Crewe, d. 1411, at Wixford, Warwick.
No. 17. Brass of John Hadresham, d. 1417, at Lingfield, Surrey.
No. 18. Brass of Richard Dixton, d. 1438, at Cirencester, Glos.

27

development, and it is only when regarded as such that they assume their true perspective.

The true wheel-pommel (Type VIII), which had a life of over two centuries, seems to have been evolved during the later 13th century from the simple disc-pommel, Type V. It does not appear to be represented among the wide variety of sword-types illustrated in such mid-13th-century manuscripts as the Maciejowski Bible. On the other hand, the earliest military brasses, e.g. Sir John D'Abernon, d. 1277, at Stoke d'Abernon, Surrey ; Sir Roger de Trumpington, d. 1289, at Trumpington, Cambs ; and Sir Robert de Bures, d. 1302, at Acton, Suffolk, all appear to portray them. Such two-dimensional representations are naturally inconclusive ; but at least they mark the transition to the true wheel-pommel of the 14th century.

The sword shown on the brass of Sir Robert de Bures (Fig. 3, No. 1) may be taken as a fairly typical example of an early 14th-century sword, although the quillons are frequently shorter and stouter. The quillons are in fact an important dating-criterion, for apart from these and from the generally more slender proportions of the sword there is very little to distinguish a sword such as this from an undoubted early 15th-century specimen such as the " Battle Abbey " sword, made during the abbacy of Thomas de Lodelow, 1417–34 (G. Laking, *European Armour and Arms*, II, Fig. 639). The " Battle Abbey " sword may be compared with specimens illustrated in contemporary brasses, e.g. of Sir Arnold Savage, d. 1420, at Bobbing, Kent ; William Wylde, d. 1422, and Sir John Cressy, d. 1444, both at Dodford, Northants, and others. In all of these the quillons are longer and more slender than those shown in representations of ordinary single-handed swords down to c. 1400.

The middle of the 15th century is marked by the general adoption of a different form of quillon. These may be more or less straight with a sharp projection upwards towards the point, often floriated at the tips, e.g. on the brasses of William Prelatte, d. 1462, at Cirencester, Glos, and of Robert Watton, d. 1470, at Addington, Kent ; or they may curve upward with a sharp hook at the ends, e.g. on the brasses of John

28

PLATE IV.

36.164/1. Part of a sword found in the Thames at Blackfriars. Late 15th
century.

PLATE V. [*To face p.* 29.

Sword, early 14th century, from the Thames at Westminster; *left,* detail
of lower scabbard-mount ($\frac{1}{1}$) (52.12).

Diggis, c. 1450, at Barham, Kent (Fig. 3, No. 5), or of John Ansty, d. 1460, at Stow-cum-Quy, Cambs. The former is the more commonly represented. In the series of brasses these curved quillons appear suddenly, c. 1440, e.g. on the brasses of Robert Greyndon, d. 1443, at Newlands, Glos, and of John Throckmorton, d. 1445, at Fladbury, Worcs. Plain straight quillons are occasionally represented after this date, e.g. on the brass of John Weston, d. 1483, at Ockham, Surrey; but they are exceptional. Neither of these forms of quillon can, however, be used with absolute confidence as a criterion of 15th-century date. Strongly arched quillons appear occasionally in the later 14th century, e.g. on the brass of Sir Edward Cerne, d. 1393–4, at Draycot Cerne, Wilts; and of Sir Reginald Cobham, d. 1403, at Lingfield, Surrey. And the sword on Sir John Gifford's brass, c. 1348, at Bowers Gifford, Essex, has straight quillons with hooked, floriated tips. These instances are, however, exceptional; they do not represent ordinary usage.

The normal form of pommel throughout the series remains the wheel-pommel, Type V. Faceted, hexagonal, and octagonal forms are obvious variants which hardly require separate classification. They seem to be specially common in the later 14th and earlier 15th centuries, although they are found earlier, e.g. on the effigy of Sir Roger de Kerdeston, d. 1337, at Reepham, Norfolk (C. A. Stothard, *Monumental Effigies*, Pl. 61). Besides those illustrated (Fig. 3, Nos. 7 and 8) there are examples on at least half a dozen other brasses of the period, ranging from that of William de Audeley, d. 1365, at Horseheath, Cambs, to that of Sir Thomas le Strange, d. 1426, at Wellesbourne Hastings, Warwickshire; most of them fall between 1395 and 1410. To roughly the same period belong also swords with elongated wheel-pommels of Type IX. These range from c. 1370 (the brass of Roger Felbrig at Felbrigg, Norfolk) to the close of the century (Fig. 3, No. 9; cf. the brass of Sir Morys Russell, d. 1401, at Dyrham, Glos). A surviving dated example is the " Mourning " sword, presented to the city of Bristol in 1373 (G. Laking, *European Armour and Arms*, II, Fig. 692).

Of the remaining pommel-forms current in the 14th century one at least, the spherical pommel, Type VI, which is very clearly shown on the brass of Sir John D'Abernon, junior, d. 1327, at Stoke d'Abernon, Surrey, is evidently a tardy relic of the preceding century. The same is no doubt true of the trefoil pommel on an effigy, c. 1350, at Clehonger, Hereford (Fig. 3, No. 11); cf. Maciejowski Bible, ff. 2a and 10a; or a painting, also c. 1250, in the Chapter House of Christ Church, Oxford (*Walpole Society*, XVI, Pl. III). The lozenge-pommel, Type X, is not common, but is found on a small group of early 14th-century effigies, those of Sir John Ifield, d. 1317, at Ifield, Sussex, and of John of Eltham, d. 1334, in Westminster Abbey (C. A. Stothard, *Monumental Effigies*, Pls. 59 and 55); and of an unknown man, c. 1320, at Halton Holgate, Lincs (*Antiquaries Journal*, XVI, 1936, Pl. 76, 2). It is, however, occasionally represented both earlier and later, e.g. on the effigy of King John at Worcester, and on that of Sir Thomas Arderne, c. 1400, at Elford, Staffs. Abroad the disc-pommel, Type V, continued in use throughout the Middle Ages; and in a somewhat elaborated form it reappears in England in the 15th century on the swords of the type of 36.164/1 (Pl. IV), and possibly elsewhere.

Contemporary with the ordinary cruciform sword is the long-hilted, hand-and-a-half sword, of which that on the effigy of the Black Prince, d. 1376, in Canterbury Cathedral (Fig. 3, No. 3), may be taken as typical, although it omits one common feature, the sharply hooked ends to the long slender quillons, which can be seen, for example, on two well-dated, surviving specimens, the " Mourning " sword of Bristol, 1373, and the oldest of the state swords of Lincoln, 1386 (G. Laking, *European Armour and Arms*, Figs. 692 and 693). The increased length of the blade demanded for balance the lengthening of the hilt and a heavy pommel, and these hand-and-a-half swords were designed for use with one hand or two as occasion arose. The earliest datable English representation of such a sword seems to be that on the brass of Sir Hugh Hastings, d. 1347, at Elsing, Norfolk (Fig. 3, No. 2), where the elongated hilt is combined with the short stout quillons of the earlier 14th century.

In the early 15th century the hand-and-a-half sword continues in common use, but there is a sudden and marked change of type during the first decade of the century. The ordinary pommel of the early 15th-century hand-and-a-half sword is the "scent-stopper" pommel, Type XI, and the quillons are now almost invariably straight. These features first appear at the turn of the century (*e.g.* on the brass of Thomas de Braunstone, d. 1401, at Wisbech, Cambs) and as they are found considerably earlier on the continent (*e.g.* on the effigy of Jacopo de Cavalli, d. 1384, in San Giovanni e Paolo, Venice), they were presumably introduced from abroad. This form of sword achieved instant popularity. Out of thirty brasses, chosen at random between 1400 and 1425, twenty-one illustrate swords of this sort. Its currency, however, at any rate in this country, was correspondingly brief, for it is hardly represented after 1440 (a very late example can be seen on the brass of Sir Thomas de St. Quinton, 1445, at Harpham, Yorks, E.R.). During this period there is little variation of type. Fig. 3, No. 18, illustrates a late variant from the brass of Richard Dixton, d. 1438, at Cirencester, Glos (*cf.* that of Richard Harwedon, d. 1443, at Great Harrowden, Northants) ; and the effigy of William, Lord Bardolf, *c.* 1430, at Dennington, Suffolk (C. A. Stothard, *Monumental Effigies*, Pl. 111) illustrates a flattened, fish-tailed form of pommel of which actual examples survive (see G. Laking, *European Armour and Arms*, II, Figs. 627 and 628. *Cf.* the "Pearl" sword presented to the city of Bristol by Sir John de Wells in 1431, Laking, *op. cit.*, Fig. 699). A well-dated specimen of the ordinary form is the earlier of the ceremonial swords of the city of York, which was originally hung above the Garter-stall of the Emperor Sigismund at Windsor in 1416.

With the disappearance of this form of hand-and-a-half sword, *c.* 1440, the single-handed sword is once more found almost exclusively in contemporary English representations. This may in part be due to brass-cutting fashion. Abroad the long-hilted sword continued in common use ; and a certain number at any rate of English examples are known, *e.g.* the state sword of Edward, Prince of Wales and Earl of Chester, 1471–83 (*British Museum Guide to Medieval Antiquities*, p. 230, Fig. 148). The cruciform sword, however, ordinarily represented on mid-15th-century brasses as slung across the body was undoubtedly of the shorter type, and it probably

31

represents at any rate a partial change of fashion. The forms of quillon in the later 15th century have already been discussed above (pp. 28–9). It is only necessary to add that, to judge from the brass-series, it is only with the closing years of the century that the increasing elaboration of Continental quillon-types is felt in this country (*e.g.* the finger-rings to the quillons shown on the brass of Nicholas Parker, d. 1496, at Honing, Norfolk). These foreign forms hardly find a place in the English medieval series. Another feature which appears towards the close of the century is the ricasso at the head of the blade. This is an Italian form ; and though it appears slightly earlier than the finger-rings on the guard it does not really belong to the English medieval sword.

The forms of pommel of the later 15th century are various, but in the main they belong to Types VI and VIII, the wheel and the spherical forms. A late example of wheel-pommel, from the brass of Henry Michell, d. 1510, at Floore, Northants, is shown in Fig. 3, No. 6 ; and up to that date instances are frequent (see also below, s.v. 36.164/1). The spherical pommel (see Fig. 3, Nos. 13–14) makes its appearance about 1450 and becomes increasingly common. A tendency to split into lobes can already be seen on the brass of Henry Grene, 1467, at Lowick, Northants, *cf.* Fig. 3, No. 15, from the brass of John Weston, 1483, at Ockham, Surrey. The increasing elaboration of pommel-forms is well illustrated on the effigy of Sir Nicholas Fitzherbert, 1473, at Norbury, Derbyshire ; and it marks the passage of the English medieval sword into the complex of fresh types that characterizes the Tudor period.

(iii) *Falchions*

Compared with the sword the falchion, which had a single curved cutting-edge, had only a restricted popularity. It was a fundamentally oriental weapon, which appeared sporadically in the West over a considerable period of time. It was in use at least as early as the 12th century, for the famous Conyers falchion (G. Laking, *European Armour and Arms*, I, Figs. 157–8), itself of 14th-century date, evidently replaces an earlier falchion of tenure which must have been at

32

least as old as the confirmation of the grant of the manor of Sockburn to the Conyers family by Henry II. This weapon continued in use until the 14th century (*e.g.* Luttrell Psalter, f. 49) and the majority of surviving specimens appear to belong to this or to the preceding century (see G. Laking, *op. cit.*, pp. 127–32).

SWORDS

A 25436. Sword with corroded disc-pommel, Type VI, medium length, straight quillons, slightly fullered blade, bearing traces of silver-inlaid scrollwork. 13th century. Over-all length 36·8 in., hilt 6·0 in. Pl. II, No. 5 ; Fig. 4, No. 1. Found in the Thames.

A 24900. Sword with a pommel transitional between the disc-pommel, Type VI, and the wheel-pommel, Type VIII. Short quillons, fullered, and slightly expanding towards the end (compare the brass of Sir John D'Abernon, 1277, at Stoke d'Abernon, Surrey). The blade is fullered with a central ridge. Late 13th century. Over-all length (point missing) 26·4 in., hilt 6·25 in. Pl. II, No. 4 ; Fig. 4, No. 2. From the Thames, Old Putney.

C 802. Sword with small, solid, faceted, spherical pommel, Type VII, bearing engraved scrollwork. Short, straight quillons, fullered blade. 13th century. Over-all length 32·6 in., hilt 5·1 in. Pl. II, No. 3 ; Fig. 4, No. 4. From Ponder's End.

C 2251. Sword, hollow spherical pommel, Type VII, with incised decoration. Long straight quillons, fullered blade. 13th century. Over-all length, 39·3 in., hilt 6·4 in. Pl. II, No. 2 ; Fig. 4, No. 3. From Cannon Street. (G. Laking, *European Armour and Arms*, I, Fig. 167.)

A 16823. Hollow spherical sword pommel, Type VII, with incised decoration. Similar to C 2251. Maximum diameter 2·3 in. From London.

B 306. Sword, with wheel-pommel, Type VIII, slender quillons, very slightly drooping towards point. Fullered blade, the fullering extending halfway up the tang (the illustration, Fig. 5, No. 1, is in error on this point) and two-thirds of the way down the blade. First half of the 14th century. Over-all length 33·0 in., hilt 5·4 in. Pl. II, No. 1 ; Fig. 5, No. 1. From the Houses of Parliament, 1838.

C 2250. Sword of a youth. Wheel-pommel, Type VIII. Medium length, slender, round-sectioned quillons, slightly drooping towards point. The blade is of plain section, lacking both fullering and a central ridge. First half of the 14th century (?). Over-all length 32·0 in., hilt 5·0 in. Pl. III, No. 3 ; Fig. 5, No. 2. From the Thames, Wandsworth. (G. Laking, *European Armour and Arms*, I, p. 134 and p. 136.)

C 2507. Sword, with wheel-pommel, Type VIII. Medium length, straight, square-sectioned quillons. Slender blade of diamond-section. Maker's mark on the tang. Late 14th century. Over-all length 35·8 in., hilt 6·0 in. Pl. III, No. 1 ; Fig. 5, No. 3. From the Thames, Blackfriars.

33

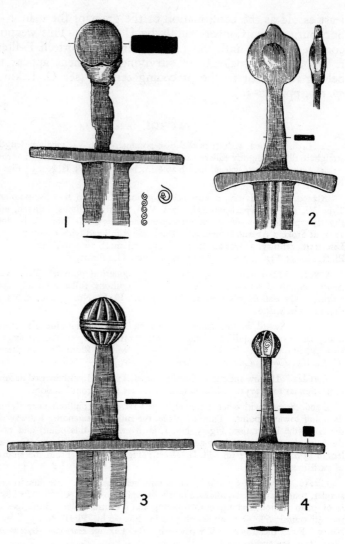

FIG. 4.—Early medieval swords from London.
1, A 25436; 2, A 24900; 3, C 2251; 4, C 802 (¼).

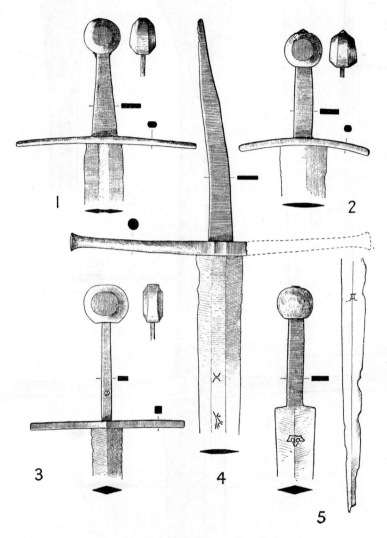

Fig. 5.—Swords from London, 14th–15th centuries.
1, B 306; 2, C 2250; 3, C 2507; 4, A 2453: 5, 36.213 (¼).

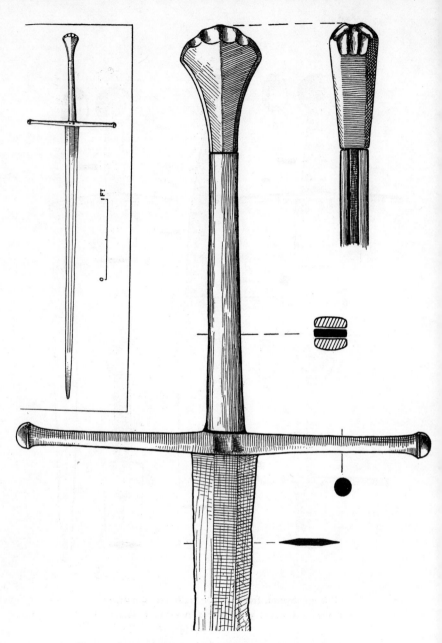

FIG. 6.—"Hand-and-a-half" sword from the Thames, Sion Reach.
Second quarter of the 15th century (⅓) (39.142).

A 2453. "Hand-and-a-half" sword. Pommel and one quillon missing. The remaining quillon is long and straight, and of circular section expanding at the point. Blade of flattened hexagonal section. Maker's mark on both faces of the blade. First half of the 15th century. Over-all length 46·9 in., hilt 10·0 in. Pl. III, No. 2 ; Fig. 5, No. 4. From the site of Holborn Tube Station.

36.213. Sword, with spherical pommel, Type VI. Quillons missing. Blade diamond-section, inlaid on either face with a crown at the top and with the latter A towards the point. Second half of the 15th century. Over-all length (about 1 in. of the point missing) 31·0 in., hilt about 5·5 in. Fig. 5, No. 5.

36.164/1. Hilt and part of the blade of a sword. The pommel is of heavy wheel type with a sunk centre and a projecting stud ; and the quillons are broad and drooping towards the point, with the broad sides set at right-angles to the blade, which has a strong central rib. All these features are characteristic of a small group of late-medieval swords, of which a fine specimen is preserved in the undercroft of Westminster Abbey. Another British example is in Whitelackington Church, Somerset (G. Laking, *European Armour and Arms*, V, 235, Fig. 1730). They can be dated with confidence to the close of the 15th century (see J. G. Mann, "A Sword and a Helm in Westminster Abbey," *Antiquaries Journal*, XI, 1931, 404 ff.). Pl. IV. From the Thames, Blackfriars Bridge.

39.142. "Hand-and-a-half" sword. The pommel is of flattened " scent-stopper " form (*cf.* the effigy of William, Lord Bardolf, *c.* 1430, at Dennington, Suffolk. Long, straight quillons, of circular section expanding at the point (*cf.* A 2453). Blade of flattened hexagonal section. Second quarter of the 15th century. Over-all length 55·4 in., hilt 13·5 in. Fig. 6. From the Thames, Sion Reach. (G. Laking, *European Armour and Arms*, II, p. 142.)

52.12. (Deposited by the Royal United Service Institution). Sword, with wheel-pommel, Type VIII, flattened at the top. Slender, curved quillons, turned back at the ends. Long slender blade of diamond-section. It retains the elaborately engraved mounts and terminal chape of its scabbard. This sword has been variously dated within the 14th century. The scabbard-mounts, however, are of a rare type illustrated on the monument of a Berkeley, *c.* 1310, in Bristol Cathedral (F. H. Crossley, *English Church-Monuments*, p. 211), and on another effigy in Gresford Church, *c.* 1331 (Crossley, *op. cit.*, p. 213). It is not likely therefore to be later than the middle of the century, if indeed it is as late. From the Thames at Westminster. (G. Laking, *European Armour and Arms*, I, pp. 131–3, Fig. 163 ; C. R. Beard, *Connoisseur*, 91, 1933, 104–6.) Plate V.

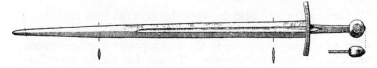

FIG. 7.—Early 14th-century sword from the Thames at Westminster (⅛).
(In the collection of the Society of Antiquaries.)

37

Also illustrated :

FIG. 2.

No. 1 (in the British Museum). Bronze openwork sword-pommel, Type VI, 12th or early 13th century.

No. 2 (in the British Museum). Bronze openwork sword-pommel, Type V, 12th or early 13th century.

No. 3 (in the British Museum). Bronze sword-pommel, Type VII, 12th century. G. Laking, *Medieval Armour and Arms*, p. 20, Fig. 25 (left).

No. 4 (in the British Museum). Bronze sword-pommel, Type VII, 13th century. G. Laking, *op. cit.*, Fig. 25 (right).

No. 5. Sword-pommel shown on the posthumous effigy of Robert of Normandy, *c.* 1290, in Gloucester Cathedral.

No. 6. Sword-pommel shown on an effigy, *c.* 1250, in Sullington Church, Suffolk.

Fig. 7 (in the collection of the Society of Antiquaries). Sword, with wheel-pommel, Type VIII. Stout, slightly curved quillons. Fullered blade, the fullering extending up the tang and halfway down the blade (*cf.* B 306, Pl. II, No. 1). Over-all length 31·2 in., hilt 5·1 in. First half of the 14th century. From the Thames at Westminster.

KNIVES AND DAGGERS

During the greater part of the Middle Ages the knife was not simply an object of domestic use. It was an essential part of a man's personal equipment. It is not easy to judge how far this was true of the 12th and 13th centuries, when such objects were worn concealed beneath the loose outer-garments and so do not appear in ordinary representations. They can, however, be seen projecting through the " pocket "-slits of civil costume in the early 14th-century Luttrell Psalter ; and it is on all grounds likely that the close continuity of type since the scramasax-knife of Saxon and Viking burials indicates also a continuity of usage.

During the late Middle Ages daggers fall into two clearly defined categories, the military weapon, which seems to have come into being in answer to the development of plate-armour, and the civilian knife-dagger. To the former group belong quillon-daggers and the majority of rondel-daggers ; to the latter, baselards, single-edged knife-daggers, and the majority of kidney-daggers. There are inevitably exceptions ; but

38

Quillon-daggers from London.
1, in the Guildhall Museum; 2, B 325; 3, B 324; 4, A 1946.

PLATE VII.   [*To face p.* 39.

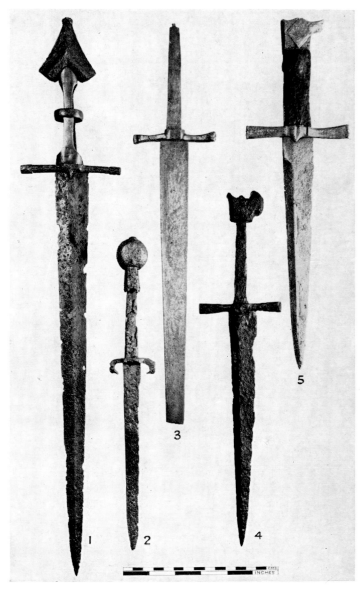

Quillon-daggers from London.
1, 33.296/1; 2, A 1947; 3, A 1783; 4, A 6617; 5, A 14620.

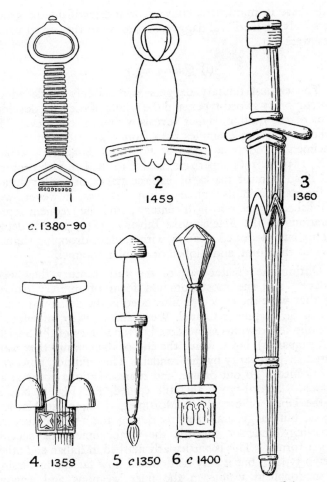

1
c. 1380-90

2
1459

3
1360

4. 1358

5 c 1350

6 c 1400

Fig. 8.—Representations of daggers on contemporary effigies.

No. 1. Effigy, c. 1380–90, at Chalgrave, Beds.
No. 2. Effigy of Sir Hugh Mortimer, d. 1459, at Martley, Worcs.
No. 3. Effigy of Maurice, 9th Lord Berkeley, d. 1360, in Bristol Cathedral.
No. 4. Effigy of Peter de Grandison, d. 1358, in Hereford Cathedral.
No. 5. Effigy, c. 1350, at Clehonger, Herefordshire.
No. 6. Effigy, c. 1400, at Much Marcle, Herefordshire.

with these in mind, it is convenient and justifiable to group the surviving medieval daggers according to the use to which they were put.

(i) *Quillon-daggers*

The earliest military daggers were closely modelled on contemporary sword-types, and the whole of the later development of the quillon-dagger reveals a similar tendency. The earliest surviving examples date from the 13th century. A specimen found in a grave at Poitiers (*Antiquaries Journal*, XIX, 1939, p. 196) is perhaps datable to the late 12th century, and if so it must mark the earliest stages of the evolution of the dagger in its military form. It was, however, well established by the mid-13th century; and the frequent representations in the Maciejowski Bible, *c.* 1250, *passim*, depict a short, sword-shaped weapon, with quillons drooping slightly towards the point, and a lobed or circular pommel.

During the greater part of the 14th century they were evidently still the most common form of military dagger (*e.g.* they were the only type illustrated in the destroyed paintings of St. Stephen's Chapel, Westminster, 1347, of which a portfolio of drawings is preserved in the library of the Society of Antiquaries), but towards the end of the century they were ousted in popularity by the rondel. They did not, however, by any means go out of use, and representations occur at all periods. Sword-types are still copied, *e.g.* Fig. 8, No. 2, on the effigy of Sir Hugh Mortimer, d. 1459, at Martley, Worcs, but in general there is during the 15th century an increasing tendency towards the establishment of specific dagger-forms. This is particularly marked in Italian and other foreign types; but it may be doubted how far the increasing internationalism visible in the finer weapons and armour affected the objects in ordinary use in this country before the close of the century.

A 365. Fragment of the tang and single-edged blade of a dagger, apparently similar to A 6617. Over-all length 7·8 in., originally about 11 in. From Westminster.

A 1946. Quillon-dagger, the quillons and pommel consisting of strips of iron curled downwards and upwards respectively at the ends. Two-edged blade. Point missing. *c.* 1400? Over-all length 11·0 in., blade 7·2 in. Pl. VI, No. 4. Found near the Bank of England. Given by Sir Guy Laking, Bart.

G. Laking, *European Armour and Arms*, III, pp. 4–6, Fig. 735 ; *cf.* Fig. 734, from Queen Victoria Street, in the Guildhall Museum.

A 1783. Quillon-dagger, pommel and point missing. Single-edged blade. The quillons have a pronounced S-curve, *cf.* A 14620, a feature possibly represented on the brass of Edward fforde, Esq., 1439, at Swainswick, Somersetshire (Fig. 9, No. 3), more certainly on a fragmentary dagger in the Leicester Museum, found on the site of the battle of Bosworth Field, 1485 (Fig. 10, No. 7), 1450–1500. Over-all length 15·0 in. Pl. VII, No. 3. From Thames Street. Given by Sir Guy Laking, Bart.

A 1947. Quillon-dagger, single-edged blade, quillons sharply down-curved, wheel-pommel continuing into an octagonal sheathe to fit over the grip. *c.* 1400? Over-all length 11·75 in., blade 7·2 in. Pl. VII, No. 2. Found near the Bank of England. Given by Sir Guy Laking, Bart.

A 4954. Quillon-dagger, pommel and point missing, two-edged blade, quillons formed from a strip of metal curved downwards and rolled back to meet the grip. Over-all length 11·75 in. From Lincoln's Inn Fields.

A 6617. Quillon-dagger, blade at first single-edged, then triangular, one side being flat, *cf.* A 14620. Plain quillons slightly broadening at ends, pommel asymmetrical, bolted in place with a brass bolt. Second half of the 15th century? Over-all length 13·25 in., blade 8·9 in. Pl. VII, No. 4. From Worship Street.

A 11886. Blade of a dagger, probably of quillon-type. For the form *cf.* A 6617. There are traces of gilding at the head of the blade. Length of blade 9·1 in. From the Wandle, Wandsworth.

A 14620. Quillon-dagger. Blade as A 6617. Quillons as A 1783. Diamond pattern on the wooden grip and on the pommel, which, like A 6617, is asymmetrical. Mid-late 15th century. Over-all length 13·0 in., blade 8·6 in. Pl. VII, No. 5. From the Thames, Mortlake.

A 22534. Portions of a small quillon-dagger, tang, blade, and quillons all fragmentary. Blade of diamond-section. The find-spot probably suggests a 15th-century date. From Finsbury Circus.

B 324. Small quillon-dagger, tang broken, pommel missing. Blade of hollowed diamond section. Knobbed quillons, a shortened version of B 325. Probably early 15th century. Length of blade 5·7 in. Pl. VI, No. 3. From Brick Hill Lane.

B 325. Quillon-dagger, complete save for grip. Blade of diamond section, slightly oval wheel-pommel, rounded quillons. Armourer's mark on tang. It is almost identical with the dagger shown on an effigy, *c.* 1380–90, in Chalgrave Church, Beds (Fig. 8, No. 1). Over-all length 13·1 in. Pl. VI, No. 2. From St. Saviour's Dock, Southwark.

C 780. Small two-edged dagger blade, from a quillon- or a kidney-dagger. The upper part of the blade is inlaid on each face with two rows of tiny brass studs. Over-all length 10·6 in., blade 6·4 in. From Chamberlain's Wharf, Thames Street.

33.296/1. Quillon-dagger with pommel of unusual form and straight quillons spirally ornamented at each end. Slender two-edged blade. The brass binding of the grip is decorated with characteristic 15th-century zigzag roulette ornament. Probably second half of the 15th century. Over-all length 20·6 in., blade 15·0 in. Pl. VII, No. 1. From Thames Street.

Also illustrated :

Pl. VI, No. 1 (in the Guildhall Museum). Quillon-dagger, complete save for grip, blade of diamond section, slightly pointed wheel-pommel, quillons plain but swelling towards the ends. Second half of the 14th century. Over-all length 12·1 in., blade 7·1 in. From London. (G. Laking, *European Armour and Arms*, III, Fig. 728.)

Fig. 10, No. 7 (in the Leicester Museum). Quillon-dagger, tang and blade fragmentary, with elaborate spirally-faceted pommel and quillons of the same form as A 1783 and A 14620. Found on the site of the battle of Bosworth Field, 1485.

(ii) *Rondel-daggers*

The term rondel-dagger should perhaps be strictly applied to those daggers only, of which both the pommel and the guard take the form of a disc set at right-angles to the tang. It is, however, convenient to include under this general heading all forms of dagger with a circular, or roughly circular guard, regardless of the form of the pommel. These daggers first appear in the mid-14th century. Fig. 8, No. 5, illustrates an example from an effigy, *c.* 1350, at Clehonger, Hereford; but it is not till about 1390 that it is commonly represented. After 1400, however, it appears on brasses practically to the exclusion of all other types, and it remains predominant throughout the century. It lasted on into the 16th century (G. Laking, *European Armour and Arms*, III, Fig. 764).

Rondel-daggers can be roughly classified in terms of the form of the pommel, the details of which, however, vary greatly from one dagger to the next. In general, too, it can be said that grips attached to the tang by large tubular rivets are later than those fastened by spiral or horizontal binding, but here again there was considerable variety of usage. The form of grip illustrated in Fig. 10, No. 5 and Fig. 9, No. 13 appear to belong exclusively to the mid-15th century.

42

PLATE VIII.

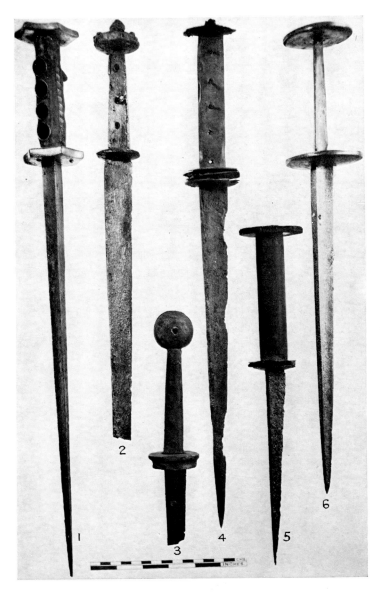

Rondel-daggers from London.

1, A 1968; 2, C 730; 3, A 22517; 4, A 1396; 5, A 1773; 6, A 16826.

PLATE IX. [*To face p.* 43.

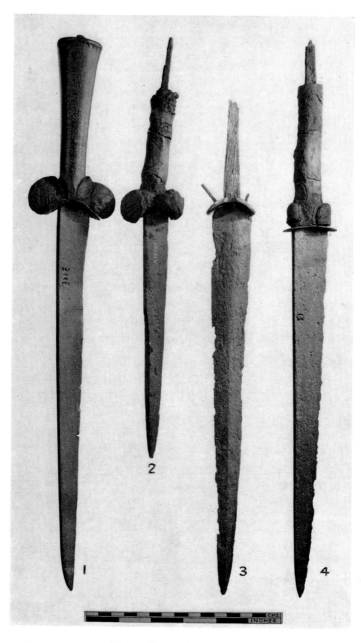

Kidney-daggers from London.
1, A 2445; 2, A 15253; 3, A 15254; 4, A 12138.

Fig. 9, No. 7, illustrates a form which appears with remarkable consistency on a great many brasses between c. 1390 and 1410. An early example is that of Robert Russell, d. 1390, at Strensham, Worcs ; a late one, that of Thomas de Crewe, d. 1411, at Wixford, Warwick. In practically every case the grip is fastened with spiral binding. Hexagonally or octagonally-faceted conical pommels are also found (Fig. 9, Nos. 8 and 10), and a later specimen with tubular rivets is shown on the brass of Simon Norwyche, d. 1476, at Brampton-by-Dingley, Northants.

Another consistent form of dagger-pommel (Fig. 9, No. 11) copies the contemporary " scent-stopper " sword-pommel, Type XI (see p. 31). It is particularly common in the decade 1415–25, e.g. on the brasses of Walter Cookesay, d. 1415, at Kidderminster, Worcs, and of John Chetwode, junior, d. 1420, at Warkworth, Northants ; but there is an example as late as 1441 on the brass of Sir Hugh Halsham at West Grinstead, Sussex. All these have plain or spirally-bound grips, but tubular-riveted grips are found with pommels of a presumably derivative, biconical form on brasses of c. 1440–50, e.g. of Robert Greyndon, d. 1443, at Newlands, Glos, and of John Daundelyon, d. 1445, at Margate, Kent.

Rondel-daggers with spherical pommels are found throughout the 15th century. The great majority of these have tubular rivets, which seem to appear first on this type of dagger. The effigy of Sir John de Cobham, d. 1407, at Cobham, Kent, has however a plain grip. Early examples with tubular rivets can be seen on the brasses of Sir John Lysle, d. 1407, at Thruxton, Cambs, and of Sir Arnold Savage, d. 1410, at Bobbing, Kent. Towards the end of the century the pommel begins to taper slightly upwards, cf. the brasses of an unknown person, c. 1470–80, at Sotterley, Suffolk (circular), and of Ralph Blenerhayset, d. 1475, at Frenze, Norfolk.

Cylindrical pommels seem to be characteristic of the mid-15th century. They normally have tubular-rivets, but that on the brass of William Prelatte, d. 1462, at Cirencester, Glos, has a spiral grip ; and the same is true of a dagger, similar, but with a projecting rivet at the end of the pommel, on the brass of Henry Grene, d. 1467, at Lowick, Northants, *cf.* that of Robert Russell, d. 1502, at Strensham, Worcs.

True rondel-daggers, with pommel and guard alike con-

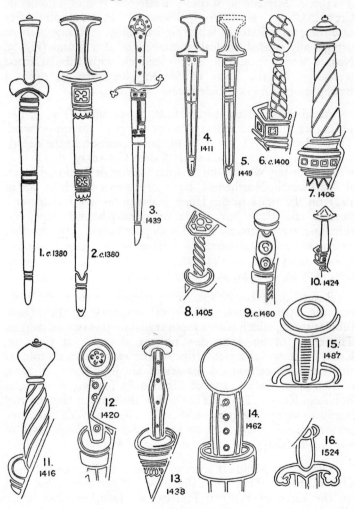

FIG. 9.—Representation of daggers on contemporary brasses.
(For list, see opposite page.)

sisting of a plain disc, are not commonly represented on brasses. They seem to belong to the latter part of the century. Examples can be seen on the brasses of Sir Walter Mauntell, d. 1487, at Heyford, Northants (Fig. 9, No. 15), and of John Boville, d. 1467, at Stokerston, Leicestershire (with tubular rivets).

A 1396. Rondel-dagger, single-edged blade. The guard and pommel are both formed of circular plates of metal originally alternate with some perishable material, the guard having two plates of brass and one of pewter, the pommel one of each. The larger faces of the tang are bound with brass strips, and the grip was fastened by five solid brass rivets. Over-all length 17·2 in., blade 12·2 in. Pl. VIII, No. 4. (G. Laking, *European Armour and Arms*, III, Fig. 782.) From Broken Wharf, Thames Street.

A 1397. Part of a dagger of composite type. Blade (broken) double-edged, save for a ricasso at the head. The pommel and quillons, of iron, are circular, but there were originally two quillons projecting slightly downward. The wooden grip, held by three unequal tubular brass rivets, widens in the middle in the characteristic mid-15th century manner. The edge of the tang is gilt and rilled diagonally. Length of hilt 4·9 in. From Finsbury Circus.

A. 1773. Rondel-dagger. Short single-edged blade, tubular wooden grip, hexagonal wooden pommel plated above with pewter, hexagonal wooden guard plated above with pewter, below with brass. Maker's mark on blade.

FIG. 9

Nos. 1–2. Brass of two civilians at King's Somborne, Hants.

No. 3.   Brass of Edward fforde at Swainswick, Somerset.

No. 4.   Brass of John Barstaple in the Trinity and Barstaple Almshouses, Bristol.

No. 5.   Brass of John Quek at Birchington, Kent.

No. 6.   Brass of William Willoughby at Spilsby, Lincs.

No. 7.   Brass of Thomas de Beauchamp, Earl of Warwick, in St. Mary's Church, Warwick.

No. 8.   Brass of Thomas de Ereville at Little Shelford, Cambs.

No..9.   Brass of an unknown man at Great Thurlow, Essex.

No. 10.   Brass of Robert Hayton at All Saints, Theddlethorpe, Lincs.

No. 11.   Brass of Sir Symon Felbrig at Felbrigg, Norfolk.

No. 12.   Brass of Sir Arnold Savage at Bobbing, Kent.

No. 13.   Brass of Sir Brian de Stapilton at Ingham, Norfolk.

No. 14.   Brass of Sir Thomas Grene at Green's Norton, Northants.

No. 15.   Brass of Sir Walter Mauntell at Heyford, Northants.

No. 16.   Brass of Philip Chatwyn at Alverchurch, Warwickshire.

Over-all length 12·2 in., blade 7·1 in.   Pl. VIII, No. 5.   (G. Laking, *European Armour and Arms*, III, Fig. 783.)   From Horseferry Road.

A 1776.   Part of a rondel-dagger.   Single-edged blade (broken), pommel missing, guard made of two iron plates, wooden grip fastened with three solid rivets.   The grip swells in the middle in the mid-15th century manner.   *Cf.* A 1397.   From Broadway, Westminster.

A 1968.   Rondel-dagger, triangular blade.   The guard and pommel are both formed of two hexagonal plates, the uppermost plate of the pommel being slightly pyramidal.   The edge of the tang is gilt and rilled diagonally, *cf.* A 1397.   The grip (missing ; in Pl. VIII it is restored) was held by four large brass tubular rivets.   Maker's mark on blade.   Mid 15th century.   Over-all length 19·0 in., blade 14·7 in.   Pl. VIII, No. 1.   (G. Laking, *European Armour and Arms*, III, Fig. 770.   *Cf.* the dagger shown in the St. William window, York Minster, *c.* 1421.   J. A. Knowles, *York Glass-Painting*, Fig. 38 (*a*).)   From Broken Wharf, Thames Street.

A 10428.   Rondel-dagger, single-edged blade (broken).   Guard and pommel alike are made of two convex plates, and the pommel is bolted in place by a brass knob.   Maker's mark on blade.   *Cf.* A 16826, probably late 15th century.   Length of hilt 4·4 in.   From Westminster.

A 15252.   Rondel-dagger, single-edged blade, back at first flat then ridged.   Guard and pommel alike made of octagonal plates of leather between plates of metal, of which the brass plate at the base of the guard alone remains.   Maker's mark on blade.   Over-all length 12·3 in., blade 7·2 in.   From Blomfield Street, London Wall.

A 16824.   Rondel-dagger, stout single-edged blade.   Circular, laminated guard and pommel ; of the pommel only the convex, iron upper plate remains, of the guard an upper plate of bone and one below of brass.   Wooden grip held by plain rivets.   Maker's mark inlaid in bronze on the blade.   Over-all length 10·4 in., blade 5·9 in.   From London.

A 16825.   Blade and hexagonal brass rondel-plate from a dagger.   Single-edged blade, with maker's mark outlined in brass on the plate.   Over-all length 14·9 in., blade 9·9 in.   From London.

A 16826.   Rondel-dagger, single-edged blade.   Guard and pommel each formed of two iron plates.   *Cf.* A 10428, probably late 15th-century.   Over-all length 16·0 in., blade 11·5 in.   Pl. VIII, No. 6.   From London.

A 17636.   Blade and circular brass rondel-plate from a dagger.   The blade is of an uneven diamond section.   Over-all length 13·85 in., blade 9·6 in.   From London.

A 22517.   Hilt and part of the blade of a rondel-dagger.   Stout, single-edged blade with an indecipherable maker's mark inlaid in base metal.   Pommel, grip, and guard are fastened by tubular brass rivets, and the junction of the two halves of pommel and grip is covered by a strip of brass.   Length of hilt 5·5 in.   Pl. VIII, No. 3.   From Finsbury Circus.

A 26278.   Blade and one circular iron rondel-plate of a dagger.   The blade is single-edged with a maker's mark inlaid in base metal.   When found

46

the rondel-plate retained the two small brass pins which joined it to the other plates of the guard. Over-all length 11·45 in., blade 6·95 in. From the Thames, Temple Stairs.

C 730. Rondel-dagger, single-edged blade. The guard is formed of two slightly convex, roughly octagonal iron plates ; the pommel is similar, with four projecting rivets and a knob on the end of the tang. Remains of wooden grip, fastened by three plain rivets ; the junction of the two halves was covered by an iron strip with serrated edges soldered on to the tang. *c.* 1400. Over-all length 14·4 in., blade 9·7 in. Pl. VIII, No. 2. (G. Laking, *European Armour and Arms*, III, Fig. 767.) From Walthamstow.

30.86. Rondel-dagger, much corroded. Single-edged blade, pommel a flattened sphere formed of two plates, the uppermost having a radiating pattern. Form of guard not recognizable. Over-all length (defective) 14·2 in., hilt 4·3 in.

37·99. Large rondel-dagger of a type approaching the baselard. Single-edged blade. Pommel and guard each made of two convex metal plates. Remains of wooden grip fastened by four large tubular brass rivets ; it swells at the centre, *cf.* A 1397 and A 1776. The joint of the two halves of the grip is covered by a diagonally rilled binding up the edges of the tang, *cf.* A 1397 and A 1968. Mid-15th century. Over-all length, 26.6 in., blade 21·5 in. Pl. X, No. 3 ; Fig. 10, No. 5. From the Thames, London. Bequeathed by G. Ward, Esq.

(iii) *Kidney-daggers*

The kidney-dagger is only occasionally found in a military context, *e.g.* on the effigies of Peter de Grandison, d. 1358, in Hereford Cathedral (Fig. 8, No. 4), and of John Fitz-Alan, Duke of Arundel, 1434, at Arundel (C. A. Stothard, *Monumental Effigies*, Pl. 119). It was almost exclusively a civilian weapon and had normally the single-edge of the civilian knife-dagger. The type had a very long life. It is worn by an archer in the Luttrell Psalter, *c.* 1335–40 (f. 45), and there is a fine example, in an ornate leather scabbard of the mid-14th century, in the National Museum at Copenhagen. After the middle of the century representations are frequent. Fig. 9, Nos. 1–2, illustrates the daggers carried by two civilians on a brass, *c.* 1380, at King's Somborne, Hants. It was evidently interchangeable with the baselard, also a civilian weapon ; and the form of this dagger differs in no essential from those illustrated in such early 15th-century manuscripts as the celebrated *Book of Hours of the Duc de Berri* (*Archæologia*, LX, 1907, 429, Fig. 3) or the Flemish *Travels of Sir John Mandeville* (British Museum Add. MSS. 24, 189).

The "kidneys" in this country are normally of wood riveted on to a transverse metal plate. A variant with metal "kidneys" seems to be foreign. It is particularly common in Scandinavia.

A 313. Fragment of the hilt of a kidney-dagger, made of jet. From Westminster. Fig. 10, No. 8.

A 1953. Straight, single-edged dagger-blade, probably from a kidney-dagger. Maker's mark on the blade. When found a fragment of the wooden grip remained on the tang. Over-all length 13·75 in., blade 9·75 in. From the Thames, Westminster.

A. 2445. Kidney-dagger. Single-edged blade, slightly curved, wooden "kidneys" and grip carved in one piece. The "kidneys" are attached to a brass quillon-plate, and there is a brass rivet at the end of the tang. Maker's mark on blade. Over-all length 16·3 in., blade 11·5 in. Pl. IX, No. 1. From Broken Wharf, Thames Street. (G. Laking, *European Armour and Arms*, III, Fig. 799.)

A 12138. Kidney-dagger. Single-edged blade with punched decoration at the top, steel quillon-plate and remains of wooden grip. Pommel missing. Maker's mark on blade. Over-all length 16·2 in., blade 10·8 in. Pl. IX, No. 4. From the Thames, Kingston.

A 13943. Kidney-dagger, two-edged blade of diamond section, steel quillon-plate with downward projections, grip missing. Over-all length 11·7 in., blade 7·4 in. *Cf.* G. Laking, *European Armour and Arms*, III, Fig. 796. From Craven Street.

A 15253. Kidney-dagger, straight, single-edged blade, flat at the back for the first 2·3 in., then tapering to a blunt back-edge. Wooden grip, "kidneys" separate, pommel missing. No quillon-plate. Over-all length 12·15 in., blade 7·24 in. Pl. IX, No. 2. From Fresh Wharf, Thames Street.

A 15254. Single-edged blade, probably of a kidney-dagger. Maker's mark. Over-all length 13·6 in., blade 9·0 in. Pl. IX, No. 3. From the Temple.

A 15464. Part of a kidney-dagger, two-edged blade of diamond section, tang broken, thick brass quillon-plate. Over-all length 14·5 in., blade 11·4 in. From the Thames, Wandsworth.

C 779. Small kidney-dagger, grip missing. Single-edged blade, strongly curved steel quillon plate. From the Thames, Millbank.

(iv) *Baselards*

The baselard is essentially a civilian weapon. It varies very considerably in size, but the form, with its H-shaped hilt, of which the quillons and pommel are often exactly balanced, is singularly constant. It seems to have had a life

48

PLATE X.

Baselard and other daggers of baselard type from London.
1, A 1780; 2, A 3092; 3, 37.99; 4, A 15251.

PLATE XI. [*To face p.* 49.

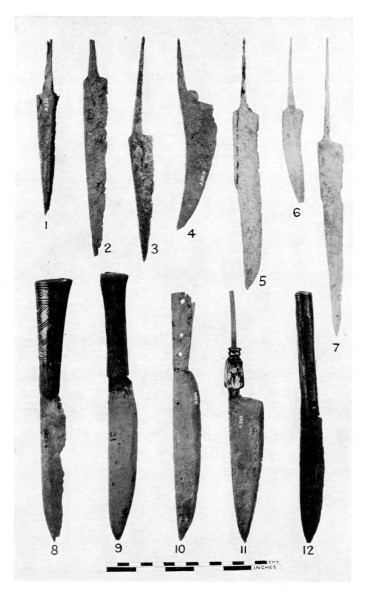

Knives from London.
1, A 236; 2, A 310; 3, A 19553; 4, A 2919; 5, C 741; 6, A 22491;
7, A 28248; 8, A 12590; 9, A 3041; 10, A 704; 11, A 349; 12, A 482.

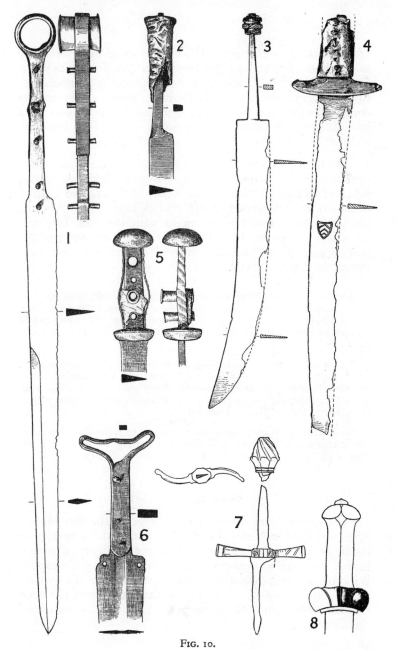

FIG. 10.

Medieval daggers from London (Nos. 1–6 and 8) and from Bosworth Field (No. 7) (⅓).

49

of rather under a century. The earliest dated examples seem to be those depicted on the brass of a civilian (*ob.* 1370) at Shottesbrook, Berks, and on a brass, probably ascribable to Roger Digges (*ob.* 1375), at Barham, Kent. They appear commonly between 1380 and 1420, and exceptionally at a later date, *e.g.* the brass of Peter Stone (*ob.* 1442) at Margate, and that of John Quek (*ob.* 1449) at Birchington.

The term " baselard " is here for convenience of reference restricted to the particular form of weapon described above, although in contemporary usage it may well have had a wider connotation. Weapons such as A 3092 and A 15251 obviously have much in common with the true baselard. They lack, however, the characteristic hilt, and are perhaps best described as " baselard-knives." They are here considered in the next section.

A 16643. Baselard, much damaged. Single-edged blade, point missing, inlaid in brass on one side with a shield of three chevrons, perhaps for Clare. Curved wooden quillons; corresponding pommel missing. Wooden grip held in place by iron rivets. Over-all length at present 17·4 in. Fig. 10, No. 4. From London Wall.

A 1780. Baselard. Blade two-edged with a shallow central groove. The tang is doubled over to form a T-shaped pommel, *cf.* a small baselard in the Guildhall Museum (G. Laking, *European Armour and Arms*, III, Fig. 751). Rivets for missing grip and quillons. Over-all length 31·75 in., blade 26·5 in. Pl. X, No. 1; Fig. 10, No. 6. From London.

For other weapons of the same general type, see 37·99 (*s.v.* Rondel-daggers) and A. 3092 and A. 15251 (*s.v.* Knife-daggers); also Fig. 10, No. 1. *Cf.* the brass of Sir Thomas Grene, d. 1461, at Green's Norton, Northants.

(v) *Knives and Knife-daggers*

The commonest form of civilian dagger in the later Middle Ages was the single-edged dagger, derived, with a greater or lesser degree of elaboration, from the ordinary domestic knife. In its most evolved form it was obviously a weapon. But often it was designed to combine the functions of a weapon and a domestic knife. It is only at the extremes of the scale that the distinction becomes more than a convenient means of classification.

(A) KNIVES

The basic forms of knife in use during the Middle Ages seem to have been few and simple. The primary type was evidently the Saxon scramasax-knife, which to judge from representations, survived relatively unaltered into the medieval period. In some cases the blade has become a short, straight-sided triangle of heavy, triangular section; but usually it retains the characteristic angle halfway down the back of the blade, as on the typical scramasax. Unfortunately most manuscript representations of knives seem to bear little detailed relation to the forms of surviving specimens; and it is hardly possible to say more than that this particular feature appears regularly right down to the 15th century. It can, for example, be seen very clearly in a Flemish early 15th-century manuscript of the Travels of Sir John Mandeville (British Museum Add. MSS. 24, 189); and it is found on several late 15th-century North German altars in Germany and Scandinavia. A derivative form with upturned point is so common in manuscript representations that it ought to represent a type in actual use; but surviving specimens are curiously elusive.

The other common medieval form of knife has a broader, more rounded blade. It is usually of narrower cross-section, and in many cases the pointed tang of the scramasax-knife is replaced by a strip-tang to which the two halves of the handle are fixed by transverse rivets. The earliest datable example comes from Rayleigh Castle, Essex, which had been abandoned by *c.* 1270, *Transactions of the Essex Archæological Society*, n.s., XII, 169, Fig. 4; and it does not seem to appear in manuscript drawings at an earlier date. A 12th-century date has been claimed for a specimen in the British Museum found in Southwark (*Antiquaries Journal*, XIV, 1934, 61) on the strength of the inlaid decoration on the blade; but the correctness of the attribution is open to doubt. Later this form appears commonly enough (*e.g.* in the Luttrell Psalter, ff. 90, 208; *cf.* f. 89, an angular scramasax-knife), and the fine carving-knives in the British Museum, which were made for John the Intrepid, Duke of Burgunday, between 1385 and 1404, are also of this form (O. M. Dalton, *Archæologia*, LX, 1907,

423 ff., with references to other datable, enamelled, 15th-century, Burgundian knives). It must be noted that in this case the blade of the carving-knives is considerably broader than that of the smaller knives which were used for eating; and although this particular distinction would probably only apply to the elaborate sets of knives demanded by courtly custom, other variations of type in surviving specimens may be due as much to differences of function as of date.

The smaller knives of the Duke of Burgundy's set already show a close approximation of shape to the types current in the early 16th-century. It is only upon certain features of form, *e.g.* the use of tubular rivets, or of decoration that 15th-century knives can with any confidence be distinguished. A feature which is apparently confined to medieval knives is the form of handle which appears on A 2989. This can clearly be seen in the Luttrell Psalter (f. 207); and in an elaborate form it appears on the Duke of Burgundy's knives. It was apparently current during the 14th and early 15th centuries.

(*a*) KNIVES OF SCRAMASAX FORM

A 236. Short scramasax-knife, plain triangular blade. Length 4·75 in. Pl. XI, No. 1. From London.

A 310. Scramasax-knife, plain triangular blade. Length (tang broken) 7·4 in. Pl. XI, No. 2. From Westminster.

A 19553. Short scramasax-knife, plain triangular blade. Length 7·5 in. Pl. XI, No. 3. From Steelyard.

A 2919. Short crescent-shaped knife. Length 6·5 in. Pl. XI, No. 4. From the Thames, Wandsworth.

C 741. Shouldered scramasax-knife. Length 8·5 in. Pl. XI, No. 5. From Moorfields.

A 22491. Short, shouldered scramasax-knife, maker's mark on blade. Length 5·6 in. Pl. XI, No. 6. From London.

A 28248. Slender, shouldered scramasax-knife, blade inlaid with bronze. Length 10·2 in. Pl. XI, No. 7. From London.

A 326. Short scramasax-knife with rough wooden handle. Length 5 in. Pl. XIII, No. 6. From Westminster.

A 13999. Knife, with heavy blade of unusual form and wooden handle. Length 7·4 in. Pl. XIII, No. 7. From Thames Street.

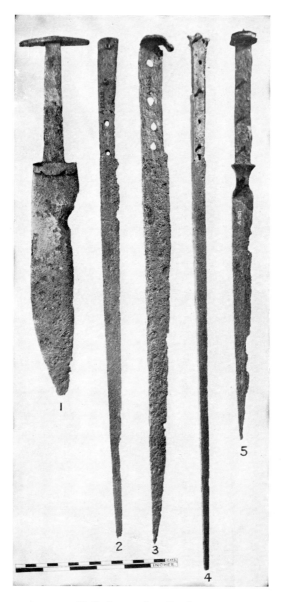

Knife-daggers from London.
1, A 4953; 2, A 12138; 3, A 4955; 4, A 358; 5, A 1951.

PLATE XIII. [To face p. 53.

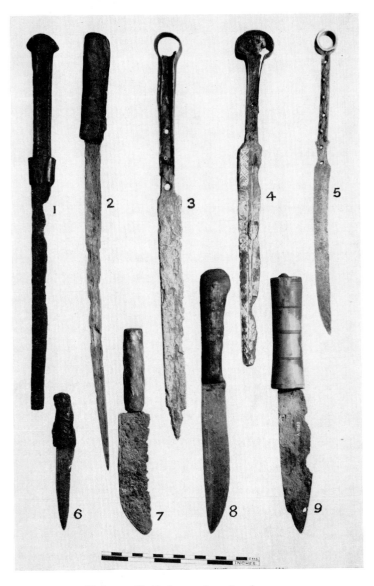

Knives and knife-daggers from London.
1, A 15255; 2, A 2362; 3, A 13924; 4, A 1955; 5, A 1952; 6, A 326;
7, A 13999; 8, A 2989; 9, A 13553.

(b) FULL-BLADED LATE MEDIEVAL KNIVES

A 2989. Knife, with flat tang and wooden handle. Bronze inlaid ornament on blade. Length 9·4 in. Pl. XIII, No. 8. From London.

A 13553. Knife, with pointed tang and turned wooden handle. Maker's mark on blade. Length 9 in. Pl. XIII, No. 9. From Whitecross Street.

A 12590. Knife, with pointed tang and decorated bone handle. Maker's mark on blade. Length 8·75 in. Pl. XI, No. 8. From Whitecross Street.

A 3041. Knife, with pointed tang and wooden handle. Maker's mark on blade. Length 9 in. Pl. XI, No. 9. From Worship Street.

A 704. Knife, with flat tang, handle missing. Maker's mark on blade. Length 8·25 in. Pl. XI, No. 10. From Copthall Court, E.C.

A 349. Knife, with pointed tang and the remains of a bone handle with bronze fittings. The blade is unusually broad. Length 8·4 in. Pl. XI, No. 11. From Farringdon Street.

A 482. Knife, with flat tang and bone handle, decorated with dot-and-circle ornament. Length 8·4 in. Pl. XI, No. 12. From Westminster.

(B) KNIFE-DAGGERS

The double character of many of these daggers assured the retention in almost all cases of the simple triangular-sectioned blade of the scramasax-knife, which was developed simply in the direction of increasing length. Even in the longest examples the hilt is often extremely simple. On the other hand, some of the 15th-century specimens are very elaborate ; and certain forms of hilt, *e.g.* those with a recess on either side at the base, as A 1951–2, are peculiar to this type of dagger. It is to this class of dagger that the great majority of the surviving leather sheaths belong. These are in the main of the 14th and 15th centuries ; but early specimens are known.

A 358. Slender, single-edged knife-dagger. The tang ends in a fish-tail ; it is bound with a strip of brass along either edge. The grip, which is missing, was secured by solid brass rivets. Over-all length 18·5 in., blade 14·3 in. Pl. XII, No. 4. From Westminster.

A 1951. Single-edged knife-dagger, with an octagonal rondel-pommel formed of two brass plates. The grip, which is missing, was secured by iron rivets ; a small portion of the recessed wooden feature at the base of the grip remains (*cf.* A 1952). Over-all length 14·0 in., blade 8·6 in. Pl. XII, No. 5. From the Thames, Westminster.

A 1952. Singled-edged knife-dagger, blade slightly curved. The pommel is formed of a very large tubular rivet. Solid brass rivets secured the grip to the tang, the base of which is shaped as A 1951. Over-all length 10·9 in., blade 6·0 in. Pl. XIII, No. 5. From the Thames, Westminster.

A 1955. Elaborate knife-dagger. The blade, which is of the same form as that of several quillon-daggers (cf. Pl. VII, Nos. 4 and 5), is decorated with engraved bronze plating, and the grip is similarly bound. Over-all length 11·8 in., blade (point missing) 8·0 in. First half of the 14th century. Pl. XIII, No. 4, and Pl. XIV (detail of the ornament on the blade). From London.

A 2362. Knife-dagger with long, slender, curving, single-edged blade. Plain wooden handle fastened by a brass rivet at the end of the tang. Over-all length 14·8 in., blade 11·5 in. Pl. XIII, No. 2. From Smithfield.

A 3092. Baselard-knife. Single-edged blade with two shallow fluted channels on one face, plain on the other. Wooden grip and short transverse pommel. "Quillons" missing, probably equally rudimentary. Over-all length 29·1 in., blade 24·2 in. Pl. X, No. 2. From Cannon Street.

A 3134. Fragment of tang and blade of a knife-dagger. One face of the blade is inlaid with two rows of small brass crosses. From London.

A 4953. Baselard-knife. The single-edged blade is unusually short and broad. Pommel a separate cross-piece. It is not clear whether there were corresponding quillons. Over-all length 12·2 in., blade 8·0 in. Pl. XII, No. 1. From the Savoy.

A 4955. Single-edged knife-dagger. The curving pommel is welded across the end. The find-spot suggests a 15th-century date. Over-all length 17·6 in., blade 13·8 in. Pl. XII, No. 3. From Finsbury Circus.

A 12138. Single-edged knife-dagger, similar to A 4955, but more slender. Small tubular brass rivets. Over-all length 17·3 in., blade 13·3 in. Pl. XII, No. 2. From the Thames, Kingston.

A 13924. Single-edged knife-dagger. The edges of the tang are bound with a strip of brass which swells to accommodate a circular pommel. This probably had a large brass tubular rivet in the centre (as A 1952), and the grip was attached by smaller rivets of the same sort. Pl. XIII, No. 3. From Fenchurch Street.

A 15251. Large, single-edged baselard-knife. Part of the round wooden grip remains; it is featureless save for a swelling towards the pommel-end. Over-all length 26·4 in., blade 21·4 in. Pl. X, No. 4, Fig. 10, No. 2. From Fresh Wharf, Thames Street.

A 15255. Single-edged knife-dagger. The wooden grip is evidently derivative from that of the kidney-dagger; the edges are bound with brass, and the grip is secured by solid brass rivets. Over-all length 13·0 in., blade (damaged) 7·9 in. Pl. XIII, No. 1. From Steelyard.

39.141. Single-edged knife with a curved blade, short tang and a bone pommel. Probably a hunting knife. Over-all length 16·8 in., blade 12·2 in. Fig. 10, No. 3. From London. Lent by the Littlehampton Museum.

Also illustrated:

Fig. 10, No. 1 (in the British Museum). Large knife-dagger, blade at first single-edged then of blunted diamond section (*cf.* A 1955). The grip was fastened by solid bronze rivets and the pommel is formed by an enormous tubular bronze rivet. There was evidently a feature at the base of the grip, probably as on A 1951 and A 1952. Over-all length 25·9 in., blade 18·3 in. Mid-15th century. Found in London, together with a portion of its decorated leather scabbard.

Pl. XIV, *left* (in the British Museum). Single-edged knife-dagger, almost identical with A 1951, but retaining the elaborately engraved fittings of the grip and pommel. From London.

AXES

(i) *Woodmen's Axes*

The woodman's axe (Type I) is a simple and efficient tool which has retained a more or less stereotyped form since the Roman period (*London in Roman Times* (*London Museum Catalogue*), Pl. XXXIV, 7 and 8; *London and the Vikings* (*London Museum Catalogue*), Fig. 8, 1 and 2). It is only upon certain detailed features, *e.g.* the approximation in shape of the socket

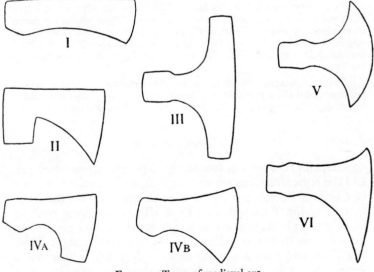

FIG. 11.—Types of medieval axe.

to other known medieval types, that individual specimens can be assigned with any confidence to the medieval period. As a general rule it would seem that the medieval axe is a larger tool than its predecessors, and that it normally had a simple socket, lacking the projecting hammer-end of many Roman examples. The butt-end could, however, if necessary be used, *cf.* an illustration in the Bible of St. Etienne Harding, *c.* 1100, in which such an axe is being used with a heavy mallet to split a log (C. Oursel, *La Miniature du XII Siècle à l'Abbaye de Cîteaux*, Pl. XXV); and in another form the axe-hammer is a known medieval tool.

A 1476. Maximum length 10·75 in., breadth at cutting edge 4·3 in. The socket has the same projecting downward wings as the axes of Type IV. Maker's mark **T** on both cheeks. Fig. 14, No. 4. From the Thames opposite the Tower.

A 2276. Maximum length 9·0 in., breadth at cutting edge 3·35 in. Socket as A 1476. Maker's mark on left cheek. From the Thames at Hammersmith.

A 13508. Maximum length 8·75 in., breadth at cutting edge 2·15 in. Very solidly made with curved wings projecting above and below the socket. Fig. 12, No. 4. From London Wall.

B 320. Maximum length 6·9 in., breadth at cutting edge 2·1 in. The blade curves downwards and the socket has a very slight tubular projection downwards. A woodman's axe with a more pronounced tubular socket from Ragnhildsholmen in Sweden (National Museum, Stockholm) can be dated between A.D. 1257 and 1308. Fig. 12, No. 1. From the Thames opposite the Tower.

A 13787. Maximum length 6·4 in., breadth at cutting edge 3·5 in. It has a pronounced tubular socket (*cf.* B 320 above), and the cutting edge is unusually broad, approximating to Type II. Fig. 12, No. 2. From Milton Street.

(ii) *Carpenters' Axes*

Carpenters' axes are frequently depicted in medieval art, and the representations are at least sufficiently detailed to show that certain stereotyped forms were in use. By far the commonest is the T-shaped axe (Type III), whose long straight blade was well adapted for such light work as dressing timber. Less common, but consistent, is the roughly straight-sided, triangular axe with a tubular socket (Type II), which was a more solid tool. Occasionally other forms are represented in

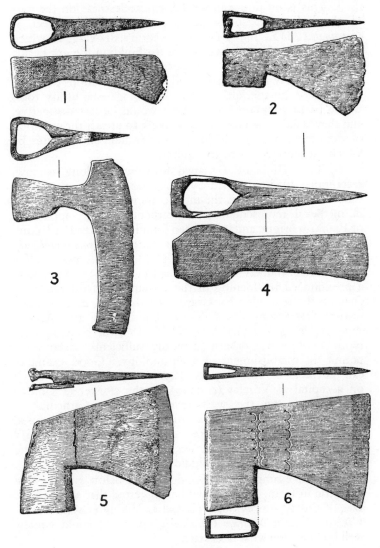

FIG. 12.—Medieval axes from London.
1, B 320; 2, A 13787; 3, A 10398; 4, A 13508; 5, B 318; 6, A 15341 (¼).

use. This is no doubt often due to carelessness on the part of the artist, but sometimes (*e.g. British Museum facs. of Illuminated MSS.*, 169, a late 13th-century drawing, in which an axe of Type V is shown in use for building the ark beside carefully drawn examples of Types II and III) these representations are clearly intentional ; and it is on all grounds probable that besides the specialized types certain general-utility tools would be in common use. These would be less distinctive, and they would therefore be less likely to attract the attention of the artist ; nor would his picture contain any features by which their use could be recognized.

(i) Type III is of T-shaped form, with a long, narrow, rectangular blade attached by a slender shank to the short, tubular socket. This is the most common type of axe shown in medieval representations of carpentry. It is apparently of Frankish origin, and it has been found in England in Viking associations (*London and the Vikings (London Museum Catalogue*), p. 24, Figs. 6 and 8, Type II), although it is not itself a recognized Scandinavian type. It had a long life ; and although a pronounced broadening of the extremities of the blade, by curving the rear edge backwards at either end, may be a late feature (Holkham MS. 666, the building of the Ark, *c.* 1325–50, *Walpole Society*, Vol. XI, Pl. IV), the contemporary representations are otherwise hardly sufficiently detailed to permit the establishment of a chronology. Good examples can be seen in the Bayeux Tapestry (late 11th century), on a capital at Vézelay (*c.* 1130), in the cloister at Gerona (*c.* 1150–70), on the west front of Wells Cathedral (*c.* 1235–40), in the Maciejowski Bible, f. 2b, where it is used for dressing planks (*c.* 1250), and in a late 13th-century Moralized Bible (*British Museum facs.* 169). It does not seem to be found much after the middle of the 14th century.

The one example from London listed below is somewhat eccentric in form. But it may be suggested that some of the axes of this type previously classed as Viking (*London and the Vikings (London Museum Catalogue*), pp. 25–6) could equally well be of a somewhat later date.

A 10398. Length of blade 7·5 in., length from blade to socket 5·2 in. The lower arm of the T is exceptionally long, the upper arm vestigial. Fig. 12, No. 3. From London.

(ii) Type II has a triangular blade and tubular socket. The socket is long and projects downwards, usually slightly pentagonal in section. The upper edge of the blade is straight and inclined slightly upwards, the lower edge is concave and curves sharply downwards.

This type of axe is common in representations of carpentry from the 13th to the 16th centuries, *e.g.* Maciejowski Bible, ff. 2b and 3b (*c.* 1250); *British Museum facs. of Illuminated MSS.*, 169 (late 13th century); *Proc. Hants Field Club*, VIII, p. 167 (a late 15th-century Miserere at Christchurch, Hants); *Twenty-Five Years of the London Museum*, Pl. XXX (a fresco from Carpenters' Hall, London, early 16th century).

A 1777. Maximum length 9·6 in., breadth at cutting edge 6·2 in. From the Thames opposite the Tower.

A 1941. Maximum length 6·1 in., breadth at cutting edge 3·9 in. From Thames Street.

A 2278. Maximum length 7·6 in., breadth at cutting edge 7·1 in.; the form is more curved than is usual in this type. Maker's mark, a four-petaled flower, on right cheek. Fig. 14, No. 1. From the Thames.

A 5472. Maximum length 6·25 in., breadth at cutting edge 4·65 in. From the Thames at Putney.

A 13788. Maximum length 6·0 in., breadth at cutting edge 3·8 in. From Milton Street.

A 13939. Maximum length 7·4 in., breadth at cutting edge 4·85 in. From Bermondsey.

A 15341. Maximum length 7·35 in., breadth at cutting edge 4·85 in. Ornamented with three lines of engrailed pattern on the right cheek. Fig. 12, No. 6. From the Thames at Lambeth.

B 318. Maximum length 6·6 in., breadth at cutting edge 4·85 in. Upper edge of blade inclined sharply upwards. The socket has a V-shaped slit in the back, the edges of which have been hammered over. Fig. 12, No. 5. From the Thames opposite the Tower.

B 319. Maximum length 4·75 in., breadth at cutting edge 3·9 in. Upper edge of blade inclined sharply upwards. From the Thames opposite the Tower.

(iii) *" Bearded " Axes and Derivatives*

At least one other class of axe is sufficiently constant to merit special classification. Its significance is best understood by a comparison of the three examples illustrated in Fig. 13, Nos.

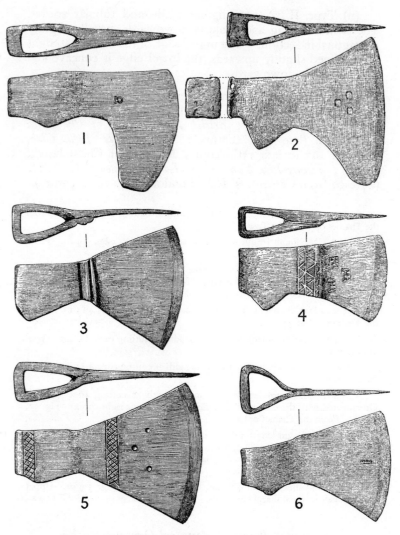

FIG. 13.—" Bearded " axes and derivative forms from London.
1, A 13507; 2, A 675; 3, A 13949; 4, B 371; 5, A 11812; 6, A 2277 (¼).

3–5. Fig. 13, No. 3, shows very clearly the method of manufacture. The socket was formed in the simplest way possible
by folding the tail of the axe over and welding it against one
cheek to form a loop. A well-defined ridge just in front of
the point of junction is clearly intended to protect this weak
point. Fig. 13, No. 4, illustrates this ridge still functional,
but serving also as a basis for decoration; while in Fig. 13,
No. 5, the ridge has vanished leaving only the now meaningless
decoration.

Axes of this type are clearly a cheap alternative to more
solidly made tools of wedge-shaped section, such as A 7673
(Fig. 14, No. 3). The origin of this latter type can, in the
absence of archæologically dated specimens, only be a matter
of conjecture. The pronounced downward projection of
the blade, however, strongly suggests a derivation from the
" bearded " form illustrated in Fig. 13, No. 1. In Scandinavia the " bearded " axe, a well-known Viking type, does
not seem to have outlasted the 10th century (*London and the
Vikings* (*London Museum Catalogue*), pp. 24–5). Elsewhere,
however, it undoubtedly continued in use. Fine examples
are to be seen on the 12th-century Tournai marble font at
Winchester and on a capital of the same century at L'Ile
Bouchard, Indre-et-Loire; and towards the close of the
Middle Ages the " bearded " axe once more becomes
common. Fig. 13, No. 2, represents a form transitional from
the " bearded " axe to the later type.

The derivative type presents no features sufficiently
striking for its identification in contemporary representations.
The frequency, however, with which it occurs and the poor
workmanship of many specimens alike suggest that it was a
cheap, general-utility tool for civil use.

A 13507. " Bearded " axe. Maximum length 7·6 in., breadth across blade
5·2 in. Winged socket and heavy square hammer-butt. Maker's mark on right
cheek. Fig. 13, No. 1. From London Wall.

A 675. " Bearded " axe of a type transitional to the succeeding examples.
Maximum length 7·0 in., breadth across blade 6·45 in. Strongly winged socket
and heavy square hammer-butt. Maker's mark, three recessed squares, on
right cheek. Fig. 13, No. 2. From Westminster.

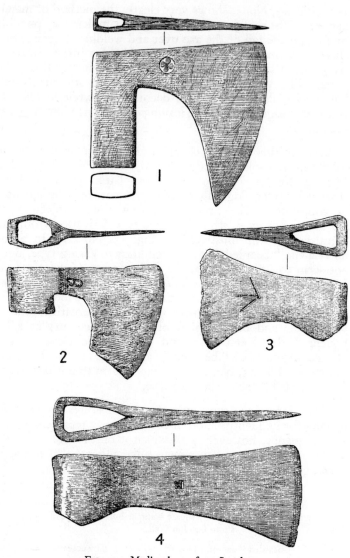

FIG. 14.—Medieval axes from London.
1, A 2278; 2, A 11467; 3, A 7673; 4, A 1476 (¼).

A 7673. Axe of Type IV. Maximum length 6·5 in., breadth across blade 4·4 in. Well-made socket on the axis of the blade. Maker's mark, a broad arrow, on the left cheek. Fig. 14, No. 3. From Westminster.

A 13949. Axe of Type IV. Maximum length 7·55 in., breadth across blade 5·3 in. Socket folded over against right cheek, with a double ridge at the junction. Fig. 13, No. 3. From Thames Street.

B 371. Axe of Type IV. Maximum length 6·5 in., breadth across blade 3·75 in. Socket as A 13949 above, the junction being decorated with three recessed zigzag lines. Maker's mark three times repeated, on right cheek. Fig. 13, No. 4. From the Thames, opposite the Tower of London.

A 11812. Axe of Type IV. Maximum length 8·3 in., breadth across blade 6·05 in. Blade unusually broad, socket folded over against right cheek. Band of incised lattice ornament across just in front of point of junction, another at back of socket, both on the right cheek. Maker's mark, three small stamped circles, on the right cheek. Fig. 13, No. 5. From Matthew Parker Street.

C 789. Axe of Type IV. Maximum length 7·3 in., breadth across blade 4·55 in. Socket as A 11812. No ornament. From London Wall.

A 2277. Axe of Type IV. Maximum length 6·55 in., breadth across blade 4·75 in. Socket folded over against left cheek. Maker's mark on right cheek. Fig. 13, No. 6. From the Thames at London.

A 11467. " Bearded " axe. Maximum length 6·8 in., breadth 5·0 in. Tubular socket, formed as in the preceding series by folding the butt-end over against the right cheek. The tubular socket is presumably an intrusive element from Type III. Indistinct maker's mark on right cheek. Fig. 14, No. 2. From Bankside, site of Globe Theatre.

(iv) *Battle-axes*

The axe was a common weapon of the Viking period ; and the battle-axes of the succeeding centuries strongly reflect the influence of Viking types. It may in fact well be doubted whether many of the surviving " Viking " axes do not really themselves belong to the 12th century. Axes of Viking, Type VI (*London and the Vikings* (*London Museum Catalogue*), p. 22) were admittedly current when the Bayeux tapestry was made ; and an even clearer example is to be seen in the Bible of St. Etienne Harding at Cîteaux (C. Oursel, *La Miniature du XII Siècle à l'Abbaye de Cîteaux*).

In Scandinavia the type lasted until a much later date, *e.g.* Mowinckel, *Vor Nationale Billedkunst : Middelalderen,* Fig. 34 (altar-front, 13th century, from ? Holtalen Church), Fig. 35 (altar-front, 14th century, from Kraefjord Church) ; see also S. Grieg, *Middelalderske Byfund fra Bergen og Oslo,* pp. 294-5. In this country fresh types were evolved. For medieval Type VI (Fig. 11) it is not easy to find a close parallel; but it is obviously a derivative of the Viking form. Type V is the ordinary battle-axe of medieval representations. Manuscript illustrations of axes are often plainly exaggerated; but this type can be seen very clearly in the trustworthy, mid-13th-century Maciejowski Bible, and again in the Luttrell

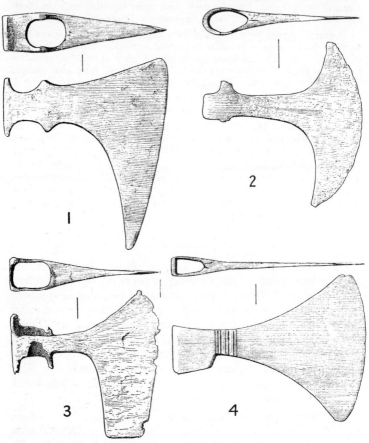

FIG. 15.—Battle-axes from London.

1, 2 and 4, battle-axes; 3, "bearded" axe. 1, A 4947; 2, A 14988; 3, 32.55; 4, A 1940 (¼).

Left: Hilt of elaborate knife-dagger from London ($\frac{1}{1}$).   (In the British Museum.)
Right: Detail of knife-dagger, A 1955 (see Pl. XIII), from London ($\frac{1}{1}$).

PLATE XV. [*To face p.* 65.

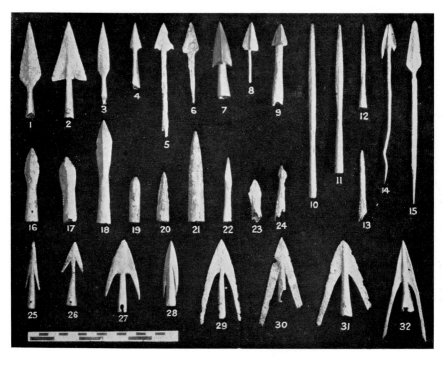

Medieval arrow-heads from London.

Psalter (*c.* 1335–40). It was probably evolved during the 13th century, for representations of battle-axes on early 13th-century enamelled Limoges caskets still retain much of the profile of the Viking prototype (*e.g. Archæologia*, LXXIX, 1929, Pl. XIX, 1–3).

Other types of axe were sometimes used in battle, particularly in the later Middle Ages, when all sorts of elaborate hafted weapons were evolved ; nor are these fighting-forms absolutely confined to warfare, *e.g. British Museum facs. of Illuminated MSS.* 169, an obviously reliable picture of 13th-century carpentry.

A 1940. Battle-axe, Type V, maximum length 8·5 in., breadth at cutting-edge 6·2 in. Fig. 15, No. 4. From Thames Street. Given by Sir Guy Laking, Bart.

A 14988. Battle-axe, Type V, maximum length 7·0 in., breadth at cutting-edge 6·8 in. Fig. 15, No. 2. From the Thames, Blackfriars.

A 4947. Heavy battle-axe, Type VI, maximum length 7·2 in., breadth at cutting-edge 8·3 in. Fig. 15, No. 1. From London.

32.55. " Bearded " axe, maximum length 6·4 in., breadth at cutting-edge 6·2 in. For the form of the socket *cf.* A 4947. Fig. 15, No. 3. From the Thames, London Bridge.

ARROW-HEADS

A variety of forms of arrow-head may be ascribed to the medieval period, but only in a few instances can they be given even an approximate date. A few have been found in this country in datable contexts ; and as the successive forms of the military arrow-head were closely determined by the development of defensive armour, which was roughly the same in all countries, the evidence of continental sites is probably broadly applicable in England. Contemporary representations, however, can hardly be expected to show much more than the presence or absence of barbs ; and even then there is often a possibility of conventionalization. The typology suggested in Fig. 16 is therefore based solely upon surviving examples, the medieval date of which can in certain cases only be regarded as proved. It may, however, serve as a convenient basis for classification.

In the later Middle Ages barbed arrow-heads were confined to the chase. The arrow used in battle had to be compact and heavy, if it was to penetrate the ever-increasing bulk of defensive armour. The Mass-Graves at Visby in

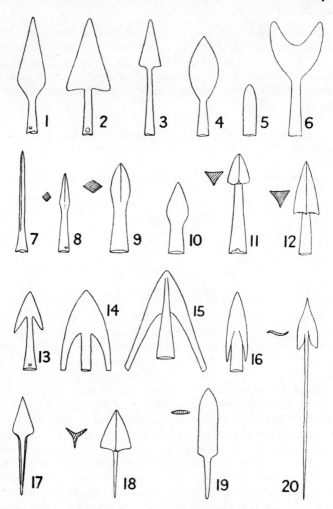

FIG. 16.—Types of medieval arrow-head.

Gotland give a clear view of 14th-century practice. In 1361, after a disastrous battle against the Danes, the citizens of Visby had to bury their dead, many of whom had received arrow wounds, armour and all, in great communal graves. The arrow-heads in the bodies with few exceptions belonged to Types 8 and 9. There was no single instance of a barbed arrow-head. At the other end of the scale the arrow-heads found on a purely civil site such as " King John's House," Tollard Royal, were mostly barbed (see A. Pitt-Rivers, *King John's House, Tollard Royal*, Pl. XX ; the finds, which were not closely dated individually, range from the 12th century onward). The same distinction can be seen in manuscript drawings, where it is almost exclusively to hunting-scenes that barbed arrow-heads are confined. It is, however, less marked in the 13th century. In the Maciejowski Bible for example, ff. 28b and 34b, barbed arrow-heads are shown in several battle-scenes. A comparison with the more pronounced barbs shown in the hunting-scenes of the same manuscript (*e.g.* f. 2a) shows that the representations are presumably intentional ; and it is therefore not necessary to consider as hunting-arrows early barbed examples such as that found on the purely military site of Dyserth Castle, Flint, occupied between the years 1241 and 1263 (*Archæologia Cambrensis*, 1915, p. 64). Barbed arrow-heads were probably used occasionally in battle as late as the 13th century ; but it is noticeable that even on early sites such as Dyserth Castle (1241–63) and Rayleigh Castle (pre-1270) they are in a minority.

The characteristic early-medieval military arrow-head had apparently a broad, flat blade with a marked shoulder (see Fig. 16, Types 1 and 2). This is a pre-conquest form which lasted on into, but probably not beyond, the 13th century. Already in the 13th century the later, more compact types have appeared in answer to the development of plate-armour ; and in the 14th century they alone are used.

The evolution of the barbed hunting-arrow is less clear. It may even be doubted whether it underwent any very coherent development. The more elaborate examples belong probably to the 14th and 15th centuries ; and it may possibly be significant that in a hunting-scene on a 12th-century (*c.* 1120–50) capital at St. Aignan, Loire-et-Cher, the arrow-head is very clearly of a broad, barbless form (P. Deschamps, *La sculpture française à l'époque romane*, Pl. 65). Even at a later date barbless arrows are occasionally so used, *e.g.* in a Book of Hours of the use of Sarum, *c.* 1330 (*Catalogue of the Burlington Fine Arts Club Exhibition*, 1908, Pl. 58), where the arrow is of the same form as one used at archery in the Luttrell Psalter, f. 147; *cf.* ff. 45 and 54. Barbed arrow-heads were, however, undoubtedly normal for hunting from the 13th century onwards.

Types 1–4.—Socketed arrow-heads with leaf-shaped or angular blades are fairly well dated to the earlier part of the Middle Ages, although a certain number may well be earlier as they are found also in Frankish graves. In this country arrow-heads approximating to Types 1 and 2 have been found in a 12th-century context at Cæsar's Camp, Folkestone (Fig. 17, No. 1) and at Marlborough (Fig. 17, No. 2), and from the 13th-century at Rayleigh Castle, Essex (Fig. 17, Nos. 3 and 5); *cf.* Fig. 17, Nos. 18 and 20, from Ragnhildsholmen, Sweden (1257–1308). Type 3 is a specialized 13th-century form; *cf.* Fig. 17, No. 12, from Dyserth Castle, Flint (1241–63); and Type 4 can be paralleled at Alsnö Hus, Sweden, a site from which a few objects belong to the late 13th century.

Type 5.—Bullet-shaped arrow-heads of this form were used with the cross-bow; *cf.* the complete arrow preserved in the British Museum. It probably represents the ultimate development of Types 7–9.

Type 6.—A hunting arrow-head of uncertain, but probably medieval, date.

Types 7–9 seem to have been developed in answer to the increasing use of defensive armour, which demanded a weapon slender enough to enter any crack, but at least sufficiently heavy to pierce cloth or leather. The transition from the earlier, bladed forms evidently took place during the 13th century, for both sorts of arrow-head are found together on two dated military sites in this country, at Rayleigh Castle, Essex, abandoned *c.* 1270 (Fig. 17, Nos. 3–7), and at Dyserth Castle, Flint, occupied 1241–63 (Fig. 17, Nos. 8–17). The same is true of the Swedish site of Ragnhildsholmen, occupied

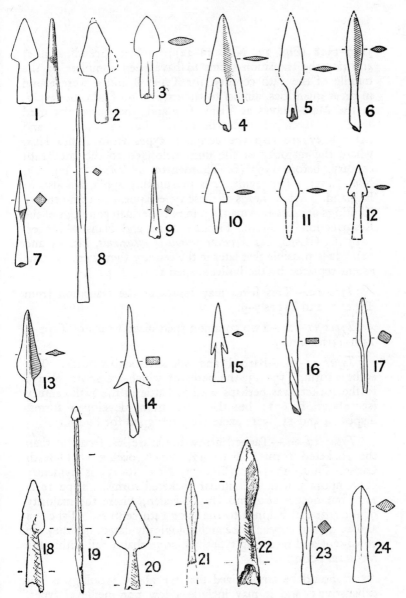

FIG. 17.—Archæologically dated medieval arrow-heads (see p. 73).
1–2, 12th century; 3–7, before c. 1270; 8–17, 1241–63; 18–22, 1257–1308; 23–4, 1361 (½).

1257–1308 (Fig. 17, Nos. 18–22); and in Scandinavia at any rate the transition seems to have been complete by the middle of the 14th century, for Types 8 and 9 were found in great quantities, almost to the exclusion of all other types, in the Mass-Graves at Visby, Gotland (the burial-pits used after the battle of Visby in 1361. Fig. 17, Nos. 23 and 24). They are also the common types from Alsnö Hus, where the majority of the finds belonged to the later 14th century, before 1390 (B. Thordeman, *Alsnö Hus*, Fig. 27, Nos. 14–5). This evidence is presumably applicable also to England. Arrow-heads of these types appear in 15th-century paintings of cross-bowmen, *e.g.* in two German paintings of the Resurrection by Master Francke, 1424, and Hans Multcher, 1437 (C. Glaser, *Les Peintres primitifs allemands*, Pls. 23 and 32). It is possible that later in the century they were to some extent replaced by the bullet-shaped form, Type 5.

Type 10.—This form may represent the transition from Types 1–2 to Types 7–9.

Types 11–12.—Two common specialized forms of Type 9, 14th–15th century.

Types 13–16.—Barbed and socketed arrow-heads. The earliest form, Type 13, the barbs of which are short relative to the socket, was perhaps used in battle in the 13th century (see above, p. 67); but the later, more developed forms, Types 14 and 15, were exclusively designed for hunting.

Types 17–20.—Tanged arrow-heads are less frequent than the socketed forms. Type 17, which occurs at Dyserth Castle, Flint, 1241–63 (Fig. 17, Nos. 10–11) is evidently contemporary with the similar socketed forms. Type 19 is rare, but occurs at Alsnö Hus, Sweden, where the majority of the material belongs to the later 14th century. Types 18 and 20 do not appear to be archæologically dated, but they are consistent and recurring types, which probably fall within the medieval period.

It should be emphasized that the above typology is not exhaustive; and it may include a few non-medieval types. It will, however, perhaps serve as a convenient basis for classification.

(a) Socketed Arrow-heads, Types 1-16

A 579. Arrow-head, Type 5, length 3·5 in. Pl. XV, No. 21. From Goswell Road.

A 1367. Arrow-head, Type 15, length of barbs 3·5 in. Pl. XV, No. 30. From Finsbury Circus.

A 1659. Arrow-head, Type 1, length 3·5 in. From London.

A 1945. Arrow-head, Type 11, length 2·4 in. Pl. XV, No. 24. From the Thames, London.

A 2363. Arrow-head, Type 9, length 2·6 in. From Christ's Hospital, Newgate Street.

A 2441. Arrow-head, Type 11, length 3 in. Pl. XV, No. 7. From London Wall.

A 2449. Arrow-head, Type 8, length 2·5 in. Pl. XV, No. 22. From Christ's Hospital, Newgate Street.

A 2462. Arrow-head, Type 2, length 4 in. Pl. XV, No. 2. From Bridge Street, S.W.1.

A 2512. Arrow-head, Type 16, length 1·8 in. From Broken Wharf.

A 3166. Arrow-head, Type 7, length 6·6 in. Pl. XV, No. 10. From Horseshoe Wharf.

A 3674. Arrow-head, Type 3, length 1·7 in. From London.

A 3675. Arrow-head, Type 13, length 2·4 in. Pl. XV, No. 26. From London.

A 3825. Arrow-head, Type 5, with two small longitudinal ridges. Length 1·9 in. Pl. XV, No. 20. From Worship Street.

A 5696. Arrow-head, Type 3, with unusually long socket, the upper half of which is of square section. Length 4·5 in. Pl. XV, No. 5. From London Wall.

A 5697. Arrow-head, Type 2, length 2·4 in. From London Wall.

A 5698. Arrow-head, Type 9, length 2·85 in. Pl. XV, No. 16. From London Wall.

A 9555. Arrow-head, Type 8, length 2·8 in. Pl. XV, No. 13. From the Thames, Battersea.

A 11855. Arrow-head, Type 13, length 2·6 in. Pl. XV, No. 25. From the Thames, Hammersmith.

A 11944. Arrow-head, Type 10, length 1·7 in. Pl. XV, No. 23. From Angel Court.

A 13718. Arrow-head, Type 16, length 2·5 in. Pl. XV, No. 28. From London Wall.

A 16113. Arrow-head, Type 16, length 1·5 in. From London.

A 16820. Arrow-head, Type 15, length of barbs 3·8 in. Pl. XV, No. 32. From London.

A 23633. Arrow-head, Type 15, length of barbs 3·5 in. Pl. XV, No. 31. From the Thames, London.

A 23635. Arrow-head, Type 10, length 1·5 in. From the Thames, London.

A 25445. Arrow-head, Type 14, length 2·75 in. Pl. XV, No. 27. From Aldersgate, Town Ditch.

A 27379. Arrow-head, Type 3, length 2·6 in. Pl. XV, No. 4. From Thames Street.

A 27387. Arrow-head, Type 14, length 3·25 in. Pl. XV, No. 29. From Lothbury.

A 27382. Arrow-head, Type 7–8, length of barbs, 5·7 in. Pl. XV, No. 11, From London.

A 27383. Arrow-head, Type 7, length 3·2 in. Pl. XV, No. 12. From Moorfields.

A 27387. Arrow-head, Type 7–8, length 3·2 in. From Lothbury.

A 27389. Arrow-head, Type 1, length 3·7 in. Pl. XV, No. 1. From Steelyard.

A 27394. Arrow-head, Type 5, length 1·75 in. Pl. XV, No. 19. From Moorfields.

C 765. Arrow-head, Types 1–2, length 3·1 in. From the Thames, Richmond.

C 2352. Arrow-head, Type 9, length 3·8 in. Pl. XV, No. 18. From London.

30.99. Arrow-head, Type 11, length 3·1 in. Pl. XV, No. 9. From London.

(b) Tanged Arrow-heads, Types 17–20

A 3673. Barbed arrow-head of unusual form with spirally-twisted tang. Length 2·9 in. From London.

A 15433. Arrow-head, Type 18, length 2·3 in. Pl. XV, No. 8. From London.

A 23634. Arrow-head, Type 17, length 3·0 in. Pl. XV, No. 6. From the Thames, London.

A 27380. Arrow-head, Type 20, length 6·4 in. From Queenhithe.

A 27381. Arrow-head, Type 20, length 6·4 in. Pl. XV, No. 14. From Queenhithe.

A 27388. Arrow-head of unusual form, with leaf-shaped head and short rather bulbous tang. Length 2·4 in. Pl. XV, No. 3. From Moorfields.

30.98. Arrow-head of unusual form, with short, flattened leaf-shaped blade and long tang. Length 6·9 in. Pl. XV, No. 15. From London.

72

Also illustrated :

SPEAR-HEADS

In the absence of archæologically-dated material the dating of medieval spear-heads is possible only in the most general terms. The forms current in Scandinavia during the Viking period are well known from grave-groups (see J. Petersen, *De Norske Vikingesverd,* Oslo, 1912); and the increasingly elaborate types in use towards the close of the Middle Ages are familiar enough from contemporary paintings. These at least provide the limits within which the medieval spear-head must fall. Representations are common, but they are rarely sufficiently detailed to be of any value.

As in the case of arrow-heads the form depended on the use to which it was put. Throughout the Middle Ages hunting-spears are generally depicted with projecting "wings" at the base of the blade. A fighting-spear of this form is shown in an early 12th-century Spanish manuscript in the British Museum (*Archæologia*, LXXXIII, 1933, Pl. 77, 3, dated 1109), but after that it only appears exceptionally in a military context, *e.g.* in the Maciejowski Bible, f. 27, where a spear of this type is carried by Goliath, whose whole armour is intentionally outlandish. The distinction is marked as early as the eleventh century. None of the spears shown in the Bayeux tapestry have "wings"; and on the late eleventh-century door at Brayton, Yorks, both types are shown, each in its proper context. "Winged" hunting spears remained in use throughout the Middle Ages.

73

Military spear-heads presumably followed the same development as arrow-heads in answer to the increased efficiency of defensive armour. Long, comparatively slender blades, such as Pl. XVI, Nos. 5 and 6, approximate to Viking types and belong probably to the earlier Middle Ages. A relatively shorter, stouter form is shown in the brass of Sir John D'Abernon, senior, d. 1277, at Stoke d'Abernon, Surrey; cf. the spear carried by the figure of Synagogue, c. 1210–35, in Strasbourg Cathedral. The solid, needle-like form illustrated on Pl. XVI, Nos. 1–4, is presumably contemporary with the similar form of arrow-head, which belongs to the period of developed plate-armour.

A certain number of spear-heads have the socket carried well up into the body of the blade. This is a feature which is certainly represented at the close of the Middle Ages, both in surviving specimens and in contemporary representations, e.g. on Bernard Notke's statue of St. George, 1489, in the Storkirke at Stockholm; and it may well prove to be a sound criterion of late medieval date.

A 510. Socketed spear-head with point of triangular section. Length 10·75 in. Pl. XVI, No. 1.

A 27384. Socketed spear-head, with point of square section. Length 7·7 in. Pl. XVI, No. 2. From Bishopsgate.

A 27378. Socketed spear-head, with point of triangular section. Length 5·0 in. Pl. XVI, No. 3. From Walbrook.

A 27385. Socketed spear-head, with point of triangular section. Length 5·0 in. Pl. XVI, No. 4. From Bishopsgate.

C 746. Socketed spear-head with slender leaf-shaped blade. Length 14·25 in. Pl. XVI, No. 5. From the Thames at Beckton.

B 321. Socketed spear-head with leaf-shaped blade. Length 15·1 in. Pl. XVI, No. 6. From the Thames at the Tower.

A 353. Tanged spear-head, heavy point with four slightly concave faces. A few spear-heads of this type were found in the Visby Mass-Graves, 1361 (see p. 67). Length 4 in. Pl. XVI, No. 7. From Westminster.

A 12240. Spear-head with wings at the heel of the blade. The socket runs into the blade. Maker's mark on the blade. Length 10·75 in. Pl. XVI, No. 8. From Worship Street.

A 1779. Spear-head with short leaf-shaped blade and hexagonal socket running the length of the blade. Length 9·25 in. Pl. XVI, No. 9. From the City.

PLATE XVI.

Medieval spear-heads from London.
1, A 510; 2, A 27384; 3, A 27378; 4, A 27385; 5, C 746; 6, B 321; 7, A 353;
8, A 12240; 9, A 1779.

PLATE XVII. [*To face p.* 75.

A 1778. Medieval mace-head from the Bank of England.

MACES

Already by the middle of the 13th century the primitive wooden club, or baston, had developed into the mace, which consisted of a knobbed or flanged iron head set on a short wooden haft. The form current in the mid-13th century (*e.g.* G. Laking, *European Armour and Arms*, I, Figs. 141-2, from a French Book of Gospels, *c.* 1250-75) suggests that its immediate predecessor was a wooden club studded with large nails. Both types can in fact be seen in simultaneous use in the Maciejowski Bible, *c.* 1250 (ff. 10a, 16a, 24b ; *cf.* f. 22a, a plain rough wooden club). Flanged forms, similar to the specimen in the Museum collection, make their appearance as early as the close of the 13th century (Laking, *op. cit.*, III, p. 90, a carving in Lincoln Cathedral), but they remained in use over a long period of time (*cf. Archæologia*, LXXIX, 1929, Pl. LXXV, 3, the tomb of Giovanni d'Antonio Maria Sala, 1527, at Bologna). It is possible that the later medieval development was influenced from the Near East, where this form of weapon was commonly used.

A 1778. Iron mace-head, with six flanges. Traces of the wooden haft remain. Pl. XVII. 14th–15th century. Found near the Bank of England. Given by Sir Guy Laking, Bart. (G. Laking, *European Armour and Arms*, II, Fig. 875.)

HAFTED WEAPONS

Besides the spear, a number of hafted, cutting or thrusting weapons, such as the glaive, the bill, the halberd, etc., were also in common use during the Middle Ages.

Of these the glaive, in its earliest form a long, single-edged weapon with a medium-length handle, somewhat resembling a large scramasax, was a regular cavalry weapon, and is shown for example so used in many scenes in the Maciejowski Bible, *c.* 1250 (*cf.* ff. 10a, 10b). The remaining hafted weapons were almost confined to the foot-soldier, and in consequence display little uniformity before the introduction of an increased standardization in infantry warfare in the later medieval and post-medieval period. They were often, in the first case, agricultural implements impressed for military

75

service; and in view of the diversity of agricultural practice from one district to another (see *The Countryman*, XIX, 1939, p. 511, six modern local variants of the bill), one can hardly expect to trace any very coherent development. Already in the 12th century a bill, shaped like an enlarged pruning knife on a long haft, can be seen depicted as a weapon on the bronze doors of Benevento Cathedral. Another, with an additional projecting point, is shown lopping a tree in the Bible of St. Etienne Harding at Cîteaux, *c.* 1100 (C. Oursel, *La Miniature du XII Siècle à l'Abbaye de Cîteaux*, Pl. XXV; *cf.* one shown in the destroyed frescoes of the Painted Chamber, Westminster Abbey, 1200–50, G. Laking, *European Armour and Arms*, II, Fig. 907). For typical 14th-century bills, see John of Gaunt's Psalter (*Burlington Fine Arts Club, Exhibition of MSS.*, 1908, Pl. 63) and Queen Mary's Psalter. The three bills in the Museum are all of very simple form, and may be of any date in the latter half of the Middle Ages. Their very crudity suggests that they could not be used by or against men in armour, but were part of the equipment of the civilian watch.

(For a general account of these hafted weapons, see G. Laking, *European Armour and Arms*, III, Chapter XX, and M. R. Holmes, *Archæological Journal*, XCI (1934), 22–31).

II. HORSE-FURNITURE

HORSES' BITS

It is only possible to speak in very general terms of the forms of horses' bits in use in the Middle Ages. Detailed representations are few, and so are archæologically dated examples. The surviving specimens are moreover bewilderingly varied in type, and it is hardly possible to do more than indicate the commoner forms and the approximate period of their use.

Snaffle-bits and curb-bits were both used throughout the Middle Ages. Actual examples of the latter are, however, extremely rare before the 15th century, although they are common in representations from the 11th century onwards. The discrepancy is due no doubt to their exclusive use for riding in its more elaborate forms, which naturally bulks disproportionately large in contemporary illustration. The draught-horse, the pack-horse, and the wayfarer's nag used some simple form of snaffle, and it is to this class that nearly all the surviving examples belong.

(i) *Curb-bits*

The medieval representations are rarely sufficiently detailed to be helpful. They do, however, show that throughout the Middle Ages the curb-bit was of a relatively simple form. It was not until the 15th century that the elaborate objects characteristic of the 16th and 17th centuries make their appearance. In the Mediterranean lands, at any rate, something of the sort can be seen in paintings of the first half of the century ; and Verrochio's statue of Bartolomeo Colleoni at Venice (1488) has a fully developed example (Fig. 18, No. 7).

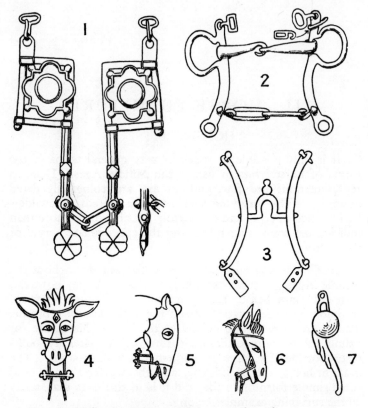

FIG. 18.—Medieval curb-bits: surviving examples and contemporary representations.

No. 1.　Elaborate bronze-gilt curb-bit in the Musée de Cluny, Paris.

No. 2.　Curb-bit from Tannenberg Castle, Prussia (R. Zschille and R. Forrer, *Die Pferdetrense*, Pl. X, No. 1).

No. 3.　From a picture of St. Siffrein, attributed to Nicolas Froment, in the Musée Calvet, Avignon, *c.* 1480.

No. 4.　From the Luttrell Psalter, f. 173 (1335–40).

No. 5.　From the Luttrell Psalter, f. 202 (1335–40).

No. 6.　From the Maciejowski Bible, f. 10a (*c.* 1250).

No. 7.　From Verrochio's statue of Bartolomeo Colleoni at Venice, 1488.

There does not seem any means of testing the date of their appearance in England, but it may well be doubted whether these elaborate forms made their appearance much before the end of the century.

Most of the earlier medieval representations show more or less plain, straight bars projecting downwards and joined by a transverse bar near the bottom (see Fig. 18, Nos. 4 and 5, from the Luttrell Psalter, c. 1335–40). There is an elaborate mid-14th century example in the Metropolitan Museum, New York (G. Laking, *European Armour and Arms*, III, Fig. 965. *Cf.* also the sculptured retable of St. Eustace from St. Denis, now in the Musée de Cluny, Paris). They must have resembled very closely the simpler forms of Roman curb-bit (*e.g.* R. Zschille and R. Forrer, *Die Pferdetrense*, Pl. IV, Nos. 2 and 3); and although there do seem to be securely dated Roman examples, it is possible that a certain number of medieval specimens have been wrongly attributed to the Roman period.

A feature of many of the medieval representations is the angular " stepped " bar. Something of the sort seems to occur as early as the Bayeux tapestry ; and a fine 13th-century specimen with enamelled bosses is preserved in the Musée de Cluny, Paris (Fig. 18, No. 1 ; the frame, behind the bosses, is a plain, open rectangle). Fig. 18, No. 2, illustrates an example from Tannenberg Castle, which was destroyed in 1399 ; it represents an obvious adaptation of a common form of medieval snaffle-bit (Type C, Fig. 19*a*). A similar specimen is shown on the brass of Martin de Visch, 1452, at Bruges (W. F. Creeny, *Facsimiles of Monumental Brasses on the Continent*, p. 28).

(ii) *Snaffle-bits*

As in the case of curb-bits, medieval representations of snaffle-bits add little to our knowledge of the incidence of particular contemporary types. The basic form in the Middle Ages, as both earlier and later, consisted of a simple mouth-piece, usually of two links, and at either end a plain ring for the attachment of the reins. Both the mouth-piece and the side-rings (or cheek-pieces) were variously elaborated, and

79

the following typology is intended to cover the commoner medieval variants of each of the two elements of the snaffle-bit.

(a) Types of Cheek-piece (Fig. 19a)

Type A.—The simple ring snaffle-bit is universal at all periods.

Type B.—Uncommon. It is found in Scandinavia as early as the 9th century (a grave-group in the Oslo University Museum, No. C 20168), but is hardly sufficiently common during the Viking period for all the British examples to be as early.

Type C.—A common medieval type, which presumably derives from the normal Viking form of cheek-piece current

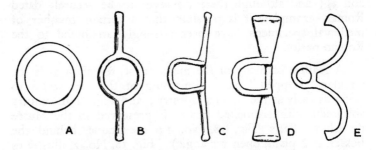

Fig. 19a.—Medieval snaffle-bits ; types of cheek-piece.

chiefly in Norway and Denmark. This is usually associated with mouth-pieces of the peculiarly Viking type illustrated in *London and the Vikings* (*London Museum Catalogue*), Fig. 20. There is, however, a 9th-century example in the Oslo University Museum (Grave-group C 6210–20) with an ordinary two-link mouth-piece (Type II) ; and the cheek-piece in .this case approximates very closely to the medieval type. From the " Old Prussian Knights' Graves " at Dolkheim, Prussia, where the coin-series lasts into the 13th century, the majority of the cheek-pieces were simple rings, Type A, a few of Type C (R. Zschille and R. Forrer, *Die Pferdetrense*, p. 9, Pl. IX, 4) ; and two cheek-pieces of Type C were found at Tannenberg Castle, destroyed in 1399 (*op. cit.*, p. 10, Pl. X, 2 and 14).

Type D.—Probably a later medieval development of C. It seems to have been specially common in London. A fine example from Moorfields in the Pitt-Rivers Museum, Farnham, dates presumably from the 15th century (Fig. 20, No. 3).

Type E.—The series of bits to which this form of cheek-piece belongs are discussed in *London and the Saxons* (*London Museum Catalogue*), pp. 150–1. Whatever their ultimate origin there is good reason to associate their appearance in the British Isles with the Vikings. Cheek-pieces of the same general type are common in Sweden; and the resemblance extends to such ornamental details as the animal-headed terminals, which appear on so many of the British examples (*e.g. London and the Saxons*, Fig. 27. Cf. P. Paulsen, " Einige Zaumzeugbeschläge aus dem Ostbaltikum," *Aratrukk Opetatud Eesti Seltsi Toimetustest*, XXX, 488–98, Fig. 4*a*, from Göksbo, Sweden, early 11th century; Fig. 4*b*, in Berlin, from the Forrer collection; Fig. 6, from Lundby, Sweden, 11th century, *Fornvännen* (1909), 246). The preponderance of Irish examples in the British Isles is compatible with a Scandinavian origin. A bit of this type from Westminster (*Antiquaries Journal*, XV, 1935, 76) has a jointed mouth-piece of a form (a variant of Type VI), for which there seems to be no evidence before the mid-15th century. The objection (*London and the Saxons*, p. 151) that the chain pendant from the central U-link prevents its identification as a bit, is hardly valid; for similar, and far more elaborate, mouth-pieces were in fact common during the 15th, 16th, and 17th centuries (R. Zschille and R. Forrer, *Die Pferdetrense*, *passim*). The type was probably in sporadic use throughout the Middle Ages.

(*b*) TYPES OF MOUTH-PIECE (Fig. 19*b*)

Type I.—The rigid-bar mouth-piece is a form which occurs sparingly at all periods, usually with some form of curb-bit.

Type II.—The ordinary two-link mouth-piece is the type most universally employed at all periods with all types of cheek-piece. It is proportionately commoner at the beginning than at the end of the Middle Ages.

Type III.—A variant of Type II with a separate central link.   Specially common with cheek-pieces of Type D.

Type IV.—A common variant of Type III.   It is found at Tannenberg Castle, before 1399 (R. Zschille and R. Forrer, *Die Pferdetrense,* p. 10, Pl. X, 2) ; *cf.* the brass of Martin de Visch at Bruges, 1452 (W. F. Creeny, *Facsimiles of Monumental Brasses on the Continent,* p. 28).   It is common on post-medieval curb-bits.

Type V.—A late variant of Type IV.   It is presumably no earlier than Type VI, and may in fact be entirely post-medieval.   A curb-bit in the Guildhall Museum, with the ends of the mouth-links cast solid with the cheek-pieces, may, however, be of 15th-century date.   It was certainly in use as late as the 18th century.

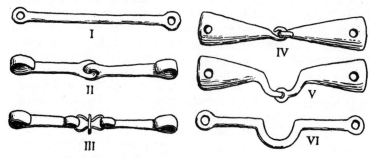

Fig. 19*b*.—Medieval snaffle-bits ; types of mouth-piece.

Type VI.—There are a large variety of mouth-pieces of this general form with a U-shaped bend in the centre.   This usually takes the form of a separate link, jointed to the side-pieces of the bar, but an early representation of a simple curb-bit in the Musée Calvet, Avignon (Fig. 18, No. 3, from a picture of St. Siffrein, attributed to Nicolas Froment, *c.* 1480), shows a solid bar.   An example, probably of the late 15th century, with swivelling centre, is preserved in the British Museum (*Antiquaries Journal,* XV, 1935, 76).

A 1514.   Iron snaffle-bit, Type II C; the links of the mouth-piece are spirally twisted.   Over-all length of mouth-piece 8·4 in.   Fig. 21, No. 1.   From London Wall.

A 2439. Iron snaffle-bit, Type III D. Over-all length of mouth-piece 9·8 in. Fig. 20, No. 1. From Butler's Wharf.

A 16814. Part of a bronze snaffle-bit, Type III D. Over-all length of mouth-piece 8·5 in. approximately. Fig. 20, No. 2. From London.

A 18787. Part of an iron snaffle-bit, Type II E, one cheek-piece missing. Over-all length of mouth-piece 6·8 in. Fig. 21, No. 3. From Old Queen Street.

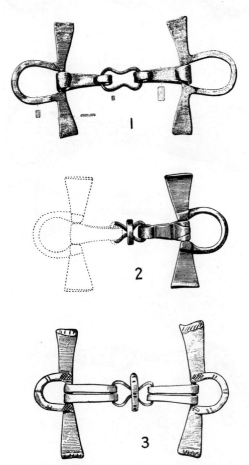

FIG. 20.—Medieval snaffle-bits from London.
1, A 2439; 2, A 16814; 3, in the Pitt-Rivers Museum, Farnham (⅓).

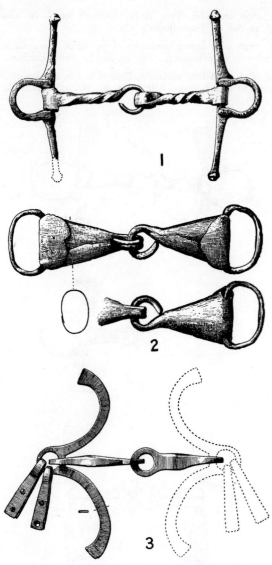

FIG. 21.—Medieval snaffle-bits from London.
1, A 1514; 2, C 728; 3, A 18787 (½).

C. 728.   Iron snaffle-bit, Type IV A.   Over-all length of mouth-piece 8·4 in. Fig. 21, No. 2.   From the Wandle at Wandsworth.

Also illustrated (from the Pitt-Rivers Museum, Farnham) :

Fig. 20, No. 3.   Iron snaffle-bit, Type III D.   Over-all length of mouth-piece 8·5 in.   From Moorfields.

BRIDLE-BOSSES

The elaborate curb-bits which made their appearance towards the close of the 15th century were usually accompanied by a pair of bowl-shaped bosses which concealed either end of the mouth-piece (see Fig. 18, No. 7).   They were the equivalent of the heraldic or decorative plaques attached to some of

Fig. 22.—Early 16th-century bridle-boss from the Thames at London.
A 7732 (⅔).

the finer medieval curb-bits of the earlier period.   An early specimen, bearing the coat of arms of Old France in enamel is illustrated by R. Zschille and R. Forrer, *Die Pferdetrense*, Pl. XI, 4 ; *cf.* the decorative plate which covers the framework of the curb-bit illustrated in Fig. 18, No. 1.

A 7732.   Bridle-boss of bronze with engraved ornament.   Early 16th century.   Fig. 22.   From the Thames at London.

A 22468.   Bridle-boss of base-metal, of plain bowl-shaped form.   Late 15th or 16th century.   From Finsbury Circus.

STIRRUPS

For the detailed development of the stirrup during the earlier medieval period we are dependent almost entirely upon foreign evidence. To judge, however, from representations and from surviving examples the various forms had a wide currency; and the typological development visible in Scandinavia and North Europe does seem to be more or less applicable to the British series.

During the Viking period in Scandinavia a number of varieties are represented; but although, particularly in a Sweden, the development is complicated by continual contacts with Eastern and South-eastern Europe, which seem to have been the effective source of most of the North-west European stirrup-types current in the Dark Ages and early Middle Ages, two basic forms can be distinguished. The first of these consists in its simplest form of a loop of wire twisted at the top to form a smaller loop for the stirrup-leather (see *London and the Vikings* (*London Museum Catalogue*), Fig. 18a). The other type is more complex (*op. cit.*, Fig. 18b). Its peculiarities have been explained in several ways. One of these is suggested in *London and the Vikings*. Alternatively they may be reminiscent in metal of simple wood and leather stirrups (R. Zschille and R. Forrer, *Die Steigbügel*, Pl. I). In any case both types are already represented in the earliest Scandinavian graves and had probably already been evolved elsewhere.

The first of these types is best represented in Norway, where it underwent little change (O. Rygh, *Norske Oldsager*, Types 587–9). The twist at the top in some of the later examples becomes a separate loop joined by a boss to the body of the stirrup; and there is an increasing tendency for the bottom to expand into a flattened foot-rest. A stirrup of the simple, early type, and one showing both these later developments were found associated together in a 9th-century grave in Westfold (Oslo University Museum, C 6461–93). The form of the body in many cases approximates to that of the second type, but a distinctive sub-group, which seems to belong to the later Viking period and to continue in use into the early Middle Ages, has a long, slender body.

86

The second type (O. Rygh, *Norske Oldsager*, Type 590) is characteristic of Viking settlement in all regions. The shape varies considerably, but the long slender form of Fig. 23, No. 4, is predominant. In some examples, in Sweden in particular (see T. J. Arne, *Das Bootgräberfeld von Tuna in Alsike*, pp. 64–6), this gives way in the 10th and 11th centuries to a more rounded form (Fig. 23, No. 1, from Tuna, grave III, *c*. 950–1000), to which seem to belong most of the British Viking stirrups (*London and the Vikings (London Museum Catalogue)*, pp. 38–41, Fig. 17).

This is almost certainly due to conflation with rounded forms of loop-stirrup in contemporary use. Fig. 23, No. 3, also from Tuna (grave I, *c*. 1000–50), is of a type well known in Russia in the 10th century, and in Hungary in the 10th and 11th centuries; and it is probably not unduly far-fetched to compare it with a Siberian stirrup of the 8th or 9th century in the British Museum, from Bjelovodsk, or with the detailed representations of similar stirrups on Chinese statuettes and reliefs of the Han and Tang periods. A third example from Tuna (Fig. 23, No. 2, grave VIII, *c*. 1000–50) is intermediate between the native and the intrusive forms.

Over the greater part of Scandinavia the spread of Christianity meant that grave-groups are rare after the 11th century. In East Prussia the practice of burying grave-furniture persisted into the 13th century; and although detailed evidence is difficult of access, the large series of stirrups from the graves at Dolkheim, published by R. Zschille and R. Forrer (*Die Steigbügel*, Pls. III and IV), show clearly enough the range of types employed. The apparent typological development from Viking types is sufficiently illustrated in Fig. 23, Nos. 4–8. The later forms are found in Scandinavia, but not in dated grave-groups; and it is evident therefore that we have here the forms of stirrup current in the later 12th and 13th centuries.

Representations of early medieval stirrups are sufficient only to show that both loop-stirrups and squared forms with a flattened foot-rest were current. Apparently the only English dated example is one found in a 13th-century pot at Knebworth,

87

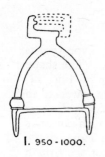

1. 950-1000.

2. 1000-50.

3. 1000-50.

1-3. FROM TUNA, SWEDEN.

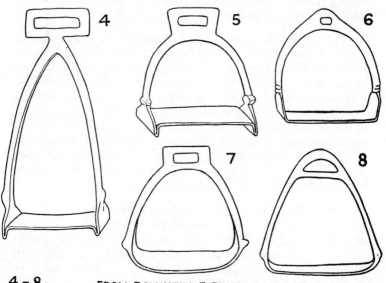

4-8. FROM DOLKHEIM, E. PRUSSIA. 11ᵀᴴ-13ᵀᴴ CENTURIES.

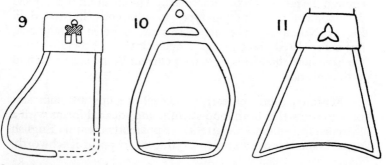

9-10. FROM TANNENBERG CASTLE. destroyed 1399.   PRAGUE, ST. GEORGE, 1373.

FIG. 23.—Dated stirrups from continental sites.

Herts (Fig. 25, No. 1 ; see further *Antiquaries Journal*, XIX, 1939, 303–5). This is of simple form with an expanded foot-rest and no suspension-loop, and it supports the suggestion that the evidence from sites such as Dolkheim is, broadly speaking, applicable to English finds.

The 14th century is marked by an elaboration of the 13th-century type, coupled with a tendency towards asymmetrical projection to one side. The sides, as well as the foot-rest, are often expanded, and the suspension-loop is in many instances masked by a superficial plate. These changes are sufficiently illustrated in Fig. 23, Nos. 9–11. The first two are from Tannenberg Castle, destroyed in 1399, the third is depicted on the bronze statue of St. George and the Dragon, 1373, in the courtyard of the Hradschin at Prague. A plain stirrup, differing only from the 13th-century form in the expansion of the sides, can be seen on the 14th-century Retable of St. Eustace, from St. Denis, now in the Musée de Cluny, Paris.

The earlier 15th century saw little change beyond the frequent addition of a small triangular " tongue " in the centre of the foot-plate, *e.g.* on a Spanish retable, *c.* 1420, in the Victoria and Albert Museum (*Archæologia*, LXXXIII, 1933, Pl. 83). A presumably 15th-century example from Moorfields in the Guildhall Museum (Fig. 26, No. 1), which has this tongue, is otherwise of purely 14th-century type. But with the advance of the century there is an ever-increasing solidity of form which foreshadows the squat Renaissance stirrup of the 16th and 17th centuries. Those shown on

---

FIG. 23

Nos. 1–3. From Viking burials at Tuna, Sweden (T. J. Arne, *Das Bootgräberfeld von Tuna in Alsike*, pp. 64–6 ; from graves III, VIII, and I respectively).

Nos. 4–8. From burials at Dolkheim, E. Prussia (R. Zschille and R. Forrer, *Die Steigbügel*, Pls. III and IV, where also many other examples from this site are figured).

Nos. 9–10. From Tannenberg Castle, Prussia (R. Zschille and R. Forrer, *op. cit.*, Pl. V).

No. 11. From the statue of St. George and the Dragon by George of Kolozvar, in the courtyard of the Hradschin at Prague.

Verrochio's statue of Bartolomeo Colleoni, 1488, in Venice, or on Bernard Notke's statue of St. George, 1489, in the

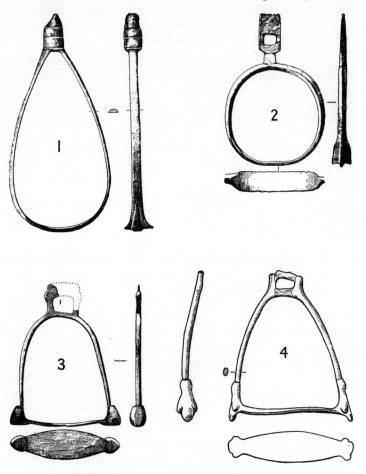

FIG. 24.—Early medieval stirrups from London.

1, B 2 ; 2, B 1 ; 3, A 2436 ; 4, in the Pitt-Rivers Museum, Farnham (¼).

Storkirke at Stockholm, are already characteristic of the later type ; but there is no evidence to show that these forms reached England before the close of the 15th century.

B 1. Iron ring-stirrup of circular form with projecting attachment. It is very like a stirrup found at Tuna in Sweden, datable to the early 11th century (T. J. Arne, *Das Bootgräberfeld von Tuna in Alsike*, Pl. IV, 15). The Tuna stirrup is noted as an East-European type, intrusive to Sweden. Fig. 24, No. 2. From London. (G. Laking, *European Armour and Arms*, I, Fig. 175 (c).)

B 2. Portion of an oval iron ring-stirrup. The loop for the stirrup-leather was joined by a boss to the body of the stirrup, probably at right-angles,

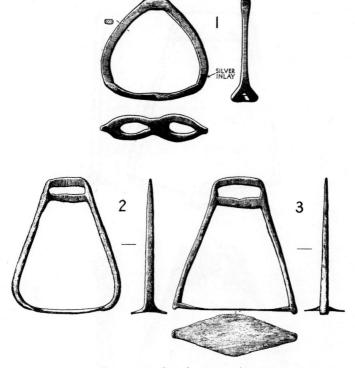

FIG. 25.—13th–14th-century stirrups.
1, from Knebworth, in the Hertford Museum ; 2, B 4 from London ;
3, B 3 from London.

but it has broken off. The type is dated in Scandinavia to the 11th and 12th centuries. Fig. 24, No. 1. From London. (G. Laking, *European Armour and Arms*, I, Fig. 175 (a).)

B 3. Trapezoidal iron ring-stirrup with slightly expanded foot-rest. Probably 14th century. Fig. 25, No. 3. From London. (G. Laking, *European Armour and Arms*, I, Fig. 175 (b).)

B 4. Iron ring-stirrup, similar to B 3, but with rounded lower corners. 13th or 14th century. Fig. 25, No. 2. From London. (G. Laking, *European Armour and Arms*, I, Fig. 175 (*d*).)

A 2436. Iron stirrup, with the foot-plate separate and welded in place by two bronze knobs. The knobs are reminiscent of the ornamental knobs on Viking stirrups, in origin themselves functional ; but the form of this stirrup can hardly be earlier than the 12th century. There is a similar stirrup, of iron

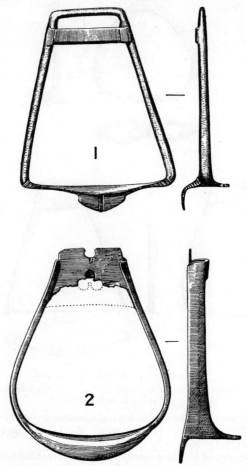

Fig. 26.—14th–15th-century stirrups from London (in the Guildhall Museum) ($\frac{1}{3}$).

plated with bronze, from London in the Pitt-Rivers Museum at Farnham (Fig. 24, No. 4) ; here the bosses are purely ornamental. Similarly bronze-plated examples with ornamental bosses are preserved in the University Museum at Oslo and in Stockholm Museum, in neither case apparently associated. From Christ's Hospital, Newgate Street. Fig. 24, No. 3.

A 1398. Iron stirrup, of typically 14th-century asymmetrical form. The presence, however, of an incipient tongue to the foot-rest and the find-spot suggest an early 15th-century date. Fig. 27, No. 2. From Moorfields.

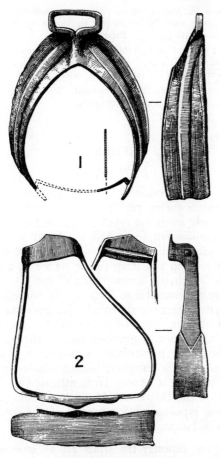

FIG. 27.—Late medieval stirrups from London.
1, A 965 ; 2, A 1398 ($\frac{1}{3}$).

93

A 965. Iron stirrup of unusual form approximating to the late 15th-century type. Perhaps mid-15th century. Fig. 27, No. 1. (G. Laking, *European Armour and Arms*, III, Fig. 962.) From Westminster.

Also illustrated :—

Fig. 25, No. 1 (in the Hertford Museum). Iron stirrup with traces of silver inlay, found in a 13th-century storage-jar at Rabley Heath, Herts. See *Antiquaries Journal*, XIX (1939), 303–5.

Fig. 24, No. 4 (in the Pitt-Rivers Museum, Farnham). Bronze-plated iron stirrup, retaining vestigial bosses just above the junction of arms and footplate. Probably 13th century. From London.

Fig. 26, No. 1 (in the Guildhall Museum). Iron stirrup from Moorfields. The find-spot and the projecting " tongue " suggest a 15th-century date, but the form is otherwise that of the 14th century. Early 15th century.

Fig. 26, No. 2 (in the Guildhall Museum). Iron stirrup from Brooks Wharf, London. Late 14th or early 15th century.

SPURS

(i) *Prick-spurs*

The spur was introduced into England by the Vikings, and Scandinavian forms played a considerable part in the evolution of early medieval types in this country. The basic Viking and Carolingian form had a tubular point (Type 1) and straight arms, which ended either in a flattened plate riveted directly on to the strap (Type A), or in a rectangular loop through which the strap passed (Type C). The point was frequently elaborated into Type 2, and sometimes further enriched with mouldings or slightly projecting spikes. Several of the more elaborate forms of points (Types 4–11) are found in Scandinavia, but not in grave-groups of the pagan period, to which they are presumably subsequent. A form of spur, however, with a flattened lozenge-shaped point set at an angle to the body is known from at least two Norwegian grave-groups (in the University Museum at Oslo), and it may possibly be the typological forerunner of the solid lozenge-shaped points of Norman France and England.

In the Bayeux tapestry the spurs are all represented with some form of expanded point, and it is therefore possible that some of the more elaborate forms were already evolved on the continent by the middle of the 11th century and introduced into England for the first time by the Normans. Conical points are shown very clearly in the S. French Apocalypse of St. Sever, 1028–72 (Ph. Lauer, *MSS. Illuminées de la Bibliothèque Nationale*, Pl. XIX), and, less clearly, on the bronze gravestone of Rudolf of Schwabia, 1080, in Merseburg Cathedral (*Die*

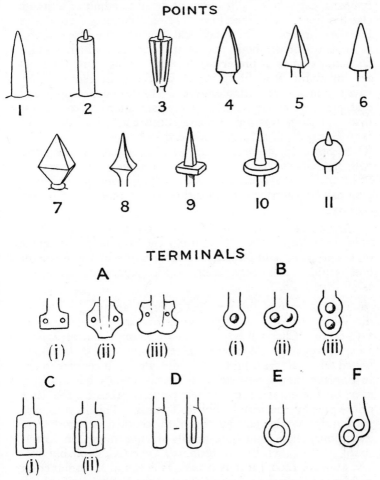

FIG. 28.—Types of prick-spur points and terminals.

Kunst des frühen Mittelalters (Propyläen-Verlag), p. 541); and they seem to be universal in 12th-century sculptural representations. In England, however, purely Viking types may well have remained in use for a considerable period.

Unfortunately, on contemporary monumental effigies the point is rarely preserved; and it does not appear on tympana, capitals, etc., in sufficient detail to admit of accurate classification. It is therefore only of secondary importance for the chronology of individual spur-types. More useful is the form of the body and of its terminals, which stand a far better chance of preservation. On Viking spurs the arms are invariably straight, whereas by the 13th century they have assumed a comfortable curve. The evidence of surviving examples and of contemporary representations alike suggest that the change was uniform and consistent. The effigies of both Henry II, d. 1189, and Richard I, d. 1199, at Fontevraud (C. A. Stothard, *Monumental Effigies*, Pls. 5 and 9), bear spurs with strongly curved arms; and in the absence of this feature from any of the spurs in pagan Viking grave-groups it is reasonable to ascribe this transition to the middle of the 12th century.

Any classification must take into account the form of both point and of terminals. The form of the latter may be different on either arm; and reference is accordingly by the forms of both terminals and of the point, *e.g.* Fig. 30, No. 2, is described as of Type DE7.

Two at least of the terminal types, A and C, go back to the Viking period. A(ii) is found, for example, in the early 11th-century Cherwell hoard (*Victoria County History, Oxfordshire*, I, 1939, p. 368); and these more or less elaborate bolted terminals are found on Scandinavian 11th-century spurs. In England they appear on straight-armed types, but rarely, if ever, on the curved arm. Their place is taken on the later prick-spur by the simple bolted Type B. This in turn was apparently obsolescent by the 14th century as, with rare exceptions, these bolted terminals are not found on rowel-spurs. The other Viking terminal, Type CC, probably survives until *c.* 1200, for it is occasionally found in conjunction with curved arms, *e.g.* on two spurs in the Victoria and Albert

96

Museum, both of Type CC(i), which appear closely to resemble the spurs on the effigies of Henry II and Richard I at Fontevraud. There is no evidence that Type C outlasted the 12th century. Vertically-slotted terminals, Type DD, appear at an early date on the continent (*e.g.* R. Zschille and R. Forrer, *Der Sporn*, Pl. III, 6, German), but they do not seem to be found on the earlier British spurs.

Of the Viking forms of point, Type I was perhaps already obsolete at the time of the Norman Conquest. Type 2, which is found only with terminals of Types A and C and straight arms, was presumably obsolete by the middle of the 12th century.

Type 3 is found on a small group of 11th-century spurs, and is, perhaps, a peculiarly English Viking type. One was found in the early 11th-century Cherwell hoard (in the Ashmolean Museum, Fig. 29, No. 3). Another, presumably from London, is in the Guildhall Museum (Fig. 29, No. 2); a third, in the Victoria and Albert Museum. These all have terminals of Type A(ii). A fourth, in the London Museum, A 4993 (Fig. 29, No. 1), has B(i) terminals, and is therefore presumably the latest of the series.

Types 4 and 5 are found almost exclusively in association with straight arms and Type B terminals; Type 6 does occur later, but is usually replaced by more elaborate forms. Types 7–11 belong exclusively to the later phase, although the plain bi-pyramidal form, Type 7, is normally found on very slightly curved spurs, which can presumably be dated *c.* 1200 or a little earlier. The spurs shown on the earliest English brasses are unfortunately mostly schematic. But there is a sufficient number of 13th-century representations to show that the later moulded forms were already current quite early in the century (see *Archæologia*, XXXI, Pl. V, 2, incised slab of ? Sir Walter de Bitton, *ob.* 1227–8, at Bitton, Glos; *Walpole Society*, XVI, Pl. XXVII, a Matthew Paris drawing, 1250–60, in the Psalter, B.M. Roy. MS. 2A, XXII, f. 220; R. Zschille and R. Forrer, *Der Sporn*, Pl. VII, 6, the 13th-century effigy of Duke Henry IV of Schleswig; and a specimen found at Rayleigh Castle, Essex (before *c.* 1270). See also the effigies in the Temple Church, London).

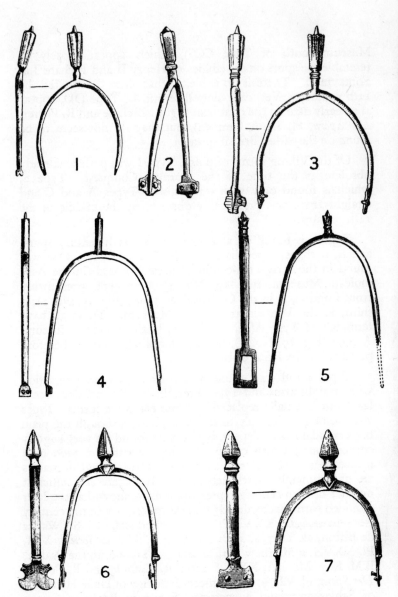

FIG. 29.—Early medieval prick-spurs from London and Oxford.
1, A 4993 ; 2, in the Guildhall Museum ; 3, in the Ashmolean Museum ;
4, A 1353 ; 5, A 1354 ; 6, A 10582 ; 7, in the Guildhall Museum (⅔).

The forms of terminal on the later prick-spurs are very varied. Type DD, with vertical slots for the passage of the straps through both arms, is not very common on surviving specimens, although it seems to be represented, for example, on several of the 13th-century effigies in the Temple Church, London. Type BB, in which the arms are both bolted to the straps, is a common 13th-century form. But although the bolted terminal remained in use into the 14th century and is, very exceptionally, found on early rowel-spurs, it had by then evidently given place in ordinary use to the ring-terminal, Type E, to which the strap was fastened by a detachable hook. Type EE, with two ring-terminals, is well illustrated by two of the later effigies in the Temple Church (*Royal Commission on Historical Monuments, London*, IV, p. 191, No. 9, late 13th century, and No. 12, *c*. 1300), and by the fine late prick-spur on the effigy of John of Eltham, d. 1334, in Westminster Abbey (Fig. 30, No. 5). As the type which was taken over by the rowel-spur, it may be assumed to have been that in common use for the prick-spur during the period of transition, *c*. 1300–50.

Complex forms, of which one terminal was slotted, Type D, the other bolted or hooked into the strap, Type B or E, were also current in the 13th and early 14th centuries. Type DE can be seen very clearly on the effigy of William Longspee, Earl of Salisbury, d. 1227, in Salisbury Cathedral (C. A. Stothard, *Monumental Effigies*, Pls. 17 and 18). The ring-terminal is worn on the outer side of the foot ; and the spurs with slotted inner terminals, which can be seen on most of the earliest brasses, may well, therefore, belong to this type, of which surviving examples are common. One of these, from Ragn-hildsholmen in Sweden, can be dated between 1257 and 1308. Another probable instance is the spur on the effigy of Edmund Crouchback, Earl of Lancaster, d. 1296, in Westminster Abbey, but the outer terminal may perhaps be bolted to the strap. This combination, Type BD, is found on at least one early rowel-spur (*Journal of the British Archæological Association*, 18 (1856), Pl. 25, 3), and may be presumed to have appeared on the contemporary prick-spurs. Yet another form, which combines the slot, Type D, and the two-holed terminal, Type F, which is found commonly on rowel-spurs, and very

99

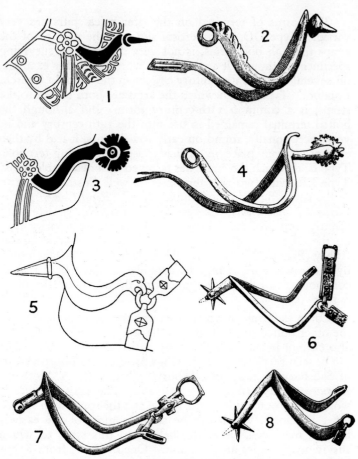

FIG. 30.—Early 14th-century spurs.

No. 1.   From the brass of Sir John D'Abernon, junior, d. 1327, at Stoke
d'Abernon, Surrey.

No. 2.   From Ragnhildsholmen, Sweden, occupied 1257–1308 (⅓).

No. 3.   From the brass of Sir John Creke, c. 1325, at Westley Waterless,
Cambs.

No. 4.   From Ragnhildsholmen, Sweden, occupied 1257–1308 (⅓).

No. 5.   From the effigy of John of Eltham, d. 1334, in Westminster Abbey.

No. 6.   From London (in the Guildhall Museum) (⅓).

No. 7.   A 5012, from Bucklersbury (⅓).

No. 8.   A 308, from Westminster (⅓).

100

occasionally on prick-spurs (*e.g.* C. Enlart, *Manuel*, Vol. III, Fig. 429), may be seen on an effigy at Dorchester, Oxon. It is evident that a great variety of detailed forms were in use during the last hundred years of the use of the prick-spur.

A 1353. Bronze prick-spur, Type AA(i)2. Straight arms. Length 5·75 in. 11th century. Fig. 29, No. 4. From Moorfields.

A 1354. Iron prick-spur, Type CC2 (point elaborated). Straight arms. Length 5·5 in. 11th or early 12th century. Fig. 29, No. 5. From London Wall.

A 4993. Iron prick-spur, point Type 3. Small bolted terminals, straight arms. Similar spurs can be seen in the Ashmolean Museum (from the early 11th-century Cherwell hoard, Fig. 29, No. 3), in the Guildhall Museum (from London, Fig. 29, No. 2), and in the Victoria and Albert Museum. Length 4·75 in. 11th century. Fig. 29, No. 1. From London.

A 10582. Iron prick-spur, Type AA(iii)4. Straight arms. Length 5·25 in. *c.* 1100. Fig. 29, No. 6. From Colman Street.

A 11004. Iron prick-spur, Type BB(ii)11. Unusually short, widely splayed, straight arms. Length 3·35 in. Mid-12th century (?). Fig. 31, No. 5. From New Bridge Street, Blackfriars.

A 1355. Iron prick-spur, Type BB(ii)7. Straight arms. Point set at a slight angle to the body. Length 3·9 in. 12th century. From Smithfield.

A 1356. Iron prick-spur, Type BB(ii)7. Arms slightly bent. Length 4·25 in. Second half of the 12th century. Fig. 31, No. 1. From Smithfield. (G. Laking, *European Armour and Arms*, I, p. 36, Fig. 36 (a).)

A 1967. Iron prick-spur, similar to A 1356, but with a moulding at the base of the point. Length 4·0 in. Second half of the 12th century. Fig. 31, No. 2. From Christ's Hospital, Smithfield.

36.43/1. Iron prick-spur, point Type 7, set on a tubular neck. Arms slightly curving, terminals broken off. Length of point 2·1 in. From London.

A 4987. Iron prick-spur, Type BB(i)6–7. Arms gently curving. Length 5·5 in. *c.* 1200. Fig. 31, No. 6. From London.

A 966–7. Two iron prick-spurs, point Type 8. Arms damaged, slightly curving. From Angel Court.

C 1220. Iron prick-spur, Type BB(ii)8. Arms gently curving. Length 4·25 in. Early 13th century. From Upper Thames Street.

A 291. Iron prick-spur almost identical with C 1220. From Westminster.

A 4994. Iron prick-spur very like C 1220 but longer in the neck. From the Thames, London.

A 10182. Iron prick-spur, Type BB(ii)7–8. Arms gently curving. Length 4·5 in. Early 13th century. From Finsbury Circus.

C 1219. Iron prick-spur, Type BB(ii)8. Arms strongly curved. Length 4·5 in. Late 13th century. Fig. 31, No. 3. From Upper Thames Street.

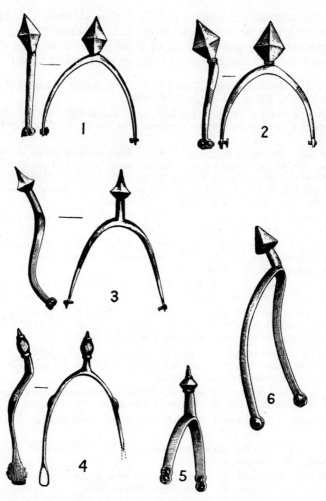

Fig. 31.—Prick-spurs from London.

1, A 1356; 2, A 1967; 3, C 1219; 4, A 4995; 5, A 11004; 6, A 4987 (½).

A 3902. Point, Type 8, of an iron prick-spur set on a long neck. Remainder missing. From London.

36.43/2. Point only, Type 8, of an iron prick-spur. From London,

102

A 4995. Iron prick-spur, one arm missing, the other arm with slotted terminal, Type D. Moulded globular point. Mouldings at the curve of the arms. Length 4·75 in. Early 14th century. Fig. 31, No. 4. From London Wall.

(ii) *Rowel-spurs*

There is considerable doubt as to the date of the introduction of the rowel-spur into this country. It is often stated that it can be clearly seen on the second seal of Henry III, A.D. 1240 ; but in view of the character of any seal-impression, confirmatory evidence would be welcome ; and this is very hard to find. The apparent representation of the rowel in several even more unexpected contexts, *e.g.* in the 9th-century Spanish Apocalypse of Valenciennes (L. de Noëttes, *L'Attelage et le Cheval de Selle à travers les Ages*, Fig. 924) and on a 12th-century leather book-binding (G. D. Hobson, " Further Notes on Romanesque Bindings," *The Library*, XV, 1934–5, 170, Fig. 6), carries still less conviction ; and the only other recorded 13th-century English example, on the slab of John Boteler, 1285, at St. Bride's, Glamorgan, is so crudely represented that it too admits of doubt.

Two mailed legs of a monumental brass with a rowel-spur, which are now in the Wallace Collection, have been quoted as evidence of a 13th-century date (Fig. 32, No. 1 ; G. Laking, *European Armour and Arms*, III, p. 164, Fig. 969). They are, however, probably foreign, and in any case of early 14th-century date.

Abroad rowel-spurs are found at the close of the 13th century, *e.g.* on the incised tomb-slab of Nenkinus de Gotheim, d. 1296, at Gotheim, Belgium (W. F. Creeny, *Incised Slabs on the Continent*, No. 27), but not earlier. It does seem, therefore, that the evidence for the use of rowel-spurs before the last years of the 13th century can only be accepted with great reserve ; and there can be no questioning that in general usage the transition from the prick-spur to the rowel-spur did not take place before the first half of the following century.

This is well marked on the series of monumental brasses. The earlier examples all have prick-spurs. But of the two contemporary brasses of Sir John D'Abernon, junior, d. 1327, at Stoke d'Abernon, Surrey, and of Sir John de Creke, at Westley Waterless, Cambs, which were certainly the product

103

of the same workshop, the former has prick-, the latter rowel-spurs (Fig. 30, Nos. 1 and 3; *cf.* Nos. 2 and 4, from Ragnhildsholmen, Sweden, occupied 1257–1308).

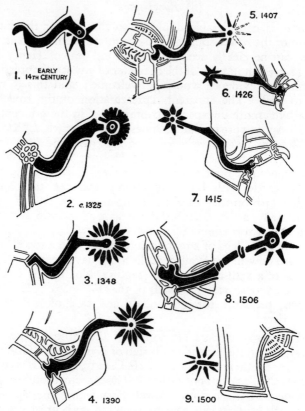

FIG. 32.—Representation of rowel-spurs on contemporary brasses.

No. 1.   Brass (legs only), early 14th century, in the Wallace Collection.
No. 2.   Brass of Sir John Creke, *c.* 1325, at Westley Waterless, Cambs.
No. 3.   Brass of Sir John Gifford, *c.* 1348, at Bowers Gifford, Essex.
No. 4.   Brass of Sir Andrew Louterell, d. 1390, at Irnham, Lincs.
No. 5.   Brass of Sir William Bagot, d. 1407, at Bagington, Warwickshire.
No. 6.   Brass of Sir Thomas le Strange, d. 1426, at Wellesbourne Hastings, Warwickshire.
No. 7.   Brass of Walter Cookesey, d. 1415, at Kidderminster, Worcs.
No. 8.   Brass of Sir Roger L'Estrange, d. 1506, at Hunstanton, Norfolk.
No. 9.   Brass of John Tame, d. 1500, at Fairford, Glos.

The later brasses all have rowel-spurs, with the exception of that of Sir Hugh Hastings, d. 1347, in Elsyng Church, Norfolk, the latest recorded instance of prick-spur. Another late specimen is that on the effigy of John of Eltham, d. 1334, in Westminster Abbey (Fig. 30, No. 5; C. A. Stothard, *Monumental Effigies*, Pl. 56). On the other hand the seals of the Baron's letter to the Pope in 1301 (see *Archæologia*, XXI, 1909, 194) all appear to depict prick-spurs. It is evident that the rowel came into general use after 1300, and was universal by 1350.

The earliest rowel-spurs are naturally very similar in form to the contemporary prick-spurs. The rowels are small, usually with six or seven points, but occasionally of the form illustrated in Fig. 30, Nos. 3–4. In the second half of the 14th century the many-pointed wheel-rowel (*e.g.* Fig. 32, Nos. 3–4; Fig. 34, No. 3) became fashionable; but throughout the Middle Ages smaller, simpler forms remained equally in common use. The body of the spur was normally uniformly curved. A few early specimens, *e.g.* Fig. 30, Nos. 6 and 8, are sharply bent; and sometimes the curve is relatively slight, *e.g.* Fig. 34, No. 1. The projecting ornamental point at the junction of the body and the shank only makes its appearance at the very close of the century, *e.g.* on the brass of John Bettesthorne, d. 1398, at Mere, Wilts.

For a short time the terminals of the arms were varied and various combinations of Types B, D, and E (Fig. 28) are found, *e.g.* Fig. 30, Nos. 2, 4, 6–8, Fig. 33, No. 1. After the transitional period, however, only Types EE and FF are found, and of these the latter is far more common. Type EE was sometimes used in the mid-14th century, *e.g.* one of the spurs from the Mass-Graves at Visby, 1361 (p. 67); and it sometimes appears on a group of spurs, usually with an elaborate decorative point at the junction of shank and body, of which representations are common, *c.* 1390–1410 (*e.g.* brasses of Robert Russell, *c.* 1390, at Strensham, Worcs, and of Sir William Bagot, d. 1407, at Baginton, Warwick. A late example is that of Robert Hayton, d. 1424, at Theddlethorpe, Lincs. This type of terminal is not found in association with the mid-15th century long shank). After the close of the Middle Ages it apparently again came into fashion ; but throughout the remainder of the 15th century Type FF was the invariable rule.

The 15th century was marked by two changes in the form of the rowel-spur, the increasing length of the shank, due to the growing use of horse-armour, and the elaboration of the body. A slight increase of length is visible on brasses of the decade 1410–20, *e.g.* on that of Sir Arnold Savage, d. 1420, at Bobbing, Kent ; and soon afterwards it becomes well marked, *e.g.* on the brass of Sir Thomas le Strange, d. 1426, at Wellesbourne Hastings, Warwickshire (Fig. 32, No. 6). By the third quarter of the century the fashion had reached its height, and it was not until the closing years of the century that these enormous spurs gave place to something different. The characteristic spur of the early 16th century had a short shank which projected very slightly from the heavy leg armour of the period. The change, which was sudden and complete, took place almost exactly at the turn of the century. Fig. 32, No. 9, illustrates an early representation of the new fashion on the brass of John Tame, d. 1500, at Fairford, Glos ; *cf.* Fig. 32, No. 8, from the brass of Sir Roger L'Estrange, d. 1506, at Hunstanton, Norfolk. The latest representations of long shanks on brasses seem to be those of Sir William Ayscough, d. 1509, at Stallingborough, Lincs, and of Robert Whyte, d. 1512, at South Warnborough, Hants ; and these are tardy survivals.

The 15th-century development of the body of the spur can only be studied in general terms. This is due to the increase in size of leg-armour, which, by the middle of the century, usually projects so as to cover all of the spur except the shank. Typologically the surviving examples seem to represent two streams of development (see Fig. 33). The one (Type A1) is well illustrated on a series of brasses ranging from *c.* 1410 to *c.* 1445, which depict a form of spur with a marked angle at the back of the ankle (see Fig. 32, No. 7). An early example of this consistent form can be seen on the brass of Sir John Chetwode, d. 1412, at Warkworth, Northants, and it is very commonly represented between 1415 and 1425, After that date it is less frequent, but it is shown as late as 1444. on the brass of Sir William and Sir Thomas Etchingham, at Etchingham, Sussex. The ornate bronze spur of this form, illustrated in Fig. 35, No. 1, was found on the field of the battle of Towton, fought March 15th, 1461. Typologically, however, it falls at least a quarter of a century earlier, and it illustrates very clearly the limitations of any attempted close

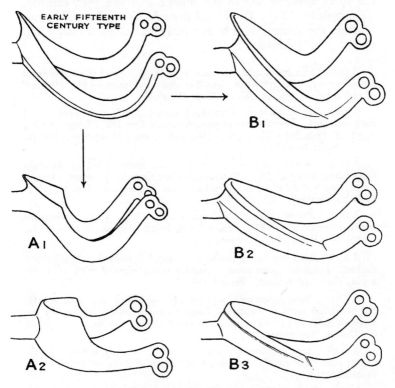

FIG. 33.—Types of 15th-century rowel-spur.

chronology. A derivative form of body (Type A2) is illustrated in Fig. 35, No. 6. It is not uncommon in conjunction with the exaggerated shanks of the late 15th century.

More characteristic, however, of these long-shanked spurs is the form of body (Type B1–3) illustrated in Fig. 35, Nos. 4, 5, and 7. It is developed directly from the plain curved body of the beginning of the 15th century, and although it did not lend itself to distinctive contemporary illustration, it can perhaps be recognized on brasses such as that of Richard Dixton, d. 1438, at Cirencester, Glos. It is extremely common in conjunction with the long shank, and it was evidently the stock form in use in the middle and late 15th century. Typologically, Type B1 should precede Types B2 and 3, but whether this corresponds to any real chronological distinction may well be doubted.

A 5016. Iron rowel-spur, terminals Type B(i)D. Short shank and small six-point rowel. Length 5·0 in., length of shank and rowel 1·3 in. First half of 14th century. Fig. 34, No. 1. From Moorfields.

A 308. Iron rowel-spur, short shank turned sharply downwards, small six-point rowel. Strongly curved arms, terminals Type DE. Length 4·4 in., length of shank and rowel 2·4 in. First half of the 14th century. Fig. 30, No. 8. From Westminster.

A 5012. Bronze rowel-spur, short shank, rowel missing. Strongly curved arms, terminals Type DE, with elaborate fittings for the straps. Length 5·0 in., length of shank 1·1 in. First half of the 14th century. Fig. 30, No. 7. From Bucklersbury.

A 2419. Bronze rowel-spur with remains of gilding. Large twelve-point rowel. Terminals Type FF. Length 6·1 in., length of shank and rowel 2·5 in. c. 1370–80. Fig. 34, No. 3. From London.

A 2418. Brass rowel-spur, similar to A 2419, but projecting slightly above the heel. Large nine-point rowel. Length 6·25 in., length of shank and rowel 2·5 in. Late 14th century. From Lothbury.

A 17351. Brass rowel-spur, with remains of gilding similar to A 2418, but projection more pronounced. Large six-point rowel. Length 6·3 in., length of shank and rowel 2·8 in. Late 14th century. Fig. 34, No. 6. From the Thames, Westminster.

A 13296. Iron rowel-spur, similar to A 2419, but more slender. Large, slender eight-point rowel. Length 6·0 in., length of shank and rowel 2·2 in. From Steelyard.

A 5005. Iron rowel-spur, medium shank, six-point rowel, long curving projection above heel. Terminals Type EE. Length 6·3 in., length of shank and rowel 2·75 in. Early 15th century. From London Wall.

A 5018. Iron rowel-spur, short shank, six-point rowel. Elaborate projection above heel. Terminals Type FF. Length 4·6 in., length of shank and rowel 1·6 in. Early 15th century. Fig. 34, No. 7. From Moorgate Street.

A 2425. Unfinished iron rowel-spur, short shank, projection above heel, terminals Type FF. Length 5·0 in., length of shank 1·6 in. Fig. 34, No. 8. From Town Ditch, Newgate.

108

A 22537. Iron rowel-spur, medium shank, slightly curved arms, terminals Type EE. Length 5·6 in., length of shank and rowel 2·2 in. Late 14th century. Fig. 34, No. 4. From Finsbury Circus.

A 8403. Iron rowel-spur, similar to A 22537, but with elaborate twelve-point rowel. Length 6·1 in., length of shank and rowel 2·4 in. Late 14th century. From London.

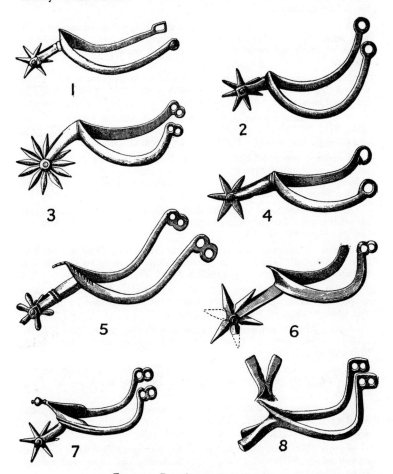

FIG. 34.—Rowel-spurs from London.
1, A 5016; 2, C 2347; 3, A 2419; 4, A 22537; 5, A 5004; 6, A 17351; 7, A 5018; 8, A 2425 (½).

C 2347. Iron rowel-spur, short shank, medium seven-point rowel, curved arms with terminals Type EE. Length 5·25 in., length of shank and rowel 1·5 in Fig. 34, No. 2. This spur, and many others like it, may belong to the late 14th or early 15th century, but the slender proportions and form of shank differ from those of the majority of specimens of that period. They should perhaps rather be assigned to the 16th century, and they are not further here listed. From London.

A 13348. Iron rowel-spur, medium shank, short curved projection above heel, arms straight and curved at ends, terminals Type EE. Length 5·7 in., length of shank and rowel 2·0 in. Early 15th century. From Leadenhall Market.

A 5004. Iron rowel-spur, medium shank, small six-point rowel. Ornamented projection above heel. Terminals Type FF. Length 6·6 in., length of shank and rowel 2·4 in. Early 15th century. Fig. 34, No. 5. From London.

A 19683. Bronze rowel-spur, with shank of medium length and plain body, Type B1. Small eight-pointed rowel. Length 6·2 in., length of shank and rowel 3·6 in. c. 1425. Fig. 35, No. 2. From London Wall.

A 18347. Iron rowel-spur, with long shank, body Type A2, but with a groove reminiscent of Type B3. Small eight-pointed rowel. Length 9·8 in., length of shank and rowel 6·2 in. Second half of the 15th century. Fig. 35, No. 6. From Old Queen Street.

A 10159. Iron rowel-spur, with long shank, body Type A2 (as A 18347). Six-point rowel. Length 7·9 in., length of shank and rowel 4·4 in. Mid-15th century. From Finsbury Circus.

A 1966. Iron rowel-spur, with very long shank, body Type B1. Medium six-pointed rowel. Length 11·3 in., length of shank and rowel 8·1 in. Mid-15th century. Fig. 35, No. 7. From Broken Wharf, Thames Street.

A 4971. Iron rowel-spur, with long shank and body Type B2. Large ten-pointed rowel. Length 8·75 in., length of shank and rowel 5·2 in. Mid-15th century. Fig. 35, No. 5. From London.

A 2420. Iron rowel-spur, rowel missing, with long shank, body Type B2. Length 9·0 in., length of shank 5·5 in. Mid-15th century. From Broken Wharf, Thames Street.

36.36. Iron spur, with long shank, body Type B2. Large eight-pointed rowel. Mid-15th century. Length 7·5 in., length of shank 4·3 in. From London.

A 2422. Iron spur, with long, slightly down-curved shank, body Type B2. Small twelve-pointed rowel. Later 15th century. Length 7·9 in, length of shank 4·3 in. Fig. 35, No. 4. From London Wall.

A 3593. Iron spur, with long shank, body (damaged) Type B2 or 3. Small six-pointed rowel. Length 7·8 in., length of shank 4·0 in. Later 15th century. From Sun Street.

A 4983. Iron spur, with long shank, body Type B3. Small eight-pointed rowel. Length 7·5 in., length of shank 4·3 in. Later 15th century. From London.

110

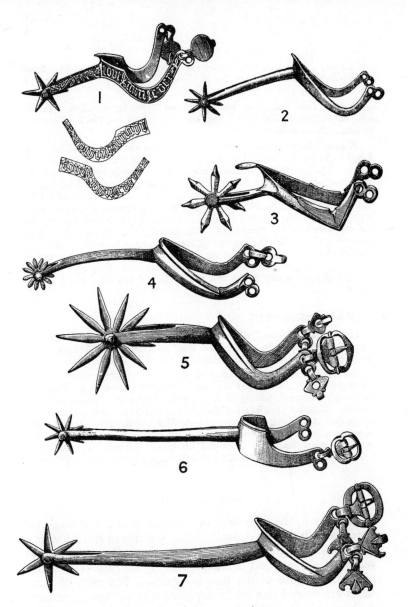

FIG. 35.—15th-century rowel-spurs.

1, from the field of Towton, 1461 (in the possession of the Society of
Antiquaries); 2–7, from London. 2, A 19683; 3, A 2423; 4, A 2422;
5, A 4971; 6, A 18347; 7, A 1966 (⅓).

A 25617. Iron spur, with medium shank, body degenerate Type B3. Small eight-pointed rowel. Length 6·4 in., length of shank 3·2 in. Later 15th century. From Thames Street.

A 437. Iron rowel-spur, body developed Type A2, terminals Type FF, long shank (incomplete) with a boss halfway; *cf.* Fig. 32, No. 8. Late 15th century. From Westminster.

A 2423. Iron rowel-spur with short shank and elaborately moulded body. Large eight-point rowel. Length 6·0 in., length of shank 2·0 in. Fig. 35, No. 3. The form is unusual, and it may provide an explanation for the otherwise meaningless ornament which occurs on the body of so many long-shanked rowel-spurs of Types B2 and B3, *e.g.* Fig. 35, No. 4. An identical spur is illustrated in Sir William Burrell's Sacrament Tapestry (*Archæological Journal*, XCIII (1936), 45–50). The figure of Abraham in that tapestry is deliberately archaised but the details are contemporary. Unfortunately the accepted date, 1439, has been queried in favour of another, *c.* 1474. It cannot be certain therefore on the evidence of this tapestry that the ornament on this spur is not simply an elaboration of a type already current. The general form of the spur, however, strongly suggests a date in the first half of the 15th century. From Thames Street.

Also illustrated :

Fig. 30, No. 6 (in the Guildhall Museum). Iron rowel-spur, angular body, terminals Type DE. Short shank and small six-point rowel. Length 4·2 in., length of shank and rowel 1·2 in. Early 14th century. From London.

Fig. 35, No. 1 (in the collection of the Society of Antiquaries). Bronze rowel-spur, fairly short shank and small six-point rowel, body Type A1. Elaborately decorated, bearing on the body the inscription : *En loial amour tout mon coer.* Length 5·9 in., length of shank and rowel 2·7 in. This spur was found on the field of the battle of Towton, fought March 18th, 1461. It was made, however, at latest, in the second quarter of the 15th century, and is typical of a group of spurs frequently illustrated on brasses between 1410 and 1445. (*Archæologia*, XI, 1808, 433, Pl. XX ; C. de L. Lacy, *History of the Spur*, Pl. 20.)

HORSESHOES

Thanks to the discovery of a certain number of medieval horseshoes in datable deposits, some features of their development are fairly clear. Nevertheless, there does not seem as yet to be any method of distinguishing the earliest medieval types from those of the Roman period. The nails of these shoes are shaped like fiddle-keys and they are accommodated in large countersunk depressions, the punching of which gives the shoes a sinuous outline. The general form is light, and so are the calkins. Shoes of this type are not

112

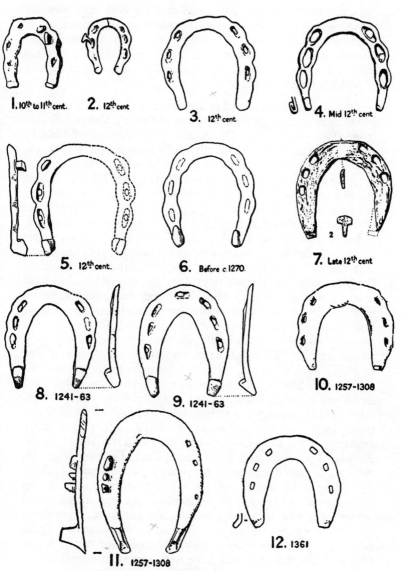

1. 10th to 11th cent.   2. 12th cent

3. 12th cent.

4. Mid 12th cent

5. 12th cent.

6. Before c. 1270.

7. Late 12th cent

8. 1241-63

9. 1241-63

10. 1257-1308

11. 1257-1308

12. 1361

FIG. 36.—Archæologically dated medieval horseshoes (¼).
(For list, see pp. 116–7.)

uncommon on Roman sites, and at least two examples are recorded from sealed Roman deposits in this country, at Colchester, and from the body of a Roman road near Gloucester. On the other hand, Roman horseshoes with plain outline are also known ; *e.g.* from a late 4th-century deposit at Maiden Castle, Dorset.

Shoes with the wavy edge are also found on Norman sites. Pitt-Rivers records a number from " Cæsar's Camp," Folke-stone (Fig. 36, No. 2). One was found at Pevensey by Mr. F. Cottrill, just above the rapid silt of the Norman ditch (Fig. 36, No. 4). Another from Kalesgrove, Reading, came from a cooking-pit with 12th-century pottery (Fig. 36, No. 5). There are also dated 12th-century examples abroad, *e.g.* from the lake-village of Lake Paladru, Isère (Fig. 36, No. 3), or from some pits at Nantes (*Bulletin de la Société des Antiquaires de Nantes*, I, 1860, p. 204, Pl. II, 8). Dr. R. W. Murray (*Journal of the British Archæological Association*, 3rd series, I, 25–6) has stated that the Norman examples can be invariably distinguished from those of the Roman period by the use of squared nails in the place of round. This thesis can, however, be main-tained only on the assumption that examples of the former type from Roman sites (*e.g.* from Hod Hill, Dorset) are in-trusive ; and several medieval specimens may well have carried rounded nails. There is not really a sufficient body of evidence to justify generalization. Still less have the proposed identifi-cations of Saxon shoe-types any objective validity. No dated pre-Norman examples are recorded from this country. Abroad their character, a rather clumsy variant of the Norman type, seems to be indicated by dated 10th–11th century examples from Brugeiroux (a fort near Murat, Cantal; in the Aurillac Museum), and from Castel-Cran, Brittany (Fig. 36, No. 1 ; C. de Keranflec'h Kernezue, *Castel-Cran* (1892), in the Vannes Museum). It is perhaps significant that in Scandinavia, where burials containing bits and stirrups, and occasionally the horses themselves, are common, horseshoes of the Viking period are not apparently recognized. There does seem to be documentary evidence of their use in Saxon England, but this may well have been somewhat restricted.

The Norman type certainly persisted into the 13th century.

114

It is found, for example, at Rayleigh Castle, Essex (destroyed 1270, *Transactions of the Essex Archæological Society*, n.s., XII, 1912, 147–85), and at Dyserth Castle, Flint (occupied 1241–63, *Archæologia Cambrensis*, 1915, p. 65). The two specimens from Dyserth are somewhat broader and heavier than usual ; and the same is true of a Swedish specimen from Ragnhilds-holmen, 1257–1308, in Stockholm Museum (Fig. 36, No. 10). They may be regarded as transitional to the heavier forms of the later Middle Ages.

The wavy edge does not seem to be found after the 13th century. An example in the Liverpool Museum from the field of Crecy, 1346, is hardly sufficient evidence of survival. There seem to be no dated English 14th-century specimens. Abroad, however, the type is clear enough. The nail-holes are no longer countersunk, and the outline is in consequence plain. The form is rather heavier than before. Of the four shoes from a pre-1350 deposit at Schloss Hallwil, Switzerland (N. Lithberg, *Schloss Hallwil*, Pl. 56, Nos. B, E, H, and J), three are of this type, the fourth has the sinuous edge of the earlier type. Another 14th-century specimen was found in the Mass-Graves at Visby, Gotland, 1361 (Fig. 36, No. 12). A light version of the type was found at Woody Bay, Isle of Wight, in a midden with 12th-century pottery (Fig. 36, No. 7 ; *Proceedings of the Isle of Wight Natural Historical and Archæological Society*, II, 1937, 681, Fig. 5, 1). The date seems remarkably early ; but the association seems to be sound, and the type may therefore have overlapped for a considerable period with the earlier form.

The 15th century seems to be marked by an increasing tendency to breadth and weight. The calkins are often very marked, though this is a feature which varies from shoe to shoe. Of the three specimens from Alsnö Hus, Sweden (abandoned in 1390 ; most of the material dates from the later 14th century, B. Thordemann, *Alsnö Hus*, Fig. 27, 6), one has very slightly upturned ends, two have heavy block-calkins. One of these latter is also " fullered," *i.e.* round the line of the nails runs a groove, a common feature of late medieval and post-medieval shoes. Its function is obscure. The specimen from Alsnö Hus seems to be the earliest recorded example. From the 15th century it can be seen, for example, on the statue of St. George, 1489, in the Storkirke, Stockholm. A fullered specimen found in the Town Ditch at Aldersgate (Fig. 37, No. 4) may belong either to the 15th or 16th century. It shows no trace of the characteristically 17th-century " key-hole " profile (found, for example, on the shoes from Prince Rupert's smithy at Gloucester), of which examples are very common and must cover a considerable period of time. In general, there is an increase of weight in the 15th and 16th centuries ; but although large calkins seem to be the rule in the 15th century, whereas in the 16th century they were frequently omitted altogether (R. W. Murray, *Journal of the British Archæological Association*, 1937, 136, quoting T. Blundevil, *The Four Chiefest Offices belonging to Horsemanship*, 1565), there seems to be no hard-and-fast distinction between the later medieval and the Tudor horseshoe.

(See also, particularly for later medieval and post-medieval types, R. W. Murray, *Journal of the British Archæological Association*, n.s., I, 1936, 14–33 ; II, 1937, 133–44 ; *Proceedings of the Cotteswold Naturalists' Field Club*, XXIII, 1927, 79–105 ; also Gordon Ward, *Sussex Notes and Queries*, VII, 1938, 38–43 ; *Transactions of the Lancashire and Cheshire Antiquarian Society*, LIII (1939), 140.)

36.217/50. Horseshoe with sinuous edge and countersunk depressions for the nail-heads. Small turn-over calkins. Fig. 37, No. 1. From Town Ditch, Old Bailey. Lent by the Caermarthenshire Antiquarian Society.

36.217/51-3. Three horseshoes similar to 36.217/50. Fig. 37, Nos. 2 (/53) and 3(/51). From London. Lent by the Caermarthenshire Antiquarian Society.

A 24957. Heavy horseshoe with plain outline and fullered groove on the line of the nail-holes. No calkins. A small sun is stamped on either end. Late 15th or 16th century. Fig. 37, No. 4. From Town Ditch, Aldersgate.

Also illustrated (from the Guildhall Museum) :

Horseshoe with heavy calkins and projecting nail-heads. 15th or early 16th century. Fig. 37, No. 5. From Moorfields.

Also illustrated (Fig. 36) from dated sites :

No. 1. From Castel-Cran, Brittany (after C. de Keranflec'h-Kernezue, *Castel-Cran* (1892), Pl. III, 5).

No. 2.   From Cæsar's Camp, Folkestone (after *Archæologia*, XLVII, 1882, Pl. XVIII).

No. 3.   From Lake Paladru, Isère (after E. Chantre, *Les Palafittes du lac de Paladru* Pl. IV, 4).

No. 4.   From the ditch-silting at Pevensey Castle.

No. 5.   From a cooking-pit at Kalesgrove, Reading (*Berkshire Archæological Journal*, XIII, 122).

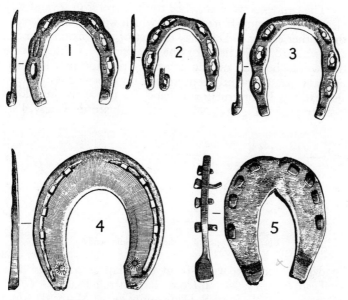

FIG. 37.—Medieval horseshoes from London.

1, 36.217/50 ; 2, 36.217/53 ; 3, 36.217/51 ; 4, A 24957 ; 5, in the Guildhall Museum.

No. 6.   From Rayleigh Castle, Essex (*Transactions of the Essex Archæological Society*, n.s., XII, 1912, Pl. E).

No. 7.   From a midden at Woody Bay, Isle of Wight (*Proceedings of the Isle of Wight Natural Historical and Archæological Society*, II, 1937, 681, Fig. 5, 1–2).

Nos. 8–9.   From Dyserth Castle (*Archæologia Cambrensis*, XV, 1915, p. 65).

Nos. 10–11.   From Ragnhildsholmen, Sweden.

No. 12.   From the Mass-Graves at Visby, Gotland (see p. 67).

117

Elaborate pendant-fittings were a regular feature of medieval horse-furniture. These commonly, but by no means invariably, included the badge or coat-of-arms of the owner, usually in enamel work or niello upon bronze or copper. The form of the pendant varies considerably, and the main types are here listed for convenience of reference.

The pendants were attached to the harness in several ways. Usually they swing from a fitting which was attached direct to the leather straps. This may consist of a horizontal bar with a downward projection for the attachment of the pendant; this would be used on the peytrel, a position in which such pendants are frequently represented on aquamaniles. It may alternatively be of cruciform shape, for use at the junction of two straps, *e.g.* Fig. 39, No. 1, in the Musée de Cluny, Paris.

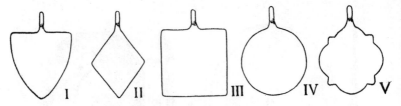

FIG. 38.—Types of medieval heraldic pendant.

Pendants were also worn from the strap across the horse's forehead (Fig. 18, No. 4, from the Luttrell Psalter. *Cf.* the S. Eustace retable from S. Denis, now in the Musée de Cluny, Paris). Salisbury Museum possesses a fine early 15th-century fitting for four pendants which projected upwards from some high point of the harness, probably the horse's head (*Proc. Dorset Field Club*, 32, 1911, 226), and there are portions of similar fittings in the British Museum. Another not uncommon form is illustrated in Fig. 40, No. 2, a pendant from London in the Guildhall Museum. The finest collection of pendants and pendant-fittings is that in the Musée de Cluny, Paris. For the latter, see also *Antiquaries Journal*, XVI (1936), 291, from Canterbury; *Ulster Journal of Archæology*, I (1938), p. 130, from Doonmore.

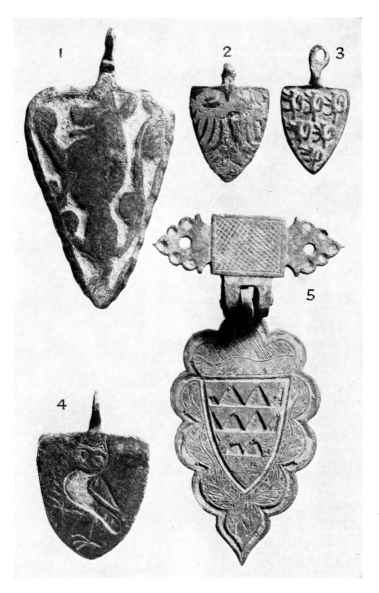

Heraldic pendants from London.
1, A 1360; 2, A 12016; 3, A 8871; 4, B 124; 5, A 1359 ($\frac{1}{1}$).

PLATE XIX.

[*To face p.* 119.

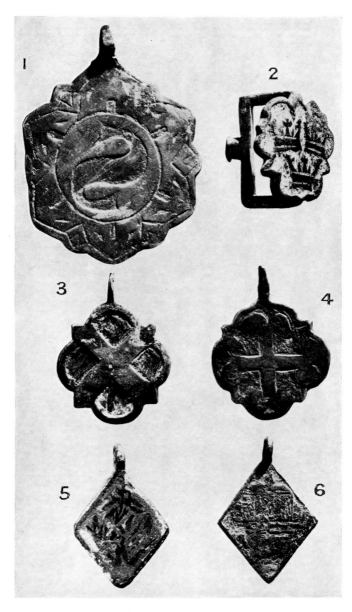

Heraldic pendants from London.

1, A 6783; 2, C 975; 3, A 2522; 4, A 6784; 5, A 8870; 6, C 483 ($\frac{1}{1}$).

The Musée de Cluny also possesses a large collection of non-heraldic pendants. These normally consist of an elaborately lobed central portion, usually of bronze-gilt, swinging within a similarly lobed frame, *e.g.* Fig. 39, No. 2, in the Musée de Cluny. These do not seem to have been common in England, but an example from St. Albans is figured in *Proceedings of the Society of Antiquaries*, 2, XXII (1908), p. 455.

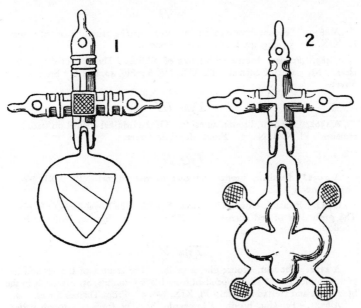

FIG. 39.—Medieval pendants and pendant-fittings (in the Musée de Cluny, Paris).

Type I

A 1359. An elaborate pendant with mounting for its attachment to a horizontal strap ; gilt bronze with remains of enamel, red round the border, blue (?) on the coat ; elaborate diaper border. The charge is possibly intended for vair. Early 15th century. Pl. XVIII, No. 5. From Basinghall Street.

A 1360. Pendant, bronze with traces of gilding, a lion rampant. The ground was enamelled. 13th century. Pl. XVIII, No. 1. From Smithfield.

A 8871 Pendant, bronze, six lioncels rampant. The background was probably enamelled. 14th century. Pl. XVIII, No. 3. From London.

A 12016. Pendant, bronze, a double-headed eagle displayed. The device itself is of red enamel, the ground of bronze. 14th century. Pl. XVIII, No. 2. From Southwark.

B 124. Pendant, bronze, an owl. It is not clear whether the body was originally enamelled. Pl. XVII, No. 4. From King Street, Kensington.

36.116/29. Pendant, bronze, with traces of gilding. The design was evidently painted or stencilled on the flat surface, an unusual technique. 13th century. Fig. 40, No. 1. From Fetter Lane. Given by H. S. Gordon, Esq.

Type II

A 8870. Pendant, bronze, a griffin segreant. The ground is of red enamel. Pl. XIX, No. 5 ; Fig. 40, No. 4. From London.

C 483. Pendant, bronze with traces of gilding. The coat-of-arms is not clear. No traces of enamel. Pl. XIX, No. 6 ; Fig. 40, No. 6. From Wood Street.

Type III

A 1362. Pendant, bronze, an eagle. Of the original enamel no trace now remains. Pl. XXI, No. 1. From Moorgate Street.

Type IV

A 3932. Pendant, bronze, an owl in red enamel. Pl. XXI, No. 4. From London Wall.

C 484. Pendant, bronze with traces of gilding, the Royal Arms of England. The ground is of red enamel. Pl. XXI, No. 2 ; Fig. 40, No. 3. From London.

Type V

A 2522. Pendant, bronze-gilt, a saltire. The enamel of the ground has gone completely. A similar pendant from Black Grounds, St. Albans, is in the St. Albans and Herts Museum. Pl. XIX, No. 3. From Thames Street.

A 6783. Pendant, bronze, a lombardic S. The form is a rough variant of Type V, and the sunk design was probably never enamelled. Pl. XIX, No. 1. From London.

A 6784. Pendant, bronze, a cross moline. The roughened ground was never enamelled. Pl. XIX, No. 4. From London.

Also illustrated :

Fig. 40, No. 2 (in the Guildhall Museum). Roundel, as Type IV, but designed for use on the upper part of the harness. From London.

Bronze discs bearing badges or coats-of-arms, sometimes in enamel-work, but more often in plain relief or impression, are quite common in the Middle Ages. Some of these show signs of attachment to a metal surface, and were presumably the fittings of mazer bowls and the like. Others have projecting studs which fastened them to leather. These, and more elaborate objects like C 975, were probably harness ornaments. Occasionally these discs bear no visible sign of

FIG. 40.—Heraldic pendants from London.

1, 36.116/29 ; 2, in the Guildhall Museum ; 3, C 484 ; 4, A 8870 ;
5, A 11069 ; 6, C 483 ($\frac{1}{2}$).

attachment to anything, *e.g.* C 2313, and it can only be assumed that they were somehow inset into leatherwork.

A 303. Plain bronze disc, bearing impressed a lion rampant within a bordure engrailed. Late 14th or 15th century. Pl. XX, No. 6. From Westminster.

A 2541. Disc of base bronze bearing in relief the Royal Arms of England and a label of three points, for Thomas de Brotherton, eldest son of Edward I

121

by his second wife. The back bears traces of solder for attachment to a metal surface. 14th century. Pl. XX, No. 2. From Broken Wharf, Thames Street.

A 6785. Bronze disc, pierced eccentrically by a single hole and bearing in relief three garbs, perhaps for the earldom of Chester. The background seems to be keyed (?) for enamel. 15th century. Pl. XX, No. 3. From London.

A 11069. Bronze disc, with a pronged attachment on the back and bearing a dove (?) and a leaf against a ground of blue enamel. Pl. XXI, No. 3; Fig. 40, No. 5. From Marshalsea Road.

A 15303. Bronze stud, bearing in repoussé a stag lodged. 14th century. Pl. XX, No. 4. From London Wall.

A 23642. Bronze stud, bearing in relief an Estoile. 15th century. Pl. XX, No. 5. From the Thames, at London.

C 975. Copper gilt badge, bearing the three crowns of East Anglia. On the back is a rectangular frame with a projecting stud. 15th century. Pl. XIX, No. 2. From London.

C 2313. Bronze disc, bearing impressed Quarterly, 1 and 4, 3 lions passant in pale, 2 and 3, a chevron ermine between 3 wings, for Nanfan. The back of the disc is smooth and bears no signs of attachment. Pl. XX, No. 7. From London.

29.201/3. Bronze disc, bearing the arms of Richard II, impaling those of his Queen, Anne of Bohemia, 1366–94. Pl. XX, No. 1. From Finsbury.

Heraldic roundels from London.
1, 29.201/3; 2, A 2541; 3, A 6785; 4, A 15303; 5, A 23642; 6, A 303;
7, C 2313 ($\frac{1}{1}$).

PLATE XXI.

To face p. 123.

Heraldic pendants and roundels from London.
1, A 1362; 2, C 484; 3, A 11069; 4, A 3932 ($\frac{1}{1}$).

III. DOMESTIC AND AGRICULTURAL OBJECTS

MISCELLANEOUS IRON IMPLEMENTS

(i) *Ploughs*

Ploughs are frequently illustrated in manuscripts, and it is evident that throughout the Middle Ages a considerable variety of forms were in simultaneous use. Typologically primitive implements continued in use for certain kinds of work side by side with others of more advanced type. It is in consequence extremely difficult to apply an absolute chronology to the development of plough-types; and the same difficulty occurs in connection with the iron plough-coulters. The Roman form, with its characteristically sharp-angled shoulder, is well known from the blacksmith's hoard at Silchester (*Antiquaries Journal*, XIII, 1933, p. 455); and it lasted well on into the Middle Ages, *e.g.* in the 11th-century manuscript, Trinity College, Cambridge, MS. R.17.1 (D. Hartley, *Medieval Costume and Life*, Pl. opp. p. 140), or in the 12th-century Canterbury Psalter (f. 62b). The later medieval curved type, however, with a slighter shoulder or no shoulder at all, certainly appears as early as the late 10th century (British Museum MS. Tib.B. V (i), fol. 3; *Antiquity*, September, 1936, Pl. 1) and is apparently universal at a later date (see, for example, the Bayeux tapestry, late 11th century; or the Luttrell Psalter, *c.* 1335–40). Both the examples in the Museum belong to the later type.

(For a full discussion of medieval and earlier ploughs, see A. Steenberg, " North-west European Plough-types of

Prehistoric Times and the Middle Ages," *Acta Archæologica*, VII, 1936, 244–80).

A 11473. Iron plough-coulter. Pl. XXII, No. 1. From King's Head Yard, Southwark.

A 25550. Iron plough-coulter. Pl. XXII, No. 2. From Town Ditch, Aldersgate.

(ii) *Sickles*

The ascription of the three sickles illustrated in Pl. XXIII to the Middle Ages rests solely upon their general similarity to the other tools of known medieval date. The sickle is a simple and efficient tool, and there is in consequence no real difference in form between those of the early 12th century (*e.g.* in the Bible of St. Etienne Harding at Cîteaux, C. Oursel, *La Miniature du XII Siècle à l'Abbaye de Cîteaux*, Pl. XXVI) and those in use at the present day. Toothed blades are illustrated in the Luttrell Psalter, *c.* 1335–40 (f. 168), but whether these were in common medieval use it is not possible to say.

A 13932. Sickle of simple form with rough wooden handle. The curve of the blade is relatively slight. Length of blade, 5·5 in., length of handle 4·2 in. Pl. XXIII, No. 3. From the Thames at Brentford.

A 13933. Sickle with short, stout handle. Length of blade 6·0 in., length of tang 4·5 in. Pl. XXIII, No. 2. From the Thames at Brentford.

A 22476. Sickle with long, slender blade. Overall length 16·4 in. Pl. XXIII, No. 1. From Finsbury Circus.

(iii) *Pruning-knives*

Knives of the form illustrated in Pl. XXIII, No. 4, are found at least as early as the 10th century (Haiman of Auxerre's Commentaries on Ezekiel, Ph. Lauer, *Les MSS. de la Bibliothéque Nationale*, Pl. VII). Though by no means confined to agricultural uses, they are conveniently classified as pruning-knives and are in fact frequently so depicted, *e.g.* in the Maciejowski Bible, f. 3a. For a more elaborate type of pruning-knife, see *Walpole Society*, Vol. XI, Pls. iii and iv, from an early 14th-century Bible Picture Book.

40.12. Pruning-knife. Length 6 in. Pl. XXIII, No. 4. From London.

PLATE XXII.

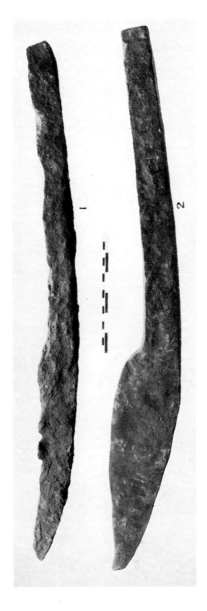

Medieval plough-coulters from London.

1, A 11473; 2, A 25550.

PLATE XXIII.

[*To face p.* 125.

Sickles and pruning-knife from London.
1, A 22476; 2, A 13933; 3, A 13932; 4, 40.12.

(iv) *Flesh-hooks*

Iron flesh-hooks were a regular feature of any medieval kitchen. They were used for examining and tasting the food while it was stewing in great cauldrons over the open fire (see, for example, the Bayeux tapestry ; or Fig. 68, No. 8, from the Luttrell Psalter). They are also often depicted in the hands of devils in manuscript representations of the Last Judgment or scenes of punishment and martyrdom (*e.g.* The Penitence of David by Jean Fouquet, 1465–70, *British Museum Reproductions of Illuminated MSS.*, III, Pl. XXV). The metal hook, with two or three prongs, has either a socket or a tang for the addition of a wooden handle, but it is not clear whether the distinction is of any chronological significance. Similar objects were current in Scandinavia in the Viking period (see T. J. Arne, *Das Bootgräberfeld von Tuna in Alsike*, p. 68, Pl. vi, 6, and refs. *ad. loc.*) and elsewhere as early as the Early Iron Age (J. Déchelette, *Manuel d'archéologie française*, 2nd ed., IV, Figs. 637–8).

A 3071. Iron flesh-hook, with socket and nail-hole for wooden handle. Three prongs. Length 10·8 in. Pl. XXIV, No. 1. From London Wall.

A 3072. Iron flesh-hook, with tang for insertion into wooden handle. The body is spirally twisted, and there are three prongs, of which the lower two are forged separately. Length 11·5 in. Pl. XXIV, No. 3. From London Wall.

C 775. Iron flesh-hook, with socket for a wooden handle. Three prongs, of which the lower two are forged separately. Length 12·2 in. From the Thames at London.

C 776. Iron flesh-hook, with socket for a wooden handle. Three prongs, of which the lower two are forged separately. Length 9·9 in. Pl. XXIV, No. 2. From the Thames at London.

(v) *Other Implements*

The implements described in the preceding sections are only a few of those that were employed by the craftsman and the farmer in the Middle Ages. There were tools for every trade and for every side of farm life, and many of these had a span of life that cannot be reckoned in archæological periods. Identical forms are in fact often in use down to the present day. It is consequently hardly practicable to do more than indicate some of the more common tools of which remains may reasonably be expected in archæological deposits.

Medieval spades were ordinarily made of wood with a metal sheath, after the Roman fashion (*e.g.* Maciejowski Bible, f. 10). It was not until the latter part of the Middle Ages that the whole blade was sometimes made of metal (*e.g.* in the early 15th century Flemish *Travels of Sir John Mandeville*, British Museum Add. MS. 24, 189, facs. Pl. XX, where the tanged metal blade is bound and riveted on to a wooden shaft). The blade might be rectangular, rounded, or pointed, but there does not seem to be any chronological distinction involved. Mattocks or picks were another common digging implement that could be used also for such varied purposes as siege warfare (Maciejowski Bible, f. 46b), agriculture, and mining (Brass of Robert Greyndon, d. 1443, at Newland, Glos). The simple form represented on the bronze doors of Hildesheim Cathedral (1015) and in the Bayeux tapestry can be seen throughout the Middle Ages (*e.g.* in the mid-13th-century Maciejowski Bible, in the early 14th-century Queen Mary's Psalter, and in the early 15th-century MS. of the *Travels of Sir John Mandeville* cited above). A more elaborate version, resembling a modern pickaxe, appears in a Matthew Paris MS., *c.* 1240 (*Walpole Society*, XIV, Pl. xix). Scythes, which are commonly shown in representations of the Seasons, were normally rather stouter in the blade than the modern implement (*e.g.* one shown on the West Front of Notre Dame, Paris), but this was not always the case (*e.g.* in Queen Mary's Psalter). Many farm-yard implements, such as rakes, were made purely from wood, but portions of metal-bound buckets, of metal-jointed flails (*e.g.* Maciejowski Bible, f. 84, Luttrell Psalter, f. 74b) and of pitchforks (*e.g.* Maciejowski Bible, f. 86) might be expected to survive. For bill-hooks, see above, *s.v.* Hafted Weapons, pp. 75–6.

The carpenter's tools were simple. Besides axes, which were used for trimming as well as for cutting wood, he had saws (usually cross-cut, *e.g.* in B.M. MS. Roy. 10.E.IV, D. Hartley and M. Elliot, *Life and Work of the People of England, 14th century*, Pl. 27 (c)), chisels (Maciejowski Bible, f. 26), hand-drills (*loc. cit.*), mallets, and hammers, of which the latter seem often to have been identical in form with those in use at the present day. The mortarer's trowel, too, was

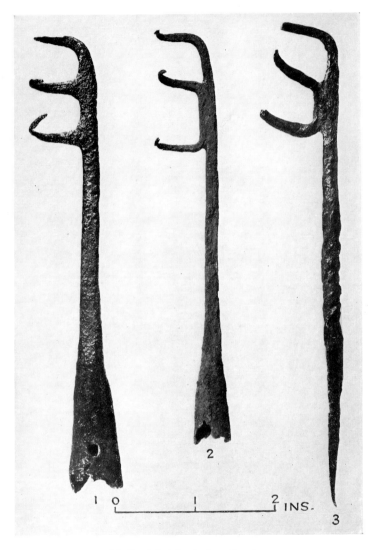

Medieval flesh-hooks from London.
1, A 3071; 2, C 766; 3, A 3072.

PLATE XXV.

[*To face p.* 127.

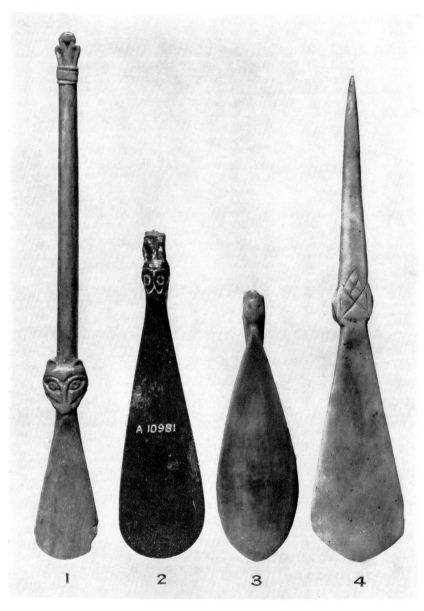

Early-medieval bone spoons from London ($\frac{1}{1}$).

the exact counterpart of its modern successor (*e.g.* Maciejowski Bible, f. 3a), as were the architect's calipers and dividers (a dated 13th-century pair of calipers was found at Dyserth Castle, 1241–63, *Archæologia Cambrensis*, 15, 1915). Of the smith's tools, bellows and tongs seem to have changed little throughout the Middle Ages. The trades, too, had their special tools. Thus, a butcher's cleaver, which was in fact a short-handled axe with a wide, straight cutting-edge (*e.g.* Maciejowski Bible, f. 23a ; *cf.* B. Berenson, *Speculum Humanæ Salvationis*, Pl. xxv, late 14th century Italian), was quite different from the sharply triangular blade of fishmonger's knife (D. Hartley and M. Elliot, *Life and Work of the People of England*, *14th century*, Pl. 27 (a) and (e), two 14th-century MSS.). The leatherdresser (D. Hartley and M. Elliot, *Life and Work of the People of England*, *11th–13th centuries*, Pl. 19 (c)), the gold-smith, the brass-founder, the barber-surgeon, every craftsman in fact had his own special tools. It is not always possible now to identify them ; but enough has been said to show the complexity of the problem, and the examples cited above at least illustrate some of the commoner forms of implement in daily use.

SPOONS

(i) *11th–13th centuries*

Spoons of the earlier Middle Ages are extremely rare. A limited number of silver examples are known of the same general form as the Coronation spoon, and some features of these, *e.g.* the form of the stem, are derived from types current in this country as early as the late 9th century. The derivation, however, of the animal's head which grips the bowl at the base of the stem is uncertain. Most of the known examples seem to belong to the close of the 12th century, but a bronze specimen in the Guildhall Museum, found in London, is of 13th-century date. In Scandinavia derivatives of the English type lasted on as late as the 15th century ; but in this country this class of spoon seems to have had a very restricted use and to have had little or no effect upon the types current in the later Middle Ages.

It is possible that in the 12th and 13th centuries spoons of bone, horn, and wood were in common use, as they were in Scandinavia (S. Grieg, *Middelalderske Byfund fra Bergen og Oslo*, pp. 102–5 ; but datable examples are rare. The four spoons from London illustrated on Pl. XXV are obviously related to the Coronation-spoon type ; but in the absence of dated examples it is hard to say whether the head at the base of the stem is the precursor of that on the 12th-century silver spoons or merely the humble contemporary.

(See J. B. Ward Perkins, " A Thirteenth Century Spoon in the Guildhall Museum," *Antiquaries Journal*, XIX, 1939, 313–6 ; P. Nørlund, En Dobbeltske i sølvefundet fra Ribe, Ostermark, *Aarbøger for Nordisk Oldkyndighed og Historie*, 1935, 117 ff.)

A 10981.   Bone spoon, stem missing, the long, narrow bowl very flat and grasped by an animal's head. Pl. XXV, No. 2.   From the Thames, Brentford. (*London and the Vikings (London Museum Catalogue)*, p. 50, Fig. 28, 6.)

A 21384.   Bone spoon, with short, pointed stem and long, narrow, flat bowl. At the junction of stem and bowl a boss derivative from an animal's head. Pl. XXV, No. 4.   From King William Street.

37.56.   Bone spoon, the stem ending in a trefoil ornament, the short, narrow, flat bowl grasped by an animal's head. Pl. XXV, No. 1.   From the City.   (*London and the Vikings*, p. 50, Fig. 28, 5.)

Also illustrated (from the collection of the Society of Antiquaries) :

Bone spoon, stem missing, the narrow, flat bowl grasped by an animal's head.   Plate XXV, No. 3.   From London.

(ii) 14th–15th centuries

Practically nothing is known about the development of the characteristic late medieval spoon, with its pear-shaped bowl, slender stem, and decorative knop, from the spoons of the preceding period.   The earliest recorded reference to silver domestic spoons is in the will of Martin de St. Cross in 1259, and it is unlikely that any of our surviving silver spoons of characteristic later medieval form date from earlier than the end of the 13th century.   Throughout the Middle Ages the spoons most generally in use must have been of wood, horn, or bone.   Silver was a rarity and an investment

128

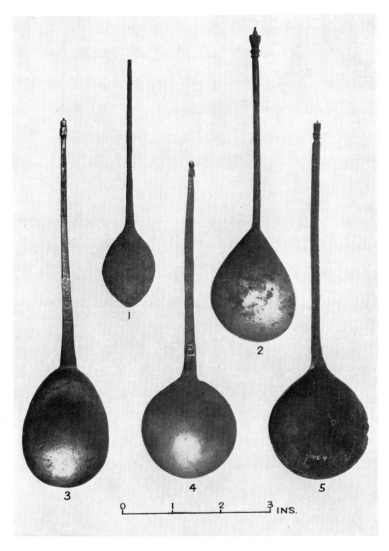

Late-medieval spoons from London.
1, A 10165; 2, A 18343; 3, A 20181; 4, A 9468; 5, A 3416.

PLATE XXVII.   [*To face p.* 129.

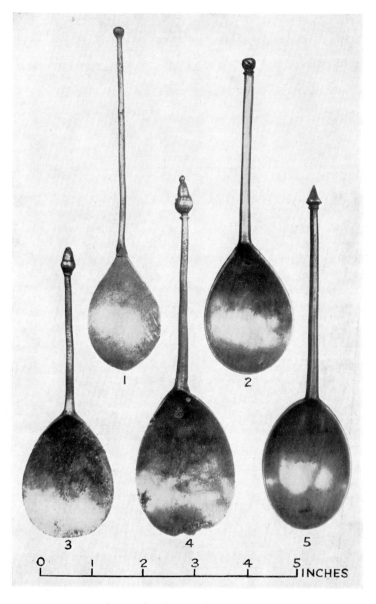

Late-medieval spoons from London.
1, A 3465; 2, A 19183; 3, A 3493; 4, A 3494; 5, 38.277.

for the average household, described and bequeathed in wills as an important part of a gentleman's estate. However, by 1481 the presumably prosperous knight, Sir Thomas Lyttelton, is the possessor of several dozen spoons of varying quality which he distributes among his heirs.

The earliest silver spoons to be described are the " twelve silver spoons with akernes " mentioned in a will of 1351. This form of knop would appear to be the earliest and most popular. Diamond points are not mentioned until the 15th century, while the first published reference to Maidenhead spoons is an inventory of Durham Priory written in 1446. This type of spoon which is very common in the 15th and 16th centuries, has a knop in the form of a female bust, supposedly the Virgin Mary. Strawberry knops are first mentioned in a will of 1440, and spoons with writhen knops are described in Robert Morton's inventory in 1487. But these are only the more common varieties. Various fancy knops were also in use, *e.g.* the " Woodwose " or wild-man spoon in the collection of the Victoria and Albert Museum. Spoons of the lion sejant type and some of the earliest Apostle spoons date from the latter part of the 15th century.

Throughout the period, pewter and latten spoons were used, but owing to the more durable nature of the material, the latter have survived more frequently than the former. One pewter spoon in the Museum, probably of the 15th century, has the stem strengthened by an iron rod, a reasonable precaution in view of the light design of so many medieval spoons. There is no reason, however, to believe that many spoons were so treated. According to Hilton Price (*Old Base Metal Spoons*, p. 20) the only surviving pewter spoon which may date from the 13th century is the ball-knop spoon in Pl. XXVII, No. 1. This leaf-shape is probably the earliest form of bowl in all metal spoons (*cf.* the Taunton spoon, *c.* 1200, *Antiquaries Journal*, X, 1930, 157), but in most of the surviving early examples it has already developed into the more characteristic pear-shape. Slender spoons with cone and finial knop— the former in latten—have survived only in base metal, but, generally speaking, they follow the same varieties as those in silver. Acorn knops and Maidenheads are common, but, according to Hilton Price (*loc. cit.*, p. 23), diamond points are

rare in pewter and unknown in latten. Some of the Maidenheads are interesting for their representations of contemporary
head-dresses, *cf.* Pl. XXVIII. Many of these spoons have the
maker's touch stamped in the bowl or on the stem, *e.g.* a crown

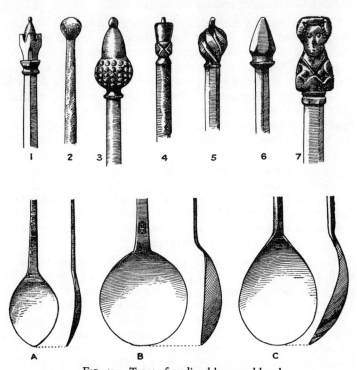

Fig. 41.—Types of medieval knop and bowl.

1, finial; 2, ball; 3, acorn; 4, acorn derivative; 5, writhen;
6, diamond; 7, maidenhead; A, leaf-shaped (early); B, circular
(possibly intermediate); C, fig-shaped (late).

or a fleur-de-lis; but no record of the touches has been
preserved, and it is impossible to trace the makers.

It is clear that a rising standard of living during the period
resulted in the possession of an increasing variety of metal
spoons among the well-to-do classes, and a sufficient number
have survived to familiarize us with the more popular types.

See F. G. Hilton Price, *Old Base Metal Spoons*; C. J. Jackson, *History of English Plate*, II, Ch. XVII; Norman Gask, *Old Silver Spoons of England;* Norman Gask, *Connoisseur*, November, 1937, p. 253, *Old Base Metal Spoons*.

FINIAL

A 16759. Latten spoon, round bowl, slender stem, stamped with two fleurs-de-lis, finial knop. Length 7·1 in. Late 14th or early 15th century. Found in London.

A 18343. Latten spoon, fig-shaped bowl, hexagonal stem, finial knop. Length 6·05 in. Pl. XXVI, No. 2. 15th century. Found in Old Queen Street.

A 3481. Latten stem of spoon, hexagonal with finial knop, maker's mark stamped at base. Length 4·7 in. 15th century. Found in London.

ACORN AND DERIVATIVES

A 3494. Pewter spoon, fig-shaped bowl, stamped with maker's mark, the initials A. B., slender round stem and acorn knop. Length 6⅜ in. Pl. XXVII, No. 4. Late 14th or early 15th century. (F. G. Hilton Price, *Old Base Metal Spoons*, Pl. III.)

A 3493. Pewter spoon, fig-shaped bowl, slender stem, acorn knop. Length 5·6 in. Pl. XXVII, No. 3. Found in London. 15th century. (F. G. Hilton Price, *Old Base Metal Spoons*, Pl. III.)

A 3497. Pewter spoon, part of pear-shaped bowl, hexagonal stem, acorn knop. Length of stem 3 in. 15th century. Found in London.

A 20181. Pewter spoon, fig-shaped bowl stamped with maker's mark, a sun in splendour, hexagonal stem with acorn knop. Length 5·35 in. Pl. XXVI, No. 3. 15th century. London Wall.

A 25421. Pewter spoon, pear-shaped bowl, hexagonal stem with acorn knop. Length 6·9 in. 15th century. Found in London.

A 3495. Pewter spoon, fig-shaped bowl, diamond-shaped stem with acorn knop. Length 5·95 in. 15th century. White's Ground, Bermondsey.

A 27684. Pewter spoon, fig-shaped bowl with hexagonal stem and modified acorn knop. Length 6·1 in. Late 15th century. Found in Wilson Street.

A 3416. Pewter spoon, flattened fig-shaped bowl, hexagonal stem, modified acorn knop, corroded. Length 7 in. Pl. XXVI, No. 5. Found in London.

A 9468. Latten spoon, oval bowl, stem stamped with maker's mark, a crown over a flower, knop derived from acorn. Length 6·1 in. Pl. XXVI, No. 4. 14th or 15th century. Found in London.

A 9469. Latten spoon, fig-shaped bowl, two illegible marks stamped on stem, knop derived from acorn. Length 7·1 in. 14th or 15th century. Found in London.

A 14422. Latten stem of spoon, four-sided, very slender, knop derived from acorn. Length 4·3 in. 15th century. Found in Tooley Street.

MAIDENHEAD

A 16756. Pewter spoon, fig-shaped bowl, stamped with maker's mark, hexagonal stem with maidenhead knop, wearing elaborate head-dress. Length 6·8 in. Pl. XXVIII, No. 2. *c.* 1450–70. Found in London.

A 3492. Pewter stem, hexagonal, with maidenhead knop. Length 3·8 in. Pl. XXVIII, No. 1. Early 15th century. Found in Worship Street.

A 3486. Pewter stem, hexagonal, with maidenhead knop. Length 4·0 in. Pl. XXVIII, No. 3. *c.* 1450–70. Found in London.

WRITHEN KNOP

A 3480 Pewter spoon, damaged fig-shaped bowl, gilt writhen knop. Length 5·8 in. Late 15th century. Found in London.

A 3304. Pewter stem ; part only, with gilt writhen knop. Length 3·25 in. Late 15th century. Found in Thames Street.

A 20174. Pewter spoon, fig-shaped bowl, stamped with maker's mark, a flower, hexagonal stem with gilt writhen knop. Length 5·8 in. Late 15th or early 16th century. London Wall.

A 19183. Pewter spoon, oval bowl stamped with maker's mark, a flower (?), hexagonal stem with writhen knop. Length 5·9 in. Pl. XXVII, No. 2. Late 15th or early 16th century. Found in Old Queen Street.

DIAMOND KNOP

A 25510. Pewter stem of spoon, hexagonal with diamond knop. Length 3·5 in. 15th century. Found in Wilson Street, Finsbury.

38.277. Pewter spoon, oval bowl, hexagonal stem with diamond knop. Length 6½ in. Pl. XXVII, No. 5. 15th century. (F. G. Hilton Price, *Old Base Metal Spoons*, Pl. IV.)

A 23693. Pewter stem of spoon, diamond shaped, with diamond knop. Length 3·2 in. 15th century. Found in London.

A 346. Pewter spoon, battered fig-shaped bowl, hexagonal stem with diamond knop. Length 6·5 in. 15th century. Found in Westminster.

A 3487. Pewter spoon, round bowl, hexagonal stem with diamond knop. Length 5·7 in. Late 15th century. Found in White's Ground, Bermondsey.

A 3504. Miniature pewter spoon, fig-shaped bowl, diamond knop, with small ring fixed to the top ; probably made as a toy. Length 2¼ in. long. 15th or 16th century. Found in Worship Street. (F. G. Hilton Price, *Old Base Metal Spoons*, Fig. 7.)

A 23693. Silver spoon, corroded and imperfect, fig-shaped bowl, four-sided stem with diamond knop. Length 6·5 in. 15th century. Found in the Thames at London Bridge.

A 2571. Silver spoon, fig-shaped bowl, diamond-shaped stem and diamond knop showing traces of gilding. Length 6·1 in. 15th century. Found in the Thames at London Bridge.

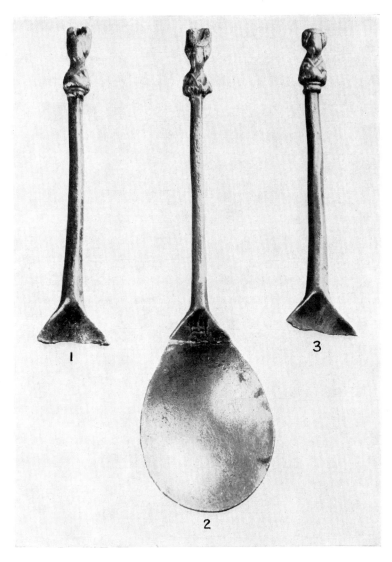

Maidenhead spoons, 15th century.
1, A 3492; 2, A 16756; 3, A 3486 (¾).

PLATE XXIX.[*To face p.* 133.]

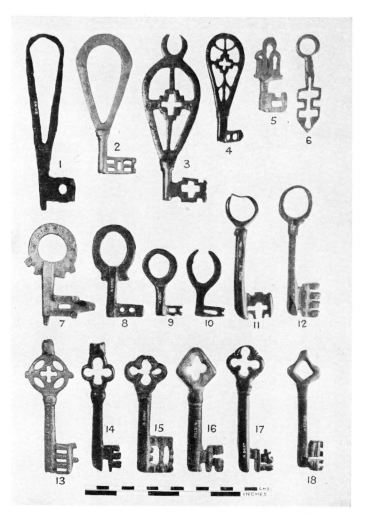

Medieval keys from London.

A 22442.   Silver spoon, fig-shaped bowl, hexagonal stem, diamond knop.
Length 6·1 in.   15th century.   Found in Moorfields.

VARIOUS

A 3465.   Pewter spoon, leaf-shaped bowl, round stem, ball knop.   Length
6·3 in.   Pl. XXVII, No. 1.   13th to 14th century.   Found on Aquarium
site, Westminster.   (F. G. Hilton Price, *Old Base Metal Spoons*, p. 21.)

A 3496.   Pewter spoon, stamped with maker's mark, a crowned T;
diamond-shaped stem with an iron rod down the middle; knop missing.
Length 5½ in.   15th century.   Found in Worship Street.

A 3491.   Pewter spoon, part of flat, fig-shaped bowl remains, stamped·with
maker's mark; round stem decorated at base and on each side of rat tail behind,
flattened lozenge knop.   Length 5·5 in.   15th century?   Found in the Thames,
London.   (F. G. Hilton Price, *Old Base Metal Spoons*, Pl. VIII.)

A 3503.   Pewter spoon, flattened circular bowl, hexagonal stem.   Length
3·75 in.   15th century.   Found in Town Ditch, Newgate.

A 13843.   Pewter spoon, fig-shaped bowl stamped with an illegible maker's
mark, unusual twisted stem, probably of foreign origin.   Length 5·5 in.   15th
century.   Found on Railway Approach, London.

A 10165.   Latten spoon, leaf-shaped bowl, flat stem, no knop, very slender.
Length 4·75 in.   Pl. XXVI, No. 1.   14th century.   Found at Finsbury Circus.
Given by W. M. Newton, Esq.

A 3489.   Latten spoon, oval bowl, flat stem stamped with maker's mark, a
crown over a flower, small ball knop.   Length 5·7 in.   Possibly 14th century,
French.   Found in London.   (F. G. Hilton Price, *Old Base Metal Spoons*,
Pl. VIII.)

KEYS

The close dating of medieval keys is a matter of great
difficulty.   A fixed point is provided by the large series discovered at Salisbury, which must post-date the foundation of the
town in 1227 (W. E. Penny, *Connoisseur*, XXIX, 1911, 11–16).
The circumstances of their discovery, however, in the accumu-
lated refuse of the old open drainage-system renders their
stratification extremely dubious : and the relative chronology
of the Salisbury series rests therefore almost entirely on
internal evidence.   Elsewhere in this country there are not
many archæologically dated medieval specimens.   Contemporary representations are common.   But the demonstrable
stylization of many examples renders the evidence of all somewhat suspect ; and the vast majority are St. Peter's door-
keys, whereas it is clear that very different forms were in

simultaneous use for different purposes. All that can here be attempted is a rough classification of the types in common use with such indications as are possible of their period of currency.

(i) *Door-keys and Chest-keys*
Type I

Type I (=O. Rygh, *Norske Oldsager*, Type 454) is a pre-Conquest form of key, which continued in use in the early Middle Ages. On the continent a large variety of sub-forms have been recognized (*Germania*, 1932, pp. 147–8), but for practical purposes they may be divided into those with a loop-shaped bow (Type I A) and those in which the bow is roughly circular (Type I B). Of these the latter appears to be the derivative form ; but Type I A has been found as late as the close of the 12th century (Fig. 43, No. 1, from King John's House, Tollard Royal). In the absence, however, of any later medieval representations it is hard to believe that either type remained in use long after that date. Archæologically dated specimens are rare, but a number of the more elaborate examples can probably be assigned to the 11th or 12th centuries, and it may be doubted whether in this country, at any rate, they were current much earlier.

A 1273. Pl. XXIX, No. 10. Bronze key with plain loop-bow, Type I B. Solid stem, bored at the end. Length 2·0 in. From the Minories.

A 2892. Pl. XXIX, No. 8. Bronze key with simple loop-bow, Type I B. Solid stem, bored at the end. Length 2·75 in. From an old pond, Clapton Common.

A 2893. Pl. XXIX, No. 9. Bronze key with plain loop-bow, Type I B. Solid stem, bored at the end. Length 2·0 in. From Fenchurch Street.

A 3086. Pl. XXIX, No. 3. Bronze key with elaborate openwork bow and loop for suspension, Type I A. Solid stem, bored at the end. Length 4·8 in. From London.

A 3087. Pl. XXIX, No. 4. Bronze key, similar to A 3086 ; loop for suspension missing. Length 3·15 in. From London.

A 9313. Pl. XXIX, No. 5. Bronze key with decorated bow. Solid stem, bored at the end. Length 2·2 in. Similar keys are often classed as Roman, but a specimen in Bergen Museum (B 4860) is probably of Viking or medieval date. From Paternoster Row.

A 12192. Pl. XXIX, No. 7. Bronze key with circular handle decorated with dot-and-circle ornament, Type I B. Solid stem and strongly projecting wards. Length 3·1 in. From Paternoster Row.

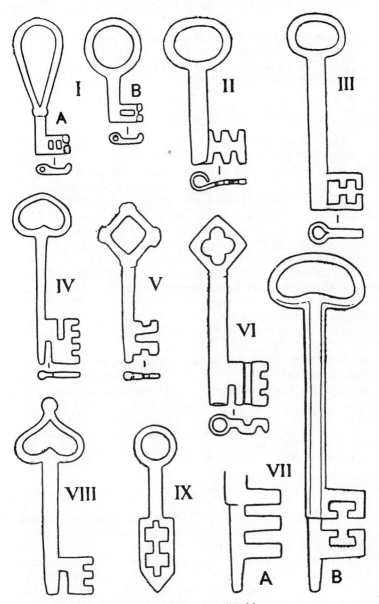

FIG. 42.—Types of medieval key.

A 13482. Pl. XXIX, No. 2. Bronze key with loop-handle, Type I A. Solid stem, bored at the end. Length 4·05 in. From Kingsway.

30.93. Pl. XXIX, No. 1. Iron key with loop-handle, Type I A. Solid stem. Length 5·0 in. From London.

Type II

Type II is distinguished by the simple method of its construction, the stem and bit being rolled out of a single sheet of metal, and the wards, instead of being filed up, are roughly cut with a chisel. The bow is almost invariably oval or circular. A few keys of this form are included in the Salisbury collection (see above, p. 133 ; Penny, *op. cit.*, Pl. I, Nos. 1–4), but their bits bear little resemblance to the more elaborate bits of the majority of the keys from that site, and they are probably rightly to be regarded as the earliest of the series. Typologically this simple form is the forerunner of Type III, and must therefore have been current at least as early as the late 11th century. It must, however, be remembered that elaborate bits were in use over a century before the crudely chiselled bits on the keys from Salisbury (*e.g.* that depicted on the sculptured tympanum at Carennac, Lot, *c.* 1150). Rough workmanship may be due as much to rusticity as to early date, and accordingly keys of Type II may belong to any date between the late 11th and the 13th centuries, possibly even later.

A 297. Pl. XXX, No. 21. Iron key, length 3·85 in. From Westminster.
A 298. Pl. XXX, No. 22. Iron key, length 3·9 in. From Tower Hill.
A 3094. Pl. XXX, No. 23. Iron key, length 2·7 in. From Crosby Hall.

Type III

Type III differs from Type II in the more solid construction of the bit, which is no longer rolled out of the stem in a single piece but is made separately and welded into place. Both types alike, however, are designed to operate a form of lock with a central projecting pin over which the open, tubular end of the key is fitted. In this they differ from Type IV, the shank of which ends in a solid and more or less tapering point, a form specially suitable for door-keys in that, given

136

symmetrical wards, it can be used equally from either side of the door. It is presumably for this reason that Types II, III, and VI, all of which have an open, tubular shank, are considerably less common than Types IV, V, and VII.

Keys of Type III are represented sporadically throughout the Middle Ages, and this range naturally covers a considerable variety of shape and size. St. Peter is a common figure in Romanesque monumental sculpture, and keys of this type can be seen for example on the tympana of the church of Ste. Foy at Conques and of Angoulême Cathedral, both dating from the first half of the 12th century, and on those of St. Trophime at Arles and of Siddington Church, Glos, which belong to the later 12th century. Keys with a solid, pointed shank are, however, considerably more common at this date. Later representations of Type III are less frequent, but they are found (*e.g.* on a 13th-century painted altar-front in Oslo Museum (Inv. No. 21973), and in other Scandinavian paintings), and surviving examples are not uncommon. A 344 and A 11884 in the Museum collections have obvious affinities with 14th- and 15th-century keys of other types ; and a number of later medieval chest-keys retain the tubular shank (*e.g.* from Salisbury, Penny, *op. cit.*, Pl. IV, No. 21 ; Pl. V, Nos. 26–9). In view of this range the dating of individual examples must depend on the form of the bow and of the bit and their resemblance to those on other, more distinctive types of key.

A 344. Pl. XXXI, No. 42. Heavy iron key with a rather flattened kidney-shaped bow. Octagonal stem. Length 3·4 in. From Westminster.

A 1868. Pl. XXX, No. 24. Iron key of unusual form ; the bit is formed from the same sheet of metal as the stem, the two edges being welded together. From Austin Friars. Given by Dr. Williamson.

A 1927. Fragmentary iron key with circular bow, and the remains of a heavy bit. Length 6·2 in. From Westminster.

A 11884. Iron key with strongly kidney-shaped bow, and the remains of an elaborate heavy bit. Length 4·75 in. From Middle Temple.

A 2866. Pl. XXX, No. 19. Iron key with oval bow and a collar round the neck ; simple toothed bit. Length 4·6 in. From Chamberlain's Wharf.

A 2916. Pl. XXXI, No. 44. Iron key with oval handle and heavy toothed bit. Length 6·1 in. From Maze Pond, S.E.

Types IV and V

Type IV and V cover a wide range of keys, all of which have in common a solid shank in place of the open, tubular shank of Type III. The common form at the beginning of the Middle Ages has a circular bow and a projecting shank. Specimens of this type, which bears a strong superficial resemblance to some 14th- and 15th-century keys, can be seen, for example, in the Bayeux Tapestry, late 11th century; on the figure of St. Peter in the cloister at Moissac, *c.* 1100; or on the early 12th-century tympanum over the south porch of St. Sernin at Toulouse. In the later 12th century the bow is still normally circular, but the projection of the shank has decreased, *e.g.* on the tympanum of St. Pierre at Vienne, Isère, *c.* 1150, or on the sculptured history of Theophilus at Souillac; and in the 13th century the shank rarely projects below the bottom of the bit. In the 14th and 15th centuries it tends once more to lengthen.

Lozenge-shaped bows are relatively common in the 13th and 14th centuries, usually on chest-keys or casket-keys. Previous to the 13th century representations (*e.g.* on the tympanum at Carennac, Lot, *c.* 1150) are infrequent. There does not seem to be any rule governing their use, and circular and lozenge-shaped bows are found indiscriminately on the same types of key, *e.g.* on a seal of the Abbey of Moissac, 1243, in which both forms are depicted side by side (E. Rupin, *L'Abbaye et les cloîtres de Moissac*, Figs. 8–9). The elaboration of the angles of the lozenge is an additional feature which appears as early as 1200 (*e.g.* on the tympanum of St. Gregor at Peterhausen) but is more frequent in the later 13th century, *e.g.* on inlaid tiles laid in the cloister at Moissac between 1260 and 1295; on the 13th-century coinage of Avignon (*Germania*, XVI, p. 218); and on a key from Salisbury (Penny, *op. cit.*, Pl. II, No. 6). The same feature occurs sporadically throughout the later Middle Ages, usually but not invariably on bows of the form of Type VI, *e.g.* on the seal of Bishop Peter Lodehat of Roskilde, 1395–1416 (in the National Museum, Copenhagen); in the arms on the Courtenay mantelpiece in the Bishop's Palace at Exeter, 1478–87 (*Archæological Journal*, LXXXIV, 382, Pl. VII); on a wooden reredos of Lübeck work

138

from Kvaefjord, Norway (in Oslo Museum). Many of the later medieval representations, however, are open to the suspicion of stylized treatment, and in general it may be said that most of the lozenge-shaped bows with elaborated angles belong to the 13th and early 14th centuries.

A surer guide to the date of individual keys is the form of the bit. Toothing along the fore edge of the bit makes a tentative appearance in chest-keys of the late 12th century (*e.g. Victoria and Albert Catalogue of Carvings in Ivory*, Vol. I, Pl. LVII), but does not really come into fashion until the 13th century. Keys similar in form and proportions to A 1517 (Pl. XXX, No. 33) and A 24639 (Pl. XXX, No. 26) can be seen very clearly on the late 13th-century floor-tiles from the Abbey of Moissac (1260–95) or on the 13th-century coinage of Avignon. On the 14th-century chest-keys this toothing reaches the extreme of elaboration, *e.g.* on the brass of Bishops Burchard de Serken and John de Mul at Lübeck, 1350 (W. F. Creeny, *Monumental Brasses on the Continent*, p. 13); *cf.* a key from Salisbury (W. E. Penny, *op. cit.*, Pl. III, Nos. 10 and 12).

(i) *Type IV*

A 304. Heavy iron key, length 3·2 in. From Westminster.

A 1364. Iron key, very similar to A 19547. Length 2·85 in. From London Wall.

A 1485. Iron key, very similar to A 1871. Length 3·15 in. From London Wall.

A 1517. Pl. XXX, No. 33. Small iron key, length 1·8 in. From London Wall.

A 1871. Iron key of simple form, circular bow, simple bit. Length 4·25 in. From London Bridge.

A 2862/2–3. Pl. XXX, No. 32. Two iron keys, lengths 2·9 in. and 3·1 in., found on a ring with A 2862/1, of Type VII A. From Fresh Wharf.

A 2869. Pl. XXX, No. 27. Iron key, length 2·65 in. From Fresh Wharf.

A 5108. Iron key, circular bow, bit damaged. Length 3·7 in. From Angel Court.

A 18350. Pl. XXXI, No. 41. Iron key, length 4·75 in. From Old Queen Street.

A 19547. Pl. XXX, No. 40. Iron key, length 3·5 in. From Barnham Street.

A 23296. Pl. XXXI, No. 45. Iron key, circular bow, simple bit. The end of the stem projects below the bit. From Old London Bridge.

A 24639. Pl. XXX, No. 26. Iron key, length 3·15 in. From Crosby Square.

(ii) *Type V*

A 2887. Pl. XXX, No. 30. Iron key, lozenge-shaped bow with foliated angles. Length 2·7 in. From Fresh Wharf.

A 2898. Pl. XXX, No. 28. Iron key, circular bow with foliated projections. Length 2·6 in. From Town Ditch, Newgate.

A 19831. Pl. XXX, No. 29. Iron key, circular bow with foliated projections. Length 2·3 in. From Royal Exchange.

Type VI

A number of closely related bronze keys of Type VI may be dated to the 14th and 15th centuries. They are characterized by the solid shank, bored at the end to leave a conical hole, by the massive bit, and by the elaborate form of the bow. The latter may be lobed or lozenge-shaped or a combination of both, and occasionally the corners of the lozenge are elaborated, as in Type V (Pl. XXIX, Nos. 15–18). The lobed form of bow is characteristic of the 14th century, *e.g.* on a number of 14th-century ivories (*British Museum Catalogue of Medieval Ivories*, p. 284, Pl. LXIV; p. 368, Pls. LXXXV and LXXXVI); on the brass of Bishops Burchard de Serken and John de Mul at Lübeck, 1350 (W. F. Creeny, *Monumental Brasses on the Continent*, p. 13); on the seal of Horseus Smetelav, *c.* 1400, in the National Museum, Copenhagen. An additional feature on a certain number of these keys is a loop at the top for suspension. This is well illustrated on the brass of Archbishop Jacobus de Sonno at Gnezen, Poland, 1480; and the late date of this example, coupled with the elaborate form of bow which it often accompanies (*cf.* Penny, *op. cit.*, Pl. III, No. 14), indicate that this feature probably belongs to the 15th century.

The following keys all have a solid shank and heavy, solid wards.

A 3866. Pl. XXIX, No. 13. Bronze key with quatrefoil bow. Length 3·65 in. From Barbican

A 4718. Pl. XXIX, No. 13. Bronze key with elaborate openwork bow and a tubular loop at the top. *Cf.* A 16116. Length 4·1 in. From Aldgate.

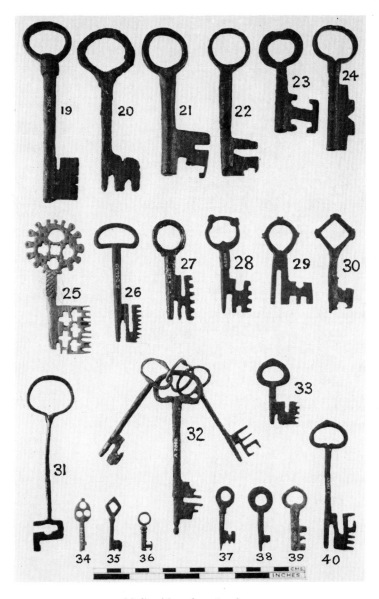

Medieval keys from London.

PLATE XXXI.

[*To face p.* 141.

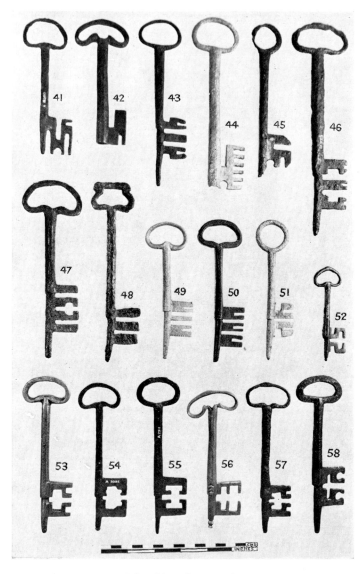

Medieval keys from London.

A 4719. Pl. XXIX, No. 12. Bronze key with plain ring-bow. Length 3·9 in. From Cheapside.

A 5760. Pl. XXIX, No. 16. Bronze key, bow lozenge-shaped, pierced with a quatrefoil. Length 3·85 in. From London.

A 5761. Pl. XXIX, No. 11. Bronze key with plain ring-bow. Length 3·75 in. From London.

A 8457. Pl. XXIX, No. 17. Bronze key with quatrefoil bow. Length 3·9 in. From London.

A 16116. Pl. XXIX, No. 14. Bronze key with quatrefoil bow and tubular loop at the top. *Cf.* A 4718. Length 4·0 in. From London.

A 17169. Pl. XXIX, No. 18. Bronze key with lozenge-shaped bow. Length 3·75 in. From London.

Type VII

A very common form of practical door-key usually made of iron. The stem, which is solid and projects to a well-defined point, usually narrows suddenly just below the head of the bit. The bit is symmetrical, for use from either side of the door, and it falls into one of two groups, Type VII A, where the general run of the wards is perpendicular to the stem, and Type VII B, where the wards surround a central opening. The two types were undoubtedly in contemporary use, but the latter does not seem to be found on the earliest examples. The bow, which may be circular but is more often oval or kidney-formed, provides the best criterion of date. The circular bow is relatively early. Keys of this type with a circular bow may be represented as early as mid-13th century on the incised 13th-century grave-slabs of the North Country (at Bakewell dated pre-1260 : *Archæological Journal*, IV, 52 ff. ; V, 252 ff.), but it is possible that these represent instead small casket-keys. One closely resembling A 1483 is however shown very clearly in the Luttrell Psalter (f. 166). A clear example can be seen on a 14th-century floor-tile in St. Mary's Church, Leicester ; and the circular bow still seems to be retained by the key depicted on the brass of William Ermyn, 1401, at Castle Ashby, Northants. The kidney-shaped bow seems to be characteristic of the 15th century, for by the early years of the 16th century it is already being superseded by the pointed heart-shaped bow, *e.g.* on the roof-bosses of Winchester Cathedral, 1503–9 *Archæologia*, LXXVI, 1926–27, Pl. XXXV ;

141

on the brass of a priest, *c.* 1520, at Tattershall, Lincs ; or in a
window of St. Michael-le-Belfrey, York, *c.* 1528–36 (J. A.
Knowles, *York Glass-Painting*, Pl. IX), which still, however,
retains the general form of Type VII.

Type VIIA

A 333. Pl. XXXI, No. 43. Iron key, length 5·85 in. Circular stem. Oval
bow. From Westminster.

A 1482. Pl. XXXI, No. 47. Iron key, length 6·3 in. Circular stem, with
mouldings. Kidney-shaped bow. The wards have a cross cut in the centre.
From London Wall.

A 1483. Pl. XXXI, No. 51. Iron key, length 5·2 in. Circular stem,
circular bow. From London Wall.

A. 1870. Iron key, length 5·4 in. Circular stem, with no marked division.
Kidney-shaped bow. From Old London Bridge.

A 1872. Iron key, length 5·2 in. Circular stem with a flat top ; no marked
division. Oval bow. From Old London Bridge.

A 2581. Pl. XXXI, No. 48. Iron key, length 6·4 in. Circular stem. Bow
folded into an unusual form. From London Wall.

A 2862/1. Pl. XXX, No. 32. Iron key, length 4·4 in. Circular stem.
Kidney-shaped bow. Found on a key-ring with A 2862/2–3, of Type IV.
From Fresh Wharf.

A 22366. Pl. XXXI, No. 50. Iron key, length 5·2 in. Octagonal stem
with mouldings. Slightly kidney-shaped bow. From Finsbury Circus.

A 26254. Pl. XXXI, No. 49. Iron key, length 4·9 in. Octagonal stem
with mouldings. Kidney-shaped bow. From Thames Street.

D 229. Pl. XXXI, No. 46. Iron key, length 7·6 in. Octagonal stem
with slightly kidney-shaped bow.

Type VIIB

A 357. Pl. XXXI, No. 57. Iron key, length 5·6 in. Octagonal stem.
Bow kidney-shaped. From Westminster.

A 1869. Iron key, length 5·6 in. Circular stem. Bow kidney-shaped.
From Old London Bridge.

A 2852. Pl. XXXI, No. 56. Iron key, length 5·1 in. Octagonal stem,
with mouldings. Bow kidney-shaped. From Worship Street.

A 2883. Pl. XXXI, No. 58. Iron key, length 5·9 in. Octagonal stem,
with mouldings. Bow, between oval and kidney-shaped. From Fresh Wharf.

A 2911. Pl. XXXI, No. 55. Iron key, length 5·75 in. Octagonal stem,
with mouldings. Bow oval. From Maze Pond, S.E.

A 5095. Pl. XXXI, No. 54. Iron key, length 5·4 in. Circular stem, kidney-shaped bow. From Sun Street.

A 15279. Iron key, length 8·25 in. From Chelsea.

A 20350. Pl. XXXI, No. 52. Iron key, length 3·5 in. Circular stem, bow kidney-shaped and slightly pointed. From Worship Street.

A 25596. Pl. XXXI, No. 53. Iron key, length 5·6 in. Octagonal stem, kidney-shaped bow. From the Thames, London Bridge.

36.146/7. Iron key, length 5·0 in. Circular stem, kidney-shaped bow. From Fetter Lane. Given by H. S. Gordon, Esq.

Type VIII

The heart-shaped bow of this form represents the final development of the kidney-shaped bow which is found on Type VII. It is possible that it occurs as early as the 15th century, but the majority of such keys are probably post-medieval. The shank may be tubular and open at the end (as Type III) or solid (as Type IV), indicating their use for chests rather than for doors. The type is well represented in the series of keys from Salisbury (W. E. Penny, *Connoisseur*, XXIX, 1911, Pl. V, Nos. 25–9).

Type IX

Casket-keys of this form were apparently in use in Roman times (*London in Roman Times* (*London Museum Catalogue*), Pl. XXX, Nos. B 9–12) and a rare Viking specimen of somewhat similar form (O. Rygh, *Norske Oldsager*, Type 458) is perhaps reminiscent of this usage. The medieval series belongs, however, to the 14th and 15th centuries. Fig. 43, No. 5, illustrates a simple iron specimen found at Alsnö Hus, Sweden (abandoned 1390; the majority of the material belongs to the later 14th century, B. Thordeman, *Alsnö Hus*, Fig. 27). The series of keys from Salisbury (see p. 133) includes several specimens (*Connoisseur*, XXIX, 1911, Pl. VI, Nos. 30–5), of which those with a simple ring-bow form a series consecutive with those with more elaborate 15th-century bows.

A 23754. Bronze casket-key. Length 2·8 in. Pl. XXIX, No. 6. From Ironmonger Row.

Some, or all of the keys of this form illustrated in *London in Roman Times* (*loc. cit.*) may be of medieval date.

A 2891. Iron key with solid moulded stem, toothed bit and heart-shaped bow. Length 3·5 in. *Cf.* W. E. Penny, *Connoisseur*, XXIX, 1911, Nos. 25–9, especially No. 27. Probably late 15th century. From Fresh Wharf.

A 11586. Pl. XXX, No. 31. Iron key of unusual design. The stem is a strip of metal which thickens laterally at the centre. Length 4·65 in. No obvious parallel is forthcoming, but it is probably of early date. From Southwark Street.

A 15279. Large key of crude form, welded in the centre to repair a break. Length 8·25 in. So crude a form may be of almost any date. From Chelsea.

A 18906. Pl. XXX, No. 25. Iron key with moulded tubular stem and elaborate bow and bit. The form of the bit with no less than ten teeth on the outer edge suggests a 15th-century date. From London.

(ii) *Casket-keys*

A number of the keys classified above as door-keys were undoubtedly used for chests and large boxes. It is, however, convenient to list separately the tiny keys, an inch or an inch and a half in length, which were used for locking small caskets. They can hardly be subdivided other than by their resemblance to the various kinds of larger key in contemporary use, and within limits the dating criteria applicable to door-keys can probably be applied here also. Several keys of this type are depicted, hanging from purses, on the 15th-century choir-screen in Albi Cathedral.

A 2894. Pl. XXX, No. 39. Bronze key, length 1·75 in. From Bear Garden, Southwark.

A 2895. Pl. XXX, No. 37. Bronze key, length 1·75 in. From City Road.

A 14921. Pl. XXX, No. 35. Bronze key, length 1·5 in. From the Thames, Richmond.

A 14922. Pl. XXX, No. 36. Bronze key, length 1·05 in. From the Thames, Richmond.

A 20818. Pl. XXX, No. 34. Bronze key, length 1·45 in. From Steel-yard.

A 23637. Pl. XXX, No. 38. Iron key, length 1·75 in. From the Thames, London.

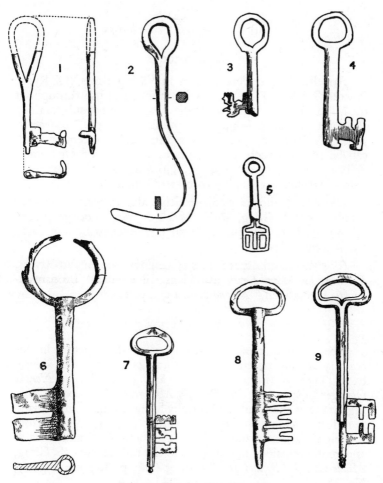

FIG. 43.—Dated medieval keys (½).

Nos. 1–2. From "King John's House," Tollard Royal, late 12th-century or later (A. Pitt-Rivers, *King John's House, Tollard Royal*, Pl. XXII).

No. 3. From Farringdon Clump, Berks (*Antiquaries Journal*, XVII, 1937, Pl. LXXXIIa, there dated to the reign of Stephen. The identification is, however, uncertain, and the associated pottery is assigned by Mr. G. C. Dunning to the late 13th century).

No. 5. From Alsnö Hus, Sweden, 1251–1390.

Nos. 4 and 6. From Ragnhildsholmen, Sweden, 1256–1319.

Nos. 7–9. From Moorfields, 15th century.

(iii) *Padlocks and Padlock-keys*

(*a*) PADLOCKS

Barrel-padlocks were known in Viking times (O. Rygh, *Norske Oldsager*, Type 452) and continued in use throughout the Middle Ages. An early medieval specimen of substantially Viking type, from London, is published in the *Antiquaries Journal*, VIII (1928), 524–6. The 14th and 15th-century form can be seen on such monuments as the brass of Sir Symon Felbrigg, d. 1416, at Felbrigg, Norfolk, or the chantry of Prince Arthur, d. 1502, in Worcester Cathedral.

Globular padlocks were probably also in use in the later Middle Ages (S. Grieg, *Middelalderske Byfund fra Bergen og Oslo*, pp. 89–90, Fig. 37), but there do not seem to be any dated English examples.

(For these and other forms of padlock, see A. Pitt-Rivers, *Primitive Locks and Keys*; also Hans Hildebrand, " Bronsnycklar fro medeltiden," *Monadsblad*, 1875, p. 166 ff.).

(*b*) PADLOCK-KEYS

The forms of medieval barrel padlock-key current in this country are illustrated in Figs. 44 and 45. The basic Viking form, Type A (Fig. 45, Nos. 1 and 5=O. Rygh, *Norske Oldsager*, Type 456; *cf. British Museum Anglo-Saxon Guide*, Fig. 218) has the shank set centrally to the wards. In England it is found as late as the 13th century (Fig. 45, No. 5, from Rayleigh Castle, abandoned *c*. 1270), and in Scandinavia it apparently remained in use down to the 14th century (S. Grieg, *Middelalderske Byfund fra Bergen og Oslo*, p. 80; see Fig. 45, No. 8).

The two common English types both have the bit set laterally to the shank, but in the one case (Type B, Fig. 45, No. 2) the wards radiate from the centre, as in the previous type; in the other (Type C, Fig. 45, Nos. 3, 4, 7, and 9) they form a loop, usually with two projections. The distinction corresponds to a difference in the internal mechanism of the padlock itself. In Scandinavia the first of these types is assigned to the 13th and 14th centuries, *e.g.* specimens from

146

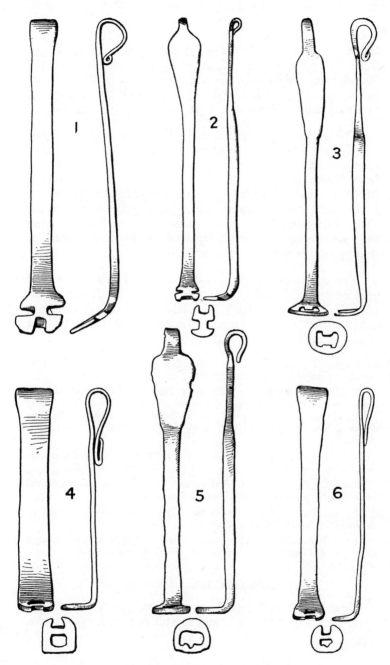

FIG. 44.—Barrel-padlock keys from London (⅓).

Lilleborg, destroyed in 1259 (in the National Museum at Copenhagen) and from Alsnö Hus, destroyed in 1390 (B. Thordeman, *Alsnö Hus*, Fig. 27, No. 10). In this country it has been found, associated with a padlock-key of Type A, in a 12th-century context at Aylesbury (Fig. 45, Nos. 1–2).

The second form, Type C, with a looped bit, is also assigned to the 13th and 14th centuries in Scandinavia, where dated examples are recorded from Lilleborg, destroyed in 1259, and from Vordingborg Castle, the 14th-century royal residence (S. Grieg, *Middelalderske Byfund fra Bergen og Oslo*, pp. 82–3). In England it would appear to be the regular type from the 13th century onwards. Both in this and in the previous types the loop-handle is frequently replaced by a hook, but it may be doubted if this is of any chronological significance.

The specimens in the London Museum collections were previously published as Roman (*London in Roman Times* (*London Museum Catalogue*), Pl. XXXI, Nos. 11–14), but from a comparison with other medieval specimens there can be little doubt of their true date and purpose.

A 2380. Fig. 44, No. 1. Padlock-key, Type B, with plain shank and hook-terminal. Length 6·5 in. From London.

A 24828. Fig. 44, No. 2. Padlock-key, Type B, with expanded shank and hook-terminal. For the form of the shank, *cf.* Fig. 45, No. 4, from "King John's House," Tollard Royal; also S. Grieg, *Middelalderske Byfunde fra Bergen og Oslo*, Fig. 29 (from Oslo). Length 5·8 in. From the Town Ditch, Aldersgate.

A 2378. Fig. 44, No. 3. Padlock-key, Type C, with expanded shank (*cf.* A 24828) and hook-terminal. Length 6·2 in. From Newgate Ditch.

A 10373. Fig. 44, No. 4. Padlock-key, Type C, with plain shank and hook-terminal. Length 4·6 in. From Westminster.

A 2379. Fig. 44, No. 5. Padlock-key, Type C, with expanded shank (*cf.* A 24828) and hook-terminal. Length 6·0 in. From London.

A 54. Fig. 44, No. 6. Padlock-key, Type C, with plain, slightly expanding shank and hook-terminal. Length 4·8 in. From Westminster.

(c) SLIDE-KEYS AND LATCH-LIFTERS

The "tumbler" lock is a primitive device, which was common in Roman times and is still not entirely obsolete.

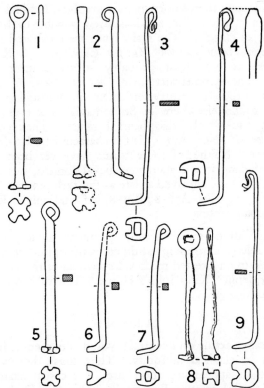

FIG. 45.—Dated examples of barrel-padlock keys ($\frac{1}{3}$).

No. 1.   Type A, found in association with 12th-century pottery on the site of a medieval hut at Aylesbury. (*Records of Bucks*, IX, 282; Aylesbury Museum.)

No. 2.   Type B, found with No. 1 at Aylesbury (Aylesbury Museum).

No. 3.   Type C, one of three similar keys, found at " King John's House," Tollard Royal.   The earliest material from this site belongs to the late 12th century. (A. Pitt-Rivers, *King John's House*, Pl. XXII, Nos. 10–12.)

No. 4.   Type C, from " King John's House," Tollard Royal (see No. 3).

No. 5.   Type A, from Rayleigh Castle, Essex (abandoned *c.* 1270, *Transactions of the Essex Archæological Society*, n.s. XII, 1912.   Southend Museum).

No. 6.   Padlock-key of simple form, from Rayleigh Castle, Essex (see No. 5).

No. 7.   Type C, from Rayleigh Castle, Essex (see No. 5).

No. 8.   Degenerate Type A, from Ragnhildsholmen, Sweden (Stockholm Museum).

No. 9.   Type C, from Dyserth Castle, Flint (*Archæologia Cambrensis*, XV, 1915 ; National Museum of Wales, Cardiff).

The slide-key, the use of which it involves, has had in consequence a very long life, and it is rarely possible to date chance finds at all closely. The main types are illustrated in *London in Roman Times* (*London Museum Catalogue*), Pl. XXX, and of these two at least probably survived until medieval times. The symmetrical form (*loc. cit.*, Nos. A, 1–2) was current in the 9th century settlement of Dorestad in Holland, and is found elsewhere in Scandinavia as late as the 11th century, after which it disappears from use. The asymmetrical form (*loc. cit.*, Nos. A, 3–4) is the characteristic English Dark-Age type. Neither of these forms have yet been recorded from England in a certainly medieval context, but they may well in fact have survived as late as the 12th century. A third form (*loc. cit.*, Nos. A, 6–8 ; B, 1–8) is found only in Roman or sub-Roman contexts.

Latch-lifters, an even more primitive device, are hardly susceptible to chronological differentiation, but attention may be called to an attested medieval specimen of the 12th century or later, from " King John's House," Tollard Royal (Fig. 43, No. 2).

SCISSORS

Scissors, acting on a central pivot, do not seem to have been known in classical antiquity. They must, however, have made their appearance soon after, for casual examples are found in north-western Europe throughout the Dark Ages. A pair were found among the secondary Saxon interments of a barrow at Driffield, Yorks (J. R. Mortimer, *Burial Mounds of East Yorkshire*, p. 286, Pl. CIV, 837), another in a barrow at Pibrac, Haute Garonne, with a Frankish burial (Toulouse, Musée S. Raymond). A third pair, with traces of silver inlay, from a woman's grave at Tuna in Sweden, are dated by the associated Islamic coins *c.* 800–50 (T. J. Arne, *Das Bootgräberfeld von Tuna in Alsike*, Fig. 27), and a fourth was found at Lastours, near Murat, in association with objects of the 11th-13th centuries (Aurillac Museum). E. E. Viollet-le-Duc (*Dictionnaire raisonné de l'Architecture française du XIe au XVIe Siècle*, II, p. 493, Fig. 1) illustrates a pair from a 10th-century Bible (MS. Bibl. Nat. Latin Bible, 6–3) ; but it is not until the 13th and 14th centuries that they make a convincing reappearance in everyday life. It is possible—and the associations of the pair from Tuna are suggestive—that their sporadic occurrence before the 13th century is due to casual importation from the Byzantine or Islamic world rather than to any local continuity of tradition.

In the later Middle Ages scissors were not common, and shears were still in normal domestic use. Scissors are mainly associated with trade. They are seen, for example, on the incised grave-slab of a 13th-century glover in St. John's Church, Chester (C. Boutell, *Christian Monuments of England and Wales*, p. 96 ; the similar monuments at Bakewell, Derbyshire, several of which depict shears, are securely dated before 1260). A large pair is used by a tailor in a 14th-century manuscript in the British Museum (Harl. 6563, D. Hartley, *Medieval Costume and Life*, title page), and another appears on the brass of Thomas Fortey and William Socors, woolmen and tailors, at Northleach, Gloucestershire, 1447 (Fig. 46, No. 1). In 1938 a pair was found at Avebury with the skeleton of a man who had been killed by the fall of one of the stones (Fig. 46, No. 2). The associated objects were a buckle, a tailor's bodkin (?), a silver sterling of the City of Toul, and two silver pennies of Edward I, 1307. For domestic work scissors were evidently established by the early 16th century, *e.g.* in Holbein's portraits of Niklaus Kratze, astronomer, 1528, and of Georg Gisze, merchant, 1532, but medieval instances are lacking.

In the Middle Ages the barber ordinarily used shears, as can be seen from frequent representations of Samson and Delilah, and these continued, exceptionally, in use as late as the early 17th century (Van Dyck, Samson, and Delilah, *c.* 1618, *Royal Academy Seventeenth Century Exhibition*, No. 68). In the 16th century shears and scissors were apparently used indiscriminately, and at least two examples of barbers' scissors can be quoted from the preceding century, the retable of SS. Claire and Marguerite, *c.* 1450, in the Museum of Catalan Art, Barcelona (*L'Art de la Catalogne*, "Cahiers d'Art," Paris, 1937, Pl. CXCIX), and a painting of Samson and Delilah on a casket by Fr. Morone at Milan (P. Schubring, *Cassoni*, No. 675, Pl. CXLVI).

The scissors used in the Middle Ages seem invariably to have had solid, circular loops set symmetrically to the axis of the handles. Open loops, formed by bending round the ends of the handles, appear however in the early 16th

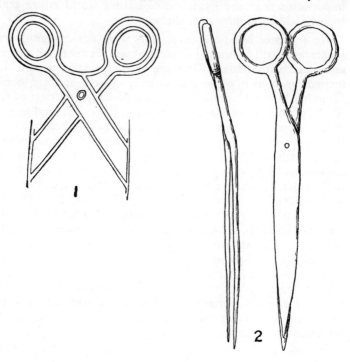

FIG. 46.—Medieval scissors.

No. 1. From the brass of Thomas Fortey and William Socors, 1447, at Northleach, Gloucestershire.

No. 2. Found at Avebury in association with two coins of Edward I, 1307. Early 14th century. (In the Avebury Museum.) (½.)

century (*e.g. Archæologia*, LXXI, 75–110, Fig. 22, No. 7, from Moorfields. *Cf. Anzeiger für Schweizerische Alterthümskunde*, 1930, p. 188, from a Swiss MS. dated 1513) and lasted into the 17th century, but there is no authority for ascribing them to the medieval period. In the case of the tailor in the

British Museum manuscript the handles are of different lengths, but this may be due to faulty drawing.

SHEARS

Shears have been in use in north-western Europe at any rate since La Tène times until the present day. Although scissors were known in the Middle Ages, shears were their ordinary everyday equivalent; and being a simple but efficient instrument there has been very little change of basic type throughout the long history of their use. Although it is possible to assign an approximate date to the introduction of certain non-essential elements, it is rarely possible to be sure that older forms did not survive. The garden shears advertised in *Harrods Catalogue* (Fig. 48, No. 10) differ in no essential from the types already established in the Middle Ages. Under these conditions of typological longevity it has seemed necessary to include with the medieval shears a certain number of examples which may well in fact be post-medieval. Of these the majority presumably belong to the sixteenth, some perhaps even to the seventeenth, century. With the increasing use of scissors shears began to drop out of domestic use, and none of the specimens in the London Museum are sufficiently large for other purposes.

Shears are normally made of iron. A certain number are in latten, or some other form of copper alloy, and from the forms it would seem that this is an indication of late medieval date. The later medieval shears seem also without exception to have a pronounced loop at the junction of the two arms (Type I B). This is a feature which appears occasionally in Scandinavia as early as the tenth century (O. Rygh, *Norske Oldsager*, Type 443), although the great majority of the shears from pagan Viking graves have the earlier and simpler form of junction (Type I A=Rygh, *op. cit.*, Type 442). A pair found in a cesspool at Old Sarum with a coin of William I have a distinct loop (Fig. 48, No. 2), but the earlier form may well have continued in use for some time. It is not, however, found in conjunction with the more developed types of blade.

153

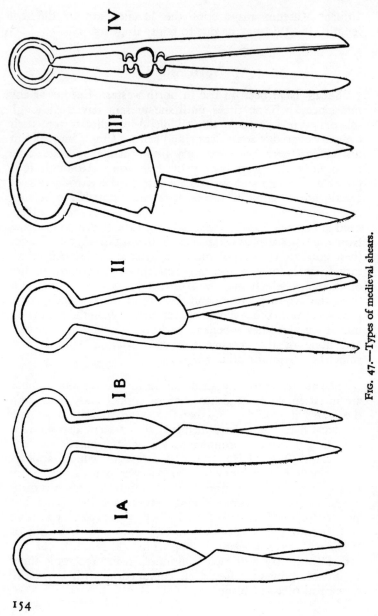

Fig. 47.—Types of medieval shears.

The form of the blade, particularly at its juncti on with the handle, provides the most effective criterion of date. The four main types are illustrated in Fig. 47. Type I preserves the simple Viking blade. Type II is characterized by a marked semicircular recess at the point of junction. Types III and IV may probably both be regarded as developments from Type II. In Type III the accentuation of the shoulder of the blade has relegated the recess into an insignificant nick and a knob at the base of the handle. In Type IV the recess is itself elaborated, and the development can be illustrated from intermediate examples.

In Scandinavia Type II occurs very exceptionally in pagan Viking associations (*e.g.* one from a tenth-century grave at Erikstein, Telemark, in the Oslo Museum), but in this country its earliest recorded occurrence is a specimen from Dyserth Castle (built 1241, dismantled 1263 ; see Fig. 48, Nos. 3–4). It can also be seen very clearly on a thirteenth-century capital, illustrating the story of Samson and Delilah, in the nave of Rouen Cathedral (Fig. 48, No. 7). Type I B evidently survived in simultaneous use, for it is depicted on a capital in the church at Aulnay, Charente-Inférieure (*c.* 1150–75, Fig. 48, No. 5), and in the Maciejowski Bible (Fig. 48, No. 6). Type III is less easily dated. The majority seem to bear a maker's mark on either blade, and in general these suggest a late- or post-medieval date. A very marked square shoulder is, however, a regular feature of the somewhat schematic shears, which, whatever their purpose, are a common item of decoration on the early medieval grave-slabs of the North Country (*Archæological Journal*, IV, 1847, 37–58, from Bakewell Church, Derbyshire, before *c.* 1260; V, 1848, 253–8; C. Boutell, *Christian Monuments of England and Wales*, pp. 85–95). An example, with characteristic square-shouldered blades but lacking the knob at their junction with the handle, was found in the (mainly) sixteenth- and early seventeenth-century deposits of the City-Ditch near All Hallows Church (Fig. 48, No. 9). It survives as the modern form (Fig. 48, No. 10).

Type IV, a specialized and therefore probably short-lived form, is well dated by the occurrence of two specimens, now in the Guildhall Museum, in the fifteenth-century Moorfields

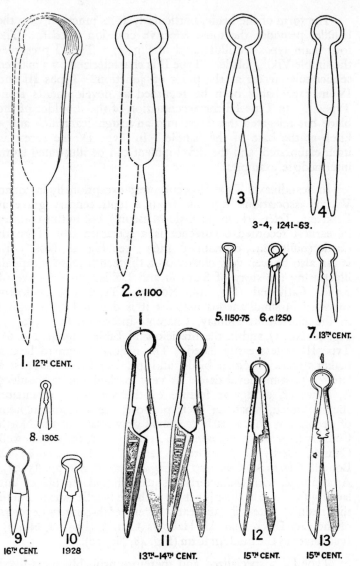

3-4, 1241-63.

2. c. 1100

5. 1150-75   6. c. 1250

7. 13TH CENT.

1. 12TH CENT.

8. 1305.

9. 16TH CENT.   10. 1928

11. 13TH-14TH CENT.

12. 15TH CENT.

13. 15TH CENT.

FIG. 48.—Dated examples of medieval shears and contemporary representations.

deposits; a third from the same source is of a simple form approximating to Type III (Fig. 48, Nos. 12–13). Fig. 48, No. 8, from the arms engraved on the tomb of Niels Manthorp (*ob.* 1305) in Skibby Church, Denmark (J. B. Løffler, *Danske Gravstene fra Middelalderen*, Pl. XVIII, 91), may illustrate an early elaboration of Type II, and other possibly intermediate forms are represented in the London Museum collections.

Type II

A 459.   Iron, length 5·4 in.   From Westminster.

A 1372.   Pl. XXXII, No. 1.   Iron, length 4·55 in.   Maker's mark on blades. From London Wall.

A 2814.   Pl. XXXII, No. 3.   Iron, length 3·9 in.   From Chamberlain's Wharf, Thames Street.

A 2815.   Iron, length 4·0 in.   Maker's mark on blades.   From Westminster.

A 2816.   Pl. XXXII, No. 2.   Iron, length 5·3 in.   From Hill Street, Finsbury.

A 2817.   Iron, length 4·9 in.   From Chamberlain's Wharf, Thames Street.

A 3142.   Iron, length 3·25 in.   From London.

A 10026.   Iron, length 4·3 in.   From Westminster Aquarium.

A 13349.   Iron, length 4·1 in.   From Carpenter's Hall.

A 18734.   Iron, length 4·1 in.   From Old Queen Street.

A 20699.   Iron, length about 6·02 in.   The handle is folded into a double loop.   From Tooley Street.

No. 1.   From Lake Paladru, Isère (E. Chantre, *Les Palafittes du lac Paladru*, Pl. III, 12).

No. 2.   From a cess-pit at Old Sarum (*Antiquaries Journal*, XV, 1935, 84).

Nos. 3–4.   From Dyserth Castle, Flint (*Archæologia Cambrensis*, XV, 1915, 65).

No. 5.   From a capital at Aulnay, Charente-Inférieure.

No. 6.   From the Maciejowski Bible, f. 15a.

No. 7.   From a capital in Rouen Cathedral.

No. 8.   From the tomb-slab of Niels Manthorp, d. 1305, at Skibby, Denmark (J. B. Løffler, *Danske Gravstene fra Middelalderen*, Pl. XVIII, Fig. 91).

No. 9.   From the Town Ditch, London, New Broad Street (*Archæologia*, IX, 1907, Pl. 29).

No. 10.   From *Harrods Catalogue*, 1928.

No. 11.   From London, inlaid with white metal (in the Guildhall Museum).

Nos. 12–13.   From Moorfields (in the Guildhall Museum).

157

A 27610. Pl. XXXII, No. 6. Iron, incomplete. The handle is elaborated into a trefoil with projecting terminal. From London.

38·2. Iron, incomplete. Handle as A 27610. From London.

Type III

A 402. Iron, length 4·6 in. Maker's mark on blades. From Westminster.

A 403. Iron, length 6·75 in. Maker's mark on blades. From Westminster.

A 457. Iron, length 8·2 in. From Goswell Road.

A 533. Iron, length 7·1 in. Maker's mark on blades.

A 591. Iron, length 7·9 in. (the form approximates to Type III). Maker's mark on blades. From Westminster.

A 594. Iron, length 4·3 in. Maker's mark on blades. From Westminster.

A 2809. Iron, length 6·9 in. Maker's mark on blades. From London.

A 2810. Pl. XXXII, No. 10. Iron, length 5·3 in. Maker's mark on blades. From Tooley Street.

A 22382. Pl. XXXII, No. 8. Iron, length 5·4 in. The slender form, approximating to that of Type IV, and the find-spot both suggest a 15th-century date. From Finsbury Circus.

Type IV

A 1387. Pl. XXXII, No. 13. Brass, length 3·8 in. From London Wall.

A 2808. Pl. XXXII, No. 11. Iron, length 5·7 in. Elaborately ornamented handles. From London.

A 2811. Pl. XXXII, No. 15. Brass, length 5·3 in. From Eldon Street, E.C.2.

A 27648. Pl. XXXII, No. 14. Brass, length 5·4 in. From Lambeth Palace.

Shears approximating to Type IV

A 2805. Pl. XXXII, No. 7. Iron, length 5·6 in. From Red Cross Street.

A 2807. Pl. XXXII, No. 12. Iron, length 5·6 in. From London.

A 10168. Pl. XXXII, No. 4. Iron, length 7·4 in. (between Types II and IV). From Finsbury Circus.

A 23531. Pl. XXXII, No. 5. Iron, incomplete. From London.

PURSES

(i) *General considerations*

Purses first made their appearance in medieval representations as simple, sack-shaped bags, tied at the neck with strings

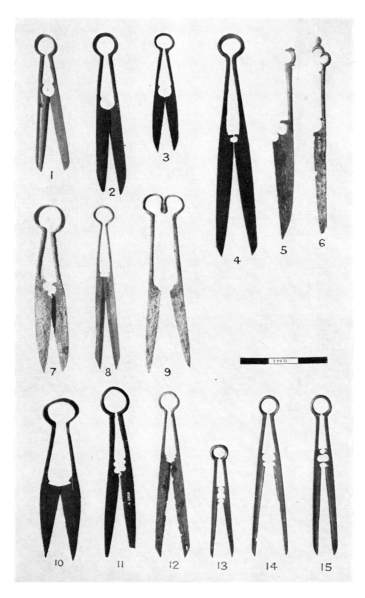

Medieval shears from London.

PLATE XXXIII. [*To face p.* 159.

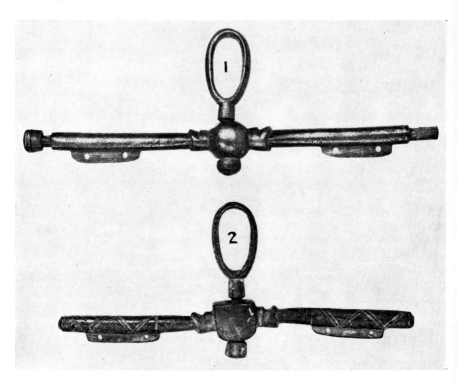

Late 15th-century purse-frames, Type A1.
1, A 9545; 2, A 13944. (Scale slightly less than ⅔.)

(see Fig. 53, No. 2, from a mid-13th-century Matthew Paris drawing, *Walpole Society*, XIV, Pl. XIII), and this simple form undoubtedly continued in use beside the more elaborate types that were evolved. It is seen very clearly, for example, on an Annunciation by Gerard David (J. Friedländer, *Die Alt-Niederlandischer Malerei*, VI, 175) and a white leather specimen was found at Newmarket containing two early 16th-century Nuremberg jettons (*Journal of the British Archæological Association*, XIV (1858), Pl. 9, 1). Usually, however, the bag is knotted at the base, sometimes with one or two, more often with three, knots. Though doubtless intended originally to make the bag hang better, these knots were retained later as a decorative feature and they were common on purses of all types until long after the close of the Middle Ages. See Fig. 53, No. 1, from the effigy of Queen Berengaria, d. 1230, at Espan (C. A. Stothard, *Monumental Effigies*, Pl. 16); No. 3 from the effigy of Philip Mede, d. 1474, in St. Mary Redcliffe, Bristol; and No. 6 from the brass of Philip Bosard, d. 1490, from Ditchingham, Norfolk. *Cf. Journal of the British Archæological Association*, XIV (1858), Pl. 9, Fig. 2, an embroidered 16th-century example.

Metal purse-frames did not come into fashion until the very end of the medieval period. These consisted of a more or less elaborate bar, slung from the belt by a central loop, and supporting from both ends one or two roughly semicircular metal arms, from which hung the bag itself. The bag hung well below the frame. The resemblance, therefore, to the elaborate purse found in the 7th century boat-burial at Sutton Hoo, Suffolk (*Antiquaries Journal*, XX, 1940, Pl. XXV, p. 170), the metal frame of which retained the outer edges of the bag, is probably quite fortuitous. The earliest English representation of a medieval metal-framed purse would seem to be that on the brass of John Browne, merchant, *c.* 1460, in All Saints, Stamford (Fig. 53, No. 5), but it is not until 1480 that they become common. From then on, until about 1520, they are, to the virtual exclusion of other types, a regular feature of civilian costume as shown on monumental brasses. After 1520 they occur only exceptionally, *e.g.* on the brass of John Cook in St. Mary-le-Crypt, Gloucester (1529), and on that of William

Hyll at Solihull, Warwick (1549). A few metal purse-frames of a devolved type are to be seen on portraits of the third quarter of the 16th century; and the miniature purses carried by ladies of the 16th century at the end of a chain slung from the clasp of the belt seem often to have had metal frames (Fig. 53, No. 11). After this date, however, it apparently became unfashionable to carry a purse, for it is never shown in 17th-century portraits; and with the lapse of fashion it presumably adopted a simpler, utilitarian form of plain leather or cloth. The great majority of surviving metal purse-frames undoubtedly belong to the period, *c.* 1475–1550.

The term " gypciere " is frequently, but wrongly, applied to these metal-framed purses. It was current in the 14th century. Chaucer's Franklin, for example, had

> " A gipciere all of silk
> Hang at his girdel, white as morwe milk,"

and the term was obsolescent by the end of the 15th century, when it was replaced by " pouch " or " purse." " Gipciere," which derives from the French *gibbecière*, a game-pouch, is applicable rather to the large flat wallets of leather or more costly material which appear as early as the 12th century (*e.g.* on the figure of Avarice on the ivory psalter-cover of Melisanda, *British Museum Catalogue of Ivories*, Pl. XV, No. 28) and continued in use throughout the Middle Ages. These might be worn slung from the shoulder like a satchel, as in the regular pilgrim's costume, or else fastened by one or two loops to the belt; and it was in this latter form that they later became assimilated to the tasselled, string-tied bag-purse to produce such types as the purse-wallet shown on an effigy, *c.* 1460, at Great Wishford, Wilts (Fig. 53, No. 4), and also many of the 15th- to 16th-century purse-types current abroad. Like the plain string-tied bag-purse, plain wallets of cloth or leather remained in use well after the end of the medieval period.

32.225. Embroidered purse. The ornament is heraldic, each face being divided into nine squares, displaying on the one side castles alternate with blank squares, on the other fleurs-de-lis alternate with swans. The embroidery no doubt originally displayed the proper tinctures, but these have faded and the devices can now only be distinguished by the variations in the stitchwork. 13th–14th century. Found in the Town Ditch at the corner of Aldersgate and Little Britain.

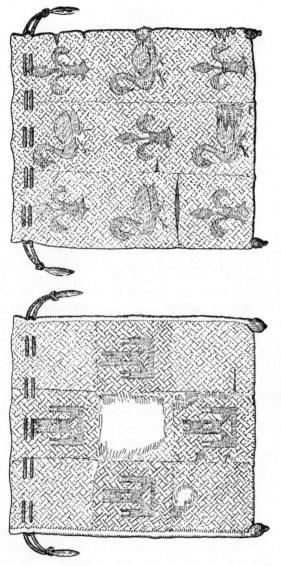

FIG. 49.—32.225. Embroidered purse, from Town Ditch, Aldersgate (⅓).

(ii) *Metal Purse-bars*

The variety of forms in which metal purse-bars are found is considerable, and in the absence of a dated series classification is bound to be somewhat arbitrary. It is, however, possible to make a broad distinction of type on the basis of the relative length of the horizontal bar, and within the limits of this distinction a certain number of specialized forms are sufficiently common and consistent to merit classification as sub-types. The classification here suggested does not claim to be exhaustive, but it probably covers most of the types that were in common use.

There is some reason to believe that the type was introduced from abroad in an already fairly elaborate form (see *s.v.* A6 below), and it is quite likely that continental fashions may also have influenced the later stages of its development. The extent of such influence it is hardly possible to assess without an unduly long discussion of the foreign material. The ordinary everyday purse in France or the Low Countries was either a string-tied bag, of the same kind as in England, or else some form of purse-wallet (somewhat as Fig. 53, No. 4; but usually with secondary pockets, like a rucksack, as carried by Dürer's Nuremberg housewives (Fig. 53, No. 12); and occasionally with metal fittings, *e.g.* on the choir-screen, *c.* 1480, in Albi Cathedral). The latter type hardly seems to be represented here. The purse of fashion abroad seems ordinarily to have been either an embroidered and tasselled rectangular wallet or else some sort of purse-wallet with elaborate metal mounts (see Flemish paintings and tapestries *passim*), and these may perhaps have played some part in the evolution of 16th-century English types. The commonest and most characteristic English forms, however (*i.e.* Types A2 and A3 and their immediate derivatives), seem to be a specifically native development and are hardly found abroad.

Type A, to which belong in general the earlier and more elaborate purses, has a bar which is usually considerably longer than the depth of the whole frame. The pendent frames are two in number. These are so often missing that generalization is dangerous, but it seems probable that on

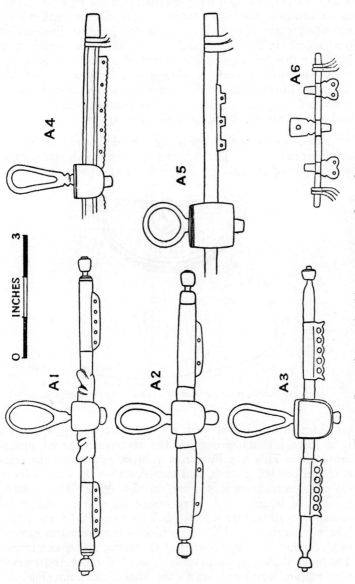

FIG. 50.—Late 15th- or early 16th-century types of purse-frame.

Types A1 and A2 they were invariably of the type illustrated in *Archæological Journal*, IV (1847), p. 361, *i.e.* the smaller loop swivelled upon two sockets set at the greatest diameter of the larger; in Types A4 and A5, on the other hand, it is probable that both invariably swivelled upon the ends of the main bar, and the same is perhaps true of type A3 and A6. The form of the frames differs correspondingly, an elaborately decorated loop of L-shaped section replacing on Types A1 and A2 the more solid form of the other types.

Type A1.—This form of purse is made entirely of bronze or of bronze alloy. The side-bars are circular in section and are gripped by animals' heads at their junction with the central

FIG. 51.—Purse, from the brass of Thomas Andrewes, *c.* 1490, at Charwelton, Northants.

boss, which is shield-shaped, or, not infrequently, spherical. It is further characterized by the invariable use of niello-ornament. This usually forms a lattice-pattern on the side-bars and pendent frames, and sometimes on the central loop. On the central boss it is more varied: AM; IHS; simple initials, of which W is very common; various forms of cross; a rudimentary scallop-shell pattern; or a tau-cross. The significance of this last, which is normally the symbol of St. Anthony of Egypt (see p. 260), it is not easy to determine. The purse shown on the brass, *c.* 1490, of Thomas Andrewes at Charwelton, Northants, bears a tau-cross at this point (Fig. 51).

Apart from a slight variety in the extent of the stylization of the animals' heads, this form is so constant as to suggest manufacture at a single centre.

A 1986. Central loop and bar only. Ends of bar missing, length originally *c.* 6·8 in. Niello-ornament, on central boss lattice and formal scallop-shell. From Finsbury.

A 2499–500. Two pendent frames of L-shaped section, swivelling the one upon the other (as *Archæological Journal*, IV, 1847, p. 361). Gilt brass with incised lattice-ornament. These belong to a purse of Type A1 or A2, and those of the latter are usually inscribed. From Worship Street.

A 9545. Central loop and bar only. Length 6·9 in. Niello-ornament, on central boss (spherical) W and * ; also on the bar zig-zag roulette-ornament of characteristic 15th-century type (*cf.* dagger, 33.296/1, p. 42). Pl. XXXIII, No. 1. From Putney Bridge Road.

A 13944. Central loop and bar and fragment of one pendent frame only. Length 6·6 in. Niello-ornament, on the central boss (shield-shaped) lattice and a tau-cross. Pl. XXXIII, No. 2. From Craven Street.

Type A2.—Like Type A1, which in general form it closely resembles, this class of purse is found only in bronze or bronze alloy, and is characterized by the invariable use of niello-ornament. It lacks, however, the animals' heads, and the greater part of the side-bars is of flat section. The central boss, which may be either shield-shaped or globular, and sometimes also the central loop and pendent loops, bears the same forms of ornament as Type A1. The side-bars, however, and often the pendent frames as well, are inscribed. The inscriptions are of a simple religious, talismanic character and are often surprisingly illiterate or incomplete. Especially common are AVE MARIA GRACIA PLENA and DOMINUS TECUM.

Like Type A1, Type A2 may well have been made at a single centre.

Type A3.—This is generally similar to the preceding types, but is made of iron with brass fittings, two on the central boss, which is invariably shield-shaped, one halfway along each arm of the bar, and a knob at each end. The pendent frames probably both hung from the central bar. The mounts bear incised ornament, that on the central boss following the forms already familiar on Types A1 and A2, with which Type A3 is doubtless contemporary.

165

A 1985. Central loop and bar only. Terminal-knobs missing. Length 7·6 in. Incised ornament on mounts, on central boss a tau-cross and a rose. Pl. XXXIV, No. 1. From Finsbury.

A 17930. Bar and pendent frames only. Central loop missing. Length 6·7 in. Incised ornament on mounts, on central boss IHC, the other face plain. Pl. XXXIV, No. 3. From Blackfriars Road.

A 23302. Central loop and bar only. Length 5·7 in. Only centre mounts (ornamented IHC and a tau-cross) and terminal knobs, other fittings missing. Pl. XXXIV, No 2. From Thames, Sion Reach.

38·227. Central loop and bar only; all fittings missing. Length 11 in. From Finsbury.

Type A4.—This class is made entirely of iron and is characterized by the length of the plates for the attachment of the bag on the under side of the bar. It is not a common type, but it is sufficiently consistent to justify a separate heading. The somewhat developed form suggests that it may perhaps be slightly later than Types A1–3.

A 13297. Central loop and most of one pendent loop missing. Length 7·5 in. Very similar to C 735. From Thames Street.

C 735. Complete. Length 8·1 in. Pl. XXXV, No. 1. From Eastcheap.

Type A5.—This class also is made entirely of iron, but the attachment plates are smaller and the central boss is roughly square, a departure from the forms of Types A1–4 perhaps indicative of late date. Like Type A4, Type A5 is not common, but it is consistent.

A 13940. Complete, length 10·5 in. Pl. XXXV, No. 3. There is a very similar purse in the British Museum. From Borough High Street.

A 19665. Bar only. Length 10·5 in. Rough lattice ornament on the central boss. From London Wall.

Type A6.—A few iron purses with bars of medium length are distinguished by the projection above the bar of the plates from which the bag is attached, and, in some cases at least, by the form of the central loop. Both pendent loops, which are of flattish section, hang directly from the bar. A simple purse of this type is shown on the brass of John Jay, *c.* 1480, in St. Mary Redcliffe, Bristol (Fig. 53, No. 8); and A 3084 strongly resembles an elaborate example, lacking the upward projections, on the brass of John Browne, *c.* 1460, in All Saints, Stamford (Fig. 53, No. 5). Elaborate purses of the same general type are shown on two paintings, *c.* 1460, by Petrus

166

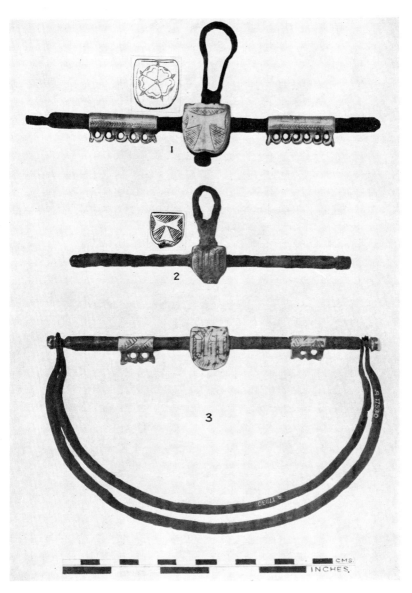

Late 15th-century purse-frames, Type A3.
1, A 1985; 2, A 23302; 3, A 17930.

PLATE XXXV. [*To face p.* 167.

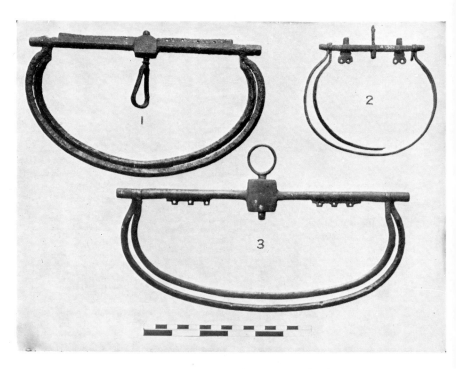

Late 15th-century purse-frames, Types A4–6.
1, C 735; 2, A 2505; 3, A 13940.

Christus, one in the National Gallery (J. Friedlander, *Die Alt-Niederlandische Malerei*, I, Pl. VIII) the other at Copenhagen (Friedländer, *op. cit.*, Pl. LXVI). It is evidently an early, and probably imported, form.

A 3084. Elaborate purse of iron with traces of tinning. Length of bar 3·9 in. Pl. XXXVI. From Sun Street.
A 2505. Plain iron purse. Length of bar 3·8 in. Pl. XXXV, No. 2. From the site of the Royal Aquarium.

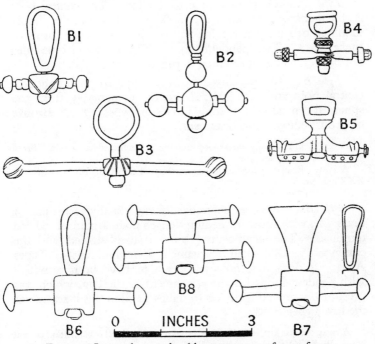

FIG. 52.—Late 15th- or early 16th-century types of purse-frame.

Type B covers a wide variety of sub-types which are distinguished in general by their small size and by the relative shortness of the bar. The pendent loops, one or two in number and regularly of circular section, hang direct from the bar; in some, probably late, examples they are absent altogether. Purses of roughly the same proportions make their appearance soon after 1500, *e.g.* that on the brass of Roger Bosard, d. 1505,

167

at Ditchingham, Norfolk (Fig. 53, No. 9); and in the absence of more detailed representations these may be presumed to have been at first mainly of Types B1–5, which more or less closely approximate to the long-barred purses of Type A, and later of the more devolved types. The isolated representation of a purse of this general form on a brass as late as 1549 shows that they did not necessarily go immediately out of use with the lapse of fashion *c.* 1520–5.

Type B1.—Of bronze or bronze alloy. The central boss is shield-shaped, as commonly on Types A1–2, and the simple moulded ornament is reminiscent of the niello-work forms of those types. Two pendent loops. This common type does not happen to be represented in the Museum's collection.

Type B2.—A specialized form of Type B1 with spherical central boss and terminals, derivative presumably from the spherical central boss of some purses of Types A1–2. Bronze or bronze alloy. No ornament.

A 2498. Gilt brass, central loop missing. Length of bar 2·2 in. From the Town Ditch at Newgate.
A 2501. Bronze, pendent loops missing. Length of bar 2·2 in. Pl. XXXVII, No. 2. From Southwark.

Type B3.—Another specialized form, usually of bronze or brass gilt, with short or medium-length plain arms and twisted terminals. The small central boss is shield-shaped, and the common " scallop-shell " ornament is reminiscent of Types A1–2. It does not, however, seem to have been provided with pendent loops for the attachment of the bag, which was presumably sewn directly on to the bar, and in this it resembles the late Types B6–8.

A 2494. Brass gilt, length of bar 4·9 in. Scallop-shell ornament on central boss. Pl. XXXVII, No. 4. From Finsbury.
A 8441. Bronze, length of bar 2·8 in. Central boss plain. Pl. XXXVII, No. 3. From London.

Type B4.—A small, cheap, and flimsy variant of Types B1 and 2, with hollow tubular bar and two pendent loops. Brass, occasionally gilt.

A 359. Central loop and one pendent bar missing. Length of bar 2·7 in. From Angel Court.

168

A 2503.   Complete.   Length of bar 1·55 in.   From Temple Avenue.
A 2506.   Complete save for one terminal.   Length of bar 2·1 in.   Additional bosses on central loop.   From Tabernacle Street.

Type B5.—A specialized but consistent form with squared central loop, two pendent loops, and moulded bar complete with plates beneath, pierced for the attachment of the bag, as on Type A. It may perhaps be regarded as a specialized derivative of Type A6.

A 2463.   Base bronze alloy.   Length of bar 2·3 in.   The bar lacks the upward " lips " of A 17155.   Pl. XXXVII, No. 1.   From London.
A 17155.   Bronze alloy.   Length of bar 2·0 in.   The " lips " on the bar and the rosette terminal are found on a purse in the British Museum.   From City Road.

Types B6–8.—These three closely related types are distinguished by the form of the boss and the absence of pendent loops. The form of the central loop marks an increasing abandonment of 15th-century types ; and the stamped ornament which is found on Types B7 and B8, *e.g.* on examples in the British Museum and in the Ashmolean Museum, Oxford, is not likely to be much earlier than the middle of the 16th century. They are, in fact, the extreme development of the late medieval purse.

Type C.—Besides the purses with a horizontal metal bar, there are a few in which bar and frames are fused into a single whole. The transition from such a form as that illustrated in *Journal of the British Archæological Association*, XIV (1858), Pl. 10, which can be dated from the decoration of the bag roughly to the middle of the 16th century, is slight ; and these purses of Type C obviously belong typologically to the very end of the series. Elaborate examples can be seen on a number of dated portraits : Maximilian II, by Antonio Moro, 1550 ; Duke Albert of Bavaria, by Hans Muelich, 1556 ; the same, by Hans Shöpfer, 1563 ; Thomas Howard, fourth Duke of Norfolk, by an unknown artist, 1562 ; Sir Thomas Gresham, by an unknown artist, *c.* 1560. The type is thus fairly securely dated to the period *c.* 1550–65. After this date metal-framed purses do not seem to have been used, and with the 17th century the girdle-purse was replaced by the pocket-purse (see H. Syer

169

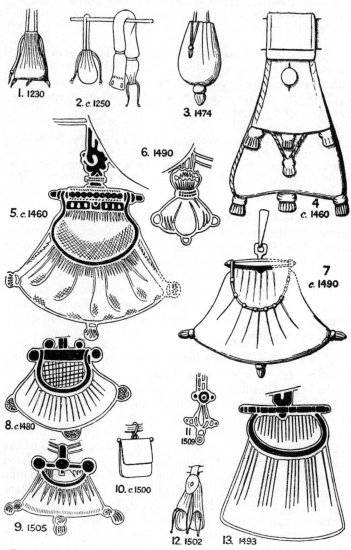

FIG. 53—Representations of purses from contemporary MSS., effigies, and brasses (see list, p. 171).

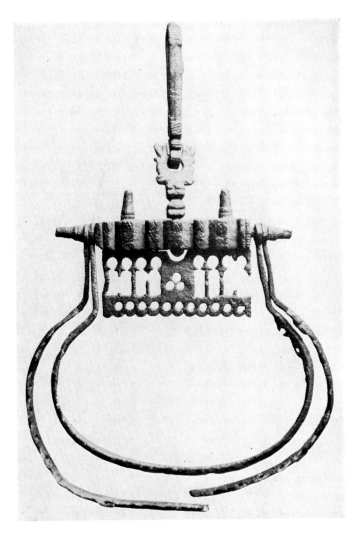

A 3084. Iron purse-frame, Type A6, *c.* 1460 ($\frac{2}{3}$).

PLATE XXXVII. [*To face p.* 171.

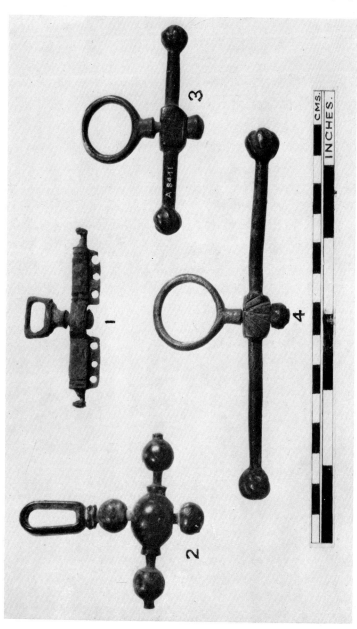

Early 16th-century purse-frames, Types B2, 3, and 5.

1, A 2463; 2, A 2501; 3, A 8441; 4, A 2494.

Cuming, *Journal of the British Archæological Association*, XIV, 1858, 131–44).

A 1987. Iron. Plain, save for mouldings on small central boss. From Finsbury.
A 18758. Iron. The frame is hinged at the point of maximum diameter, otherwise plain. From Old Queen Street.
A 18901. Iron, with brass central boss of the same form as Type B2. From Old Queen Street.

STEELYARD-WEIGHTS

During the medieval period the most common instrument for weighing was the equal-armed balance. During the later Middle Ages the steelyard also was employed, but it is doubtful if it was known before that date. It had been in common use in Roman times ; but, with the exception of a sub-Roman specimen from the Isle of Man (F. G. Skinner and R. L. S. Bruce-Mitford, " A Celtic Balance-beam of the Christian Period," *Antiquaries Journal*, XX, 1940, 87–102, containing a useful account of Dark Age measures and weighing-devices), there does not seem to be any subsequent record until its

No. 1. From the effigy of Queen Berengaria, *c.* 1230, at Espan, near le Mans (Stothard, *Monumental Effigies*, Pl. 16).

No. 2. From MS. of Matthew Paris, *Historia Major, c.* 1250 (*Walpole Society*, Vol. XIV, Pl. 13).

No. 3. From the effigy of Philip Mede, d. 1474, in St. Mary Redcliffe, Bristol.

No. 4. From an effigy, *c.* 1460, at Great Wishford, Wilts.

No. 5. From the brass of John Browne, d. 1460, in All Saints' Church, Stamford, Lincs.

No. 6. From the brass of Philip Bosard, d. 1490, at Ditchingham, Norfolk.

No. 7. From the effigy of John Cammell, d. 1487, in the Church of St. John the Baptist, Glastonbury, Somerset.

No. 8. From the brass of John Jay, *c.* 1480, in St. Mary Redcliffe, Bristol.

No. 9. From the brass of Roger Bosard, d. 1505, at Ditchingham, Norfolk.

No. 10. From Mostaert's " Tree of Jesse," *c.* 1500 (J. Friedlander, *Die Alt-Niederlandische Malerei*, X, 23).

No. 11. From a brass.

No. 12. From a drawing by Dürer in the Ashmolean Museum.

No. 13. From the brass of John Caysell, d. 1493, at Todmorton, Northants.

sudden reappearance in the 13th century, from the latter half of which over fifty examples are known. These have been exhaustively studied by Dr. G. Dru Drury (*Proceedings of the Dorset Natural Historical and Archæological Field Club*, XLVII, 1926, 1–24; LII, 1931, xlix–li; LVIII, 1937, 35–42) and it is here necessary only to summarize the evidence as to their character and date.

These steelyard-weights, which are made of latten with a lead core, are regularly of globular shape, flattened at the top, with a triangular projection for suspension and bearing round the girth two, three, or four shields charged with heraldic devices. In most cases (Class I) the devices are embossed in relief. Sometimes, however (Class II), the shields are cast plain and subsequently incised with armorial, or pseudo-armorial devices; and these weights, which are of inferior workmanship, are probably rightly to be considered as provincial imitations of Class I.

No two of the weights are exactly similar. This is due to their method of manufacture by the *cire perdue* process, which involved modelling afresh each time upon a friable core a waxen image of the bronze casing. The whole was then encased in clay, the wax was melted out and in its place was run the bronze. To complete the weight, the core was extracted through a hole at the bottom, and replaced with the necessary quantity of lead.

The heraldry employed upon weights of Class II varies considerably, but upon Class I the arms displayed are invariably, in some form or other, those of Richard, Earl of Cornwall and Poitou, younger brother of Henry III, or of his son Edmund, the second Earl. Richard's arms were: argent a lion gules crowned or, within a bordure sable besanty (Poitou within a bordure Cornwall); and, after his election as King of the Romans in 1257, or a double-headed eagle displayed sable. Richard died in 1272 and was succeeded by his son, Edmund, who continued to use both his father's devices. He married Margaret de Clare in 1272 and himself died in 1300, when the earldom became extinct. Weights therefore which bear the double-headed eagle can be dated after 1257, and those with the Clare arms after 1272. One weight, in

172

the British Museum, bears Leon and Castile quarterly, the arms of Queen Eleanor (1272–90) ; and the arms of England also commonly appear.

No absolutely convincing reason has been put forward for the monopoly apparently possessed by the family of Richard, Earl of Cornwall. In 1244 he received from his brother the right of farming the new coinage, and this control of the Mint might be presumed to indicate some additional authority over weights and measures. The appearance of the eagle, however, on four-fifths of the known examples clearly indicates a date after 1257. The most attractive suggestion is that of Dr. E. C. Curwen (*Sussex Archæological Collections*, LXVII, 1926, 193), who connects them with the German merchants of the Hanse. These had long been settled in London, but it was not till 1260 that they received from Henry III their first charter " at the instance of the most serene Prince of the Roman Empire, our Brother." Their Guildhall stood on the site of Cannon Street Station, and was known as the Steelyard. The derivation of the word is disputed ; but it seems to be generally agreed that it was originally the name of a place rather than of a thing. There were commercial centres so-named in a number of medieval English towns, and the name " Steelyard " would be applied by easy transference from the place to the official weighing-beam which was its most important furnishing. This explanation is not without its difficulties. In particular it still leaves unexplained the virtual monopoly apparently enjoyed by these weights of Class I. In the absence, how-ever, of any confirmatory historical record further discussion is hardly profitable.

A 2487. Steelyard weight of Class I, charged in relief with three shields : (i) lion rampant, (ii) lion rampant sinister, (iii) eagle displayed, *i.e.* after 1257. Height 3·4 in. ; maximum diameter 2·1 in. ; weight 2 lb., less 1 drachm. Round the shoulder there is an incised border of double-lined triangles within lines. Pl. XXXVIII, No. 2. *Proc. Dorset N.H. and A.F.C.*, LVIII (1937), 36. Given by Sir Guy Laking. Not certainly from London.

C 2381. Steelyard weight of Class I, charged in relief with two shields : (i) lion rampant, (ii) De Clare, *i.e.* between 1272 and 1300. Round the shoulder there is an incised border of triangles within parallel lines. Height 2·5 in.; maximum diameter 1·95 in. ; weight 1½ lb., less 2 drachms. Pl. XXXVIII, No. 1. *Proc. Dorset N.H. and A.F.C.*, LVIII (1937), 36. From the Laking Collection ; not certainly from London.

29.175/3. Steelyar weight of Class I, charged in relief with three shields each bearing a double-headed eagle displayed. Height 2·75 in.; maximum diameter 2·1 in.; weight 2 lb. 6 oz. No decoration on shoulder. Pl. XXXVIII, No. 3. *Proc. Dorset N.H. and A.F.C.*, LII (1930), p. L. Found during the construction of the Victoria Embankment.

LIGHTING

(i) *Cresset-lamps*

The commonest form of artificial lighting during the early medieval period was the open cresset-lamp. This took the form either of a bowl standing on some form of foot, or of a funnel-shaped bowl with a downward projection, for insertion in a bracket or for hanging in a loop from the ceiling.

In French and English manuscripts and sculpture the commonest type is the hanging lamp. Some of those in use as late as the 12th century are simply open bowls in the Dark Age tradition (*e.g.* on the tympanum of Ste. Foy at Conques); but the ordinary medieval funnel-shaped type (see Fig. 57, No.1, from the Psalter of Queen Ingeburga of Denmark, *c.* 1200) is seen as early as the 12th century (*e.g.* in a window, *c.* 1175, in Chartres Cathedral, R. de Lasteyrie, *L'Architecture réligieuse en France à l'époque romane*, Fig. 567) and certainly lasts into the 15th century (*e.g.* an unknown coat-of-arms in Prior Chillendon's Cloister, 1405–11, at Canterbury Cathedral, *Archæologia*, LXVI, 1915, Pl. XXVII, 3). Glass lamps of the same form were used in the Eastern Church from a very early date (F. Rademacher, *Die Deutschen Gläser des Mittelalters*, Berlin, 1933, pp. 77 ff.; see also *Journal of Egyptian Archæology*, XVIII, 1931, 196) and continued in use, scarcely altered, even beyond the end of the Middle Ages (*op. cit.*, Figs. 20a and 20d). Hanging lamps are normally shown in an ecclesiastical context. Examples do, however, sometimes appear in scenes of civil life, *e.g.* in the late 12th-century Huntingfield Psalter (Pierpont Morgan Library, Bennett Collection manuscripts, No. 16); and there are a number of surviving specimens of a purely domestic nature. It would seem, therefore, that the emphasis on ecclesiastical use is due rather to the character of the scenes usually depicted than to any restriction of actual usage.

The same considerations account, no doubt, for the rarity of representations of the even commoner form of cresset-lamp with a foot for standing on a shelf or table. These are found both in pottery and in stone. The former seem to be developed from a Frankish pottery-type and are common in the Low Countries in the 9th and 10th centuries (*e.g.* at Haithabu, early 9th–mid 11th century, Jankuhn, *Haithabu,* second edition 1938, Fig. 142). In England they have been found in 10th–11th century associations at Northampton and Norwich, and they lasted well on into the medieval period.

In Scandinavia these pottery lamps are replaced by more or less elaborate lamps in stone (S. Grieg, *Middelalderske Byfund fra Bergen og Oslo,* pp. 91–7). Stone lamps are occasionally found in England, but they seem to be exceptional. Both the examples here illustrated from the London Museum were apparently made from re-used capitals. Two other London specimens (Fig. 54, Nos. 3 and 4; in the Guildhall Museum) were designed in the first instance as lamps ; and there is a fine late 12th- or early 13th-century font-shaped stone lamp in Coventry Museum (*Trans. and Proc. Birmingham Arch. Soc.,* LVIII, 1934, Pl. xx).

A 16412. Fig. 54, No. 1. Broken cresset-lamp of soft stone, made from a reused 12th-century capital. Height 5·5 in. From the site of the General Post Office. Given by the Postmaster-General.

A 26228. Fig. 54, No. 2. Broken cresset-lamp of soft stone, made from a reused 12th-century capital. Height 5 in. From the corner of Wood Street and Gresham Street.

A 5201. Fig. 54, No. 5. Cresset-lamp of hard, sandy, hand-made grey pottery containing a little crushed shell. From London Wall.

A 25740. Fig. 54, No. 8. Funnel-shaped cresset-lamp of hard, red, hand-made pottery, with a patch of pale green glaze. 13th century. From an ashpit in Nicholas Lane.

A 28385. Fig. 54, No. 7. Small cresset-lamp of hard, coarse, hand-made gritted grey pottery. From Snow Hill.

29.94/28. Fig. 54, No. 6. Cresset-lamp of hand-made, hard, coarse, grey pottery containing crushed shell. From the Midland Bank, Princes Street, E.C.4.

Also illustrated, from the Guildhall Museum :—

Fig. 54, No. 3. Stone cresset-lamp from London.

Fig. 54, No. 4. Stone cresset-lamp from the site of the Old General Post Office.

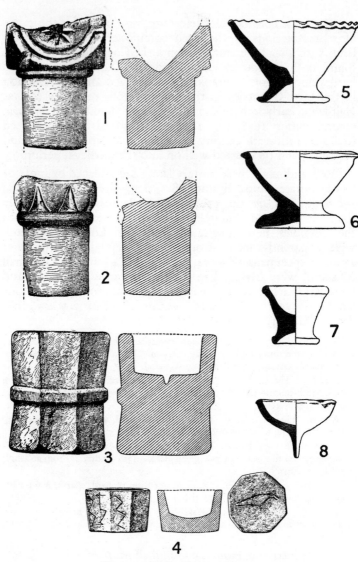

FIG. 54.—Medieval cresset-lamps.
1–2, 5–8, in the London Museum ; 3–4 in the Guildhall
Museum (¼).

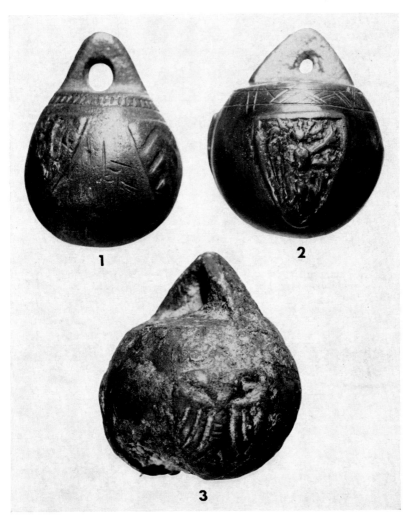

13th-century steelyard weights.
1, C 2381; 2, A 2487; 3, 29.175/3. (Scale slightly less than life-size.)

PLATE XXXIX.   [*To face p.* 177.

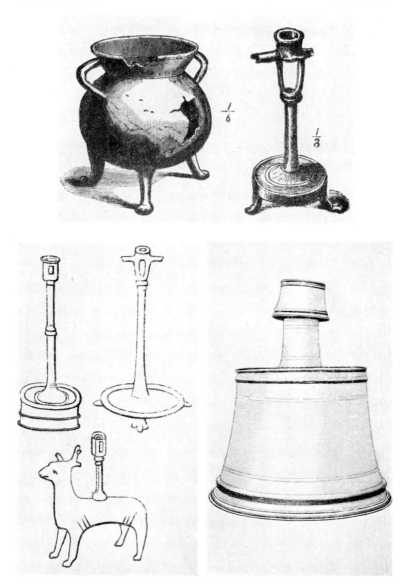

Top: Part of a hoard found at Les Loges (Seine Inférieure, canton Fécamp). 14th century.   After Cochet, *La Seine Inférieure*, p. 207.   (Cauldron $\frac{1}{6}$; Candlestick $\frac{1}{3}$.)

Bottom left: Three brass candlesticks found in a wooden bucket at Yébleron (Seine Inférieure, canton Fauville).   14th century.   The remaining items from this hoard appear to be intrusive.   After Cochet, *La Seine Inférieure*, p. 297 ($\frac{1}{3}$).

Bottom right: Arabic brass candlestick, dated 1297.   After G. Wiet, *Catalogue du Musée Arabe: Objets en cuivre*, Pl. XXX.   The elaborate ornament has been omitted from the illustration.

(ii) Candlesticks

Candles were in use throughout the Middle Ages. They varied however in quality from the fine wax candle set on an elaborate candlestick in church or palace to the peasant's simple rush-light burning in an iron holder. Ornate candlesticks of bronze-work or of enamel are a familiar feature of medieval archæology that falls outside the scope of this catalogue (see O. von Falke and E. Meyer, *Bronzegeräte des Mittelalters*, Berlin, 1935, Vol. I). They give small indication of the types of candlestick in everyday use. Fig. 56, No. 2, is a typical specimen of a class of object that was common in the Middle Ages and remained in use until almost within living memory. They might either be of pricket type, in which the end of the candle is impaled on an upright spike, or contain a loop, which gripped the body of the candle. The latter type was better adapted to the poor quality of candle in everyday use. In the absence of dated medieval specimens they belong rather to folk-study than to archæology. But it must be borne in mind that it is such objects which formed the background of everyday practice to the more determinate luxury-forms, of whose medieval status there can be no doubt.

(For a good account of these iron candlesticks, see H. Swainson Cooper, " The Domestic Candlestick of Iron in Cumberland, Westmorland and Furness," *Transactions of the Cumberland and Westmorland Antiquarian and Archæological Society* (1829), 105–27 ; also H. Syer Cuming, " On some Early Candlesticks of Iron," *Journal of the British Archæological Association*, 25 (1869), 54–60, illustrating several London specimens. Dated medieval examples are recorded from Scandinavia, S. Grieg, *Middelalderske Byfund fra Bergen og Oslo*, pp. 97–8.)

It was not until the later Middle Ages that domestic brass candlesticks became relatively common. The earlier medieval candlesticks were all of pricket type, but the later forms are socketed. The transition is well illustrated by two candlesticks of the familiar type representing Samson strangling the lion, both of very similar German workmanship, c. 1300. One of these (O. von Falke and E. Meyer, *op. cit.*, No. 221, in the Victoria and Albert Museum) has a pricket-spike, the other

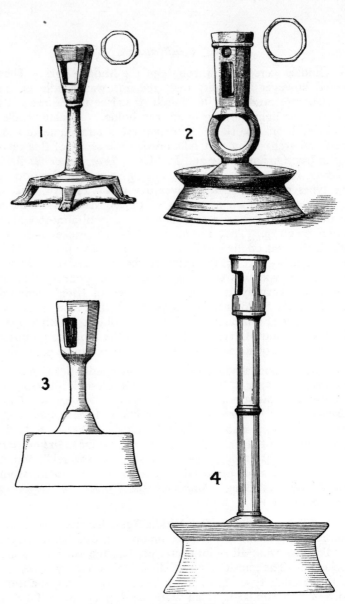

FIG. 55.—Late medieval candlesticks.
1-2 from London, in the Guildhall Museum. 3-4 in the Musée
de Cluny, Paris (½).

FIG. 56.—Medieval candlesticks from London.
1, A 2647 ; 2, A 27533 (½).

(*op. cit.*, No. 222, in the Rouen Museum) has a socket; *cf.* No. 220, late 13th-century socketed, and No. 223, early 14th century with pricket-spike. The socket is not found on these and on similar zoomorphic candlesticks before the closing years of the 13th century. It probably makes an appearance on simpler types at about the same date.

The development of the socketed brass candlestick is complicated by the interplay of two typological currents. Type I developed out of the ordinary 13th–14th-century pricket-candlestick of Western Europe, whereas Type II apparently originated in the Near East. Broadly speaking, it was the native type which dominated the development of stem and socket, whereas the base rapidly approximated to that of the intruder.

The early medieval candlestick had three legs, either straight (as Fig. 56, No. 1) or, more commonly, slightly down-curved and springing from a flattened triangular base. From the latter form was evolved, perhaps already under the influence of Type II, the flattened disc with three projecting feet illustrated in Fig. 55, No. 1. A form, typologically intermediate though probably of 15th-century date, is illustrated by A. O. Curle, " Domestic Candlesticks from the Fourteenth to the End of the Eighteenth Century," *Proc. Soc. Ant. Scot.*, LX (1925–6), 187, Fig. 1, No. 2 (in the Musée de Cluny, Paris). The final absorption of the three feet leaves a simple discoid base current in the late 15th and 16th centuries (Curle, *op. cit.*, p. 188, Fig. 2, Nos. 2, 5, 7 and 8). These tripod candlesticks of Type I are recorded from at least two small 14th-century hoards, both in Normandy (Pl. XXXIX), in one case in association with a candlestick with a cordoned cylindrical base which must already indicate the impact of Type II. It will be seen that they retain a lengthy stem, in one case with the central knop which appears on many pricket-candlesticks (*e.g.* Fig. 56, No. 1). The socket is large and has a large hole on either side for the extraction of the candle-end. In later specimens these holes grow increasingly smaller, and by 1500 usually consist of two small, horizontal, rectangular apertures near the base of the socket. A certain number of sockets with elaborate openings do, however, belong to the mid-15th century (Fig. 55, No. 2. *Cf.* Carlo Crevelli's " Annunciation "

(1485) in the National Gallery. Curle, *op. cit.*, Fig. 4, No. 1).
Many early sockets are octagonal in section (*e.g.* Fig. 55,
Nos. 1–3), and in some cases they have two horizontal forked
projections (*e.g.* Pl. XXXIX). The purpose of these projections is unexplained, but as they appear also on several
pricket candlesticks (Fig. 56, No. 1) they are presumably a
sound criterion of early date.

As early as the 13th century there was in use in the Near
East a form of brass candlestick with a high cylindrical, or
slightly conical base, surmounted by a flat, circular wax-pan
and a short, circular stem with a slightly larger socket.
(See Pl. XXXIX, bottom right, dated 1297; the ornament is
here omitted. The earliest dated specimen is half a century
earlier, and this simple basic form remained in use, beside
more elaborate specimens, for several centuries. See also
Arthur U. Pope, *A Survey of Persian Art*, Vol. vi (1939),
Pls. 1364, 1375, and others). With only the slightest variation
this form reappears in Europe in the 14th century, through
the medium of oriental craftsmen working in Venice (for an
early 16th-century damascened candlestick made at Venice by
Mahmud al-Kurdi, see *British Museum Guide to the Medieval
Collection*, p. 162). The base first assumes the 15th-century
waisted form illustrated in Fig. 55, Nos. 2 and 4, and passes
thence to the elaborately moulded forms of the 16th and 17th
centuries. Simultaneously the stem, under the influence of
Type II, increases in length. First one knop appears ; by
the end of the 15th century several are sometimes found (see
Curle, *op. cit.*, Fig. 4, No. 2, after Ghirlandaio's fresco of
" St. Jerome in his study," *c.* 1480) ; and by the mid-16th
century elaborate baluster-moulded stems are common (see
Vincenzo di Biagio's " St. Jerome in his study " in the National
Gallery ; he died in 1531. *Cf.* Curle, *op cit.*, Figs. 8 and 10,
reproducing other contemporary illustrations). A chronology
based on Italian illustrations cannot safely be applied to the
English series, which probably lagged considerably. But
the characteristic Tudor type, similar to Fig. 55, No. 4, but
with smaller openings in the socket and with several knop-
mouldings on the stem, is well illustrated by a specimen in
the Museum collections found with a mid-16th-century bronze
flagon in Trinity Lane (30.126).

(For an excellent account of late medieval brass candle-sticks, see A. O. Curle, "Domestic Candlesticks from the Fourteenth to the end of the Eighteenth Century," *Proceedings of the Society of Antiquaries of Scotland*, LX (1925–6), 183–214. His remarks on the use of the terms " copper," " brass," and " latten " (p. 184) deserve attention in a wider context. See also F. B. Wallem, *Lys og Lysstell i norske Kirke og Hjem* (Norske Folkesmuseum publication) and S. Grieg, *Middelal-derske Byfund fra Bergen og Oslo*, pp. 99–100. For late medieval candelabra, which seem to have been in fairly common domestic use, see C. C. Oman, " English Brass Chandeliers," *Archæological Journal*, XCIII (1936), 265–6.)

A 2647. Pricket-candlestick, bronze, with folding legs. The use of the V-shaped projection is uncertain, but the ring-socket opposite to it was probably intended to hold a rush, for there is a candlestick in the Musée de Cluny, Paris, identical save that it lacks the central point, which alone could be used to hold a candle. Another similar candlestick in the same collection has a central point and two of the V-shaped projections. These candlesticks were used for travel-ling and were sometimes very elaborate with enamelled armorial bearings. (See W. L. Hildburgh, " A medieval enamelled travelling-candlestick," *Proceedings of the Society of Antiquaries*, XXXII (1920), 132–5, Fig. 8 (early 14th century) and refs. *ad loc.*) Fig. 56, No. 1. From London.

A 27533. Iron candlestick of primitive form. It was probably used for holding a rush, and could either be stood upon a shelf or fastened by the spike into the wall. Fig. 56, No. 2. From the Wallbrook, Tokenhouse Yard.

Also illustrated :

FIG. 55

No. 1. Brass candlestick, from London, 14th century, in the Guildhall Museum. Curle, *op. cit.*, Fig. 1, No. 4.

No. 2. Brass candlestick from London, 15th century, in the Guildhall Museum. For the ring stem, *cf.* the candelabrum in Temple Church, Bristol, probably Flemish, *c.* 1460 (illustrated by J. C. Cox, *English Church Fittings, Furniture and Accessories*, 1923, p. 220). Curle, *op. cit.*, p. 197, Fig. 1, No. 10. He quotes three candlesticks with similar stems and sockets illustrated by Dr. Hefner-Alteneck in *Trachten Kunstwerke*, Vol. V, Pl. 297. A very similar socket can be seen as early as the closing years of the 13th century (O. von Falke and E. Meyer, *Bronzegeräte des Mittelalters*, Berlin, 1935, Vol. I, No. 220, a "Samson" candlestick of German manufacture in private possession at Amsterdam).

No. 3. Brass candlestick, late 14th century, in the Musée de Cluny, Paris.

No. 4. Brass candlestick, mid-15th century, in the Musée de Cluny, Paris.

(iii) *Lanterns*

Lanterns appear in manuscript illustrations at least as early as the 13th century. They seem at times to have been made

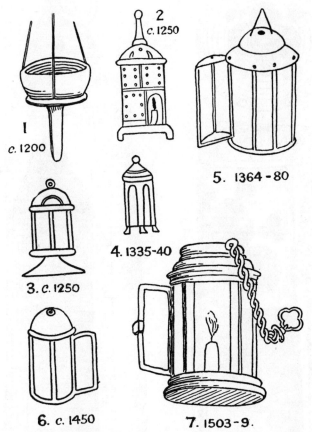

FIG. 57.—Lamp and lanterns illustrated in contemporary representations.

No. 1. From the Psalter of Queen Ingeborga at Chantilly (*Archæological Journal*, XCII, 1935, 259, Pl. VIII).

No. 2. From a mid-13th-century missal (M. R. James, *Catalogue of the Latin Manuscripts in the Sir John Rylands Library*, II, Pl. 55).

No. 3. From the Maciejowski Bible, f. 13*a*.

No. 4. From the Luttrell Psalter, f. 91.

No. 5. From the Parement d'Autel of Narbonne, now in the Louvre.

No. 6. From a mid-15th-century manuscript, Pierpont Morgan Library, Bennett Coll. MS., No. 78. The shutters are of glass.

No. 7. From a roof-boss in Winchester Cathedral (*Archæologia*, LXXVI, Pl. XXIX).

183

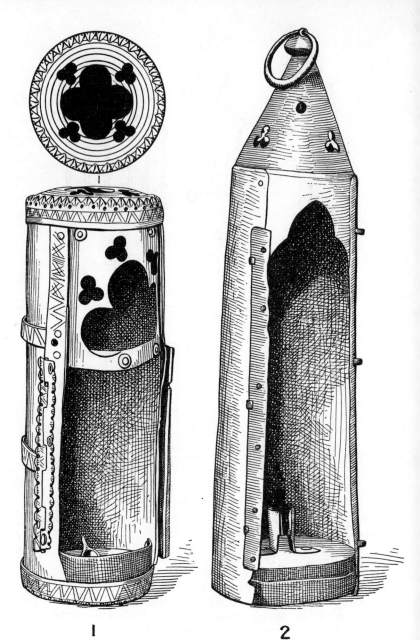

FIG. 58.—Medieval lanterns from Smithfield.

1, A 1366; 2, A 1365 (½).

184

completely of metal with a small opening in one side for the light, at times to have had panels of horn or glass. The latter are common in the later Middle Ages, but both types are represented in the mid-13th century, *e.g.* M. R. James, *Catalogue of the Latin Manuscripts in the Sir John Rylands Library*, II, Pl. 55 (metal plates) ; and Maciejowski Bible, f. 13*a* (transparent sides). The utilitarian cylindrical form with a conical top for suspension is very constant.

A 1365. Fig. 58, No. 2. Lantern of base copper alloy with a conical top ; door missing. Height 8·5 in. Probably 14th century. Found in Smithfield.

A 1366. Fig. 58, No. 1. Lantern of base copper alloy with a low openwork top ; door missing. Height 11·5 in. Probably 14th century. Found in Smithfield.

LEATHERWORK

Leather was extensively and variously used in the Middle Ages, and a considerable number of medieval sheaths, straps, shoes, book-bindings, and other objects have survived. Much of this work was, of course, plain ; but decoration was common, even on the most utilitarian objects, and at least four different techniques, used alone or in combination, may be distinguished :

Engraving with a blunt tool on leather which had probably been well damped (as Pl. XL). This technique was commonly employed in conjunction with stamps, and was often used to outline an embossed design (as Pl. XLI, No. 2).

The use of metal stamps.—An actual example of one used in book-binding may be seen in the British Museum. (For another, picked up at Belvoir Priory, see *Antiquaries Journal*, IV, 1924, 272.)

Embossing.—This might be done either from the back, the softened leather being pressed up to the required design (as Pl. XLII, No. 2), or by pressure from the front (as Pl. XLIX).

Incision with a sharp knife, a characteristically late medieval technique often used to outline lettering (Pl. XLVI).

The term *cuir bouilli*, so often applied to medieval leather-work, is difficult to define. It is frequently used in contemporary medieval documents, the earliest allusion dating from 1185, " son poitrail lui laça qui fu de cuir bolis " (*Chanson d'Antioche*, quoted by V. Gay, *Glossaire Archéologique*, p. 515). It is now supposed that the process adopted was not to boil the leather, but to soak it in wax or oil. This process rendered it supple and easy to work, but after drying it became once more hard and stiff, ensuring the permanence of the shape and decoration. While specially suited for the manufacture of cases or covering wooden chests, leather so treated was clearly useless when the finished article had to be reasonably supple. A good example of *cuir bouilli* in the London Museum is a small leather inkwell, A 28570, dating from the late 15th or early 16th century (Pl. XLV).

Probably highly decorated leatherwork was originally painted, like a 15th-century coffer in Hamburg Museum (A. Brinkmann, *Führer durch das Hamburgische Museum für Kunst und Gewerbe*, 1894, p. 116), which is still gaily coloured. Remains of red paint are observable on a sheath, bearing a late medieval engraved design, in the Guildhall Museum (Inv. No. 1934-127).

Of the four different decorative techniques employed in the Middle Ages, two are known to have been in use before the Norman Conquest. The few examples of pre-Conquest leatherwork which have been preserved, *e.g.* the Stonyhurst Gospels and some scramasax-sheaths, of which examples can be seen in the British Museum, and the Guildhall and York Museums, all bear decoration modelled in relief or engraved with a blunt tool (see Janet Russell, *Archæological Journal*, XCVI, 1939, 134). Incision and the use of metal stamps both appear to be post-Conquest practices; and a brief survey of the incidence of these four processes within the medieval period itself shows that in some cases their use was still further restricted.

Engraving with a blunt tool continued in use throughout the Middle Ages. There are a number of late 12th-century sheaths from London, which have been treated in this

Early-medieval leather sheaths.
1, A 3684, 14th century; 2, A 3664, 15th century; 3, A 3760, 12th century.

PLATE XLI. [*To face p.* 187.

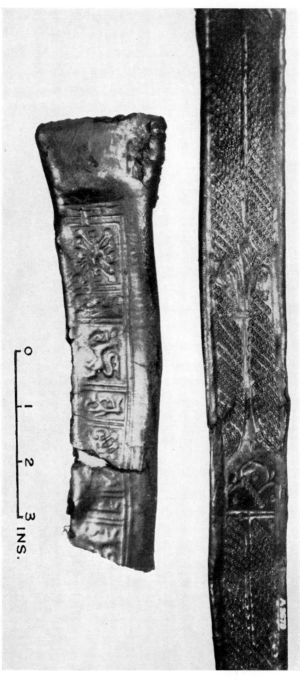

Leather sheaths, 14th–15th century.
1, A 7294, 14th century; 2, A 3678, 14th–15th century.

way ; and examples are recorded from Coventry (P. B. Chat-win, *Trans. and Proc. Birmingham Arch. Soc.*, LVIII, 1934, 60) and from Scandinavia (R. Blomqvist, " Medeltida Svärd Dolkar och Slidor funna in Lund," *Kulturen*, 1938, 189–219). The design on the front is based on the acanthus-scroll filled with monstrous birds or animals (see Pl. XL, No. 3), while the back is plain save for engraved semicircular spandrels. In all cases the position of the handle of the knife is marked, both front and back, by a distinct panel, a conventional division of the design which was retained in many cases to a considerably later date. A combination of this type of design and of engraved armorial bearings is also found, and in the 13th century armorial bearings alone were popular (Pl. XL, No. 2). The enclosed armorial motif persisted, however. It may be seen, for example, on a late 13th- or early 14th-century book-cover in the London Museum (Fig. 64) ; and a common late medieval design, in which animals are enclosed in a lozenge with a trefoil at each corner (*e.g.* Pl. XLIV, No. 2, a 15th-century sheath in the Guildhall Museum) is reminiscent of the same motif. Another pre-Conquest decorative motif, which appears also on medieval leatherwork, is the interlace. In a modified form it is found as late as the 13th–14th century on sheaths of the type illustrated in Pl. XL, No. 1, and Pl. XLIV, No. 1, which are characterized by a fold, pierced for thongs, projecting from the handle-panel. An example of this distinctive type, presumably of English origin, is recorded from Lund (R. Blomqvist, *op. cit.*, Fig. 25, and p. 155).

Metal stamps were commonly employed in the 12th century for decorating leather book-covers (G. D. Hobson, *English Binding before* 1500, and *The Library*, Vols. XV and XIX). They were also used, however, on everyday objects, such as sheaths, and this usage is on the whole characteristic of the 14th and 15th centuries. The stamps used on domestic leather-work were ordinarily neither as large nor as elaborate as the average book-binder's stamps, and they were generally heraldic in subject, *e.g.* fleurs-de-lis, lions passant, eagles displayed, etc. A typical decorative lay-out is illustrated in Pl. L, Nos. 1–2, where the stamped patterns are bordered by lozenge-shaped, engraved frames, while in each of the triangular spaces between the frames and the edges of the sheath is engraved a degenerate fleur-de-lis. This arrangement is common and consistent. From the 14th century onwards single-punch stamps were used to give a granulated effect (*e.g.* Fig. 61, No. 2). More important, however, was the stamped diaper background obtained by the use of a punch with a small repeated design, generally a fleur-de-lis or a tiny four-petalled flower (*e.g.* Pl. XLI, No. 2, and Fig. 60, No. 2). Backgrounds of this type seem to belong to the 14th and 15th centuries.

Embossing from the back was not a process commonly employed. It is illustrated from the Museum collections by two fragments of a sword-sheath, and the leather is so thin that it seems that it must originally have been backed with a wooden frame (Pl. XLII, No. 2). According to Blomqvist *op. cit.*, p. 155) this practice was customary in the case of large sheaths. Usually, however, the design was worked from the front (Pl. XLI, No. 2). Zoomorphic motifs, in the form of strange Gothic birds and beasts, are general, and they may be combined with pricked or punched backgrounds (*e.g.* Pl. XLIV, No. 3). This form of embossing appears to belong principally to the 14th and 15th centuries.

In late medieval leatherwork the outline of the design was often obtained by cutting the leather through for about half its thickness (*e.g.* Pl. XLVI, *right,* a belt carved with the motto " Love me truly, Love me, bind fast " against a punched ground). The ornament on this belt is typical of that found on a series of late medieval boxes, of which there is a fine example in the British Museum. See also Fig. 59, the sheath of a 15th-century rondel dagger, the characteristic budded-whorl ornament of which can be matched on French and Flemish leatherwork.

Two common types of leather objects call for brief separate discussion, sheaths and costrels. Leather shoes are common, but they fall outside the scope of this catalogue (see R. Blomqvist " Medeltida skor i Lund," *Kulturen*, 1938, pp. 189–219).

Of the sheaths which have survived, the majority undoubtedly belonged to small knives or knife-daggers and were worn with civilian dress. As far as can be judged from contemporary monuments and brasses, military sword- and dagger-sheaths were plain, but more or less elaborately mounted in metal. Occasionally, however, metal fittings and decorated leatherwork are found in conjunction, *e.g.* a pewter chape in the British Museum (Fig. 88, No. 2). In almost all cases the leather is sewn together up the back, as distinct from the pre-medieval practice whereby it was riveted up one side. The frequent conventional division of the ornament into two sections, corresponding to handle and blade, has already been noted. Another common, though wholly unpractical, feature is the widening of the lower part of the sheath to conform with a widening towards the point of the knife-blade (Pl. L, No. 2). Such sheaths for knives or bodkins were frequently incorporated with larger ones, *e.g.* the sheath for hunting-knives in the Museum (Fig. 62, No. 1). An example of this practice is illustrated on the effigy of Sir Hugh Mortimer, d. 1459, at Martley, Worcs.

Early military daggers appear to have been slung from the belt by an elaborate arrangement of knotted leather thongs (*e.g.* C. A. Stothard, *Monumental Effigies*, Pl. 120), and this method was still used in the 15th century. But from the 14th century onwards they might alternatively be slung from a ring on the sheath. Most of the ordinary civilian sheaths are simply provided with four slits at the back near the top, through which presumably was passed a thong, which was attached to the belt. These slits are variously arranged, and generally look as if they had been roughly effected by the owner—an observation borne out by Blomqvist (*op. cit.*, p. 164), who says that the English leather sheaths found in Sweden seem to have been fastened to the belt after the German rather than the English manner.

Costrels, presumably of leather, are frequently illustrated in medieval manuscripts, *e.g.* in a 13th-century English Bible Picture Book (Holkham MS. 666, f. 15a, *Walpole Society*, X, pl. X), or in the psalter of Queen Ingeborga at Chantilly, also of the 13th century (Musée Condé MS., 1695, f. 18). They could be carried slung, as in these illustrations, or stood upright upon their flattened undersides. The typical medieval form is recorded in the arms of the Horners' Company.

Of the two examples in the Museum, the smaller is so tiny that it can hardly have contained liquor for drinking (Pl. XLIX). The other was very much larger, but of the elaborate decoration, which dates probably from the 15th century, little can now be distinguished (Fig. 61, No. 4). As on the smaller specimen it seems to have consisted of a type of vine- or trefoil-arabesque which was a popular late-medieval leatherwork motif, *cf.* a sheath from Coventry (P. B. Chatwin, *Trans. and Proc. Birmingham Arch. Soc.*, XVIII, 1934). It may be noted in this context that in general the designs on the leatherwork found on provincial sites bear a striking resemblance to those found in London, although presumably most of it was of local workmanship. Similarly, a great deal of Scandinavian medieval leatherwork was influenced by England, if indeed it was not of English origin (R. Blomqvist, *op. cit.*).

(a) Leather Sheaths

A 3760. Sheath decorated with acanthus scrolls enclosing birds, outlined with a blunt tool. Length 8 in. Pl. XL, No. 3. 12th century. Found in Westminster.

A 3761. Imperfect sheath, decorated with acanthus scrolls enclosing birds, armorial bearings on upper part, outlined with a blunt tool. Length 6¼ in. 12th or 13th century. Found in Westminster.

A 3664. Sheath, decorated with armorial bearings outlined with a blunt tool. Length 7 in. Plate XL, No. 2. 13th century. Found on the site of the Royal Aquarium, Westminster.

A 3680. Sheath, imperfect, decorated with armorial bearings, outlined with a blunt tool. Length 5½ in. 13th century. Found in Temple Avenue.

38.316. Part of sword-sheath, decorated with armorial bearings, outlined with a blunt tool. Length 4½ in. Fig. 60, No. 1. 14th century. Found in London.

A 10636. Part of sword-sheath in two fragments, decorated with embossed animals. Lengths 3·8 in. and 4·4 in. Plate XLII, No. 2. 13th century. Found in the Town Ditch, Old Bailey.

A 3681. Fragment of sheath, decorated with zoomorphic design in slight relief with pricked background. Length 4½ in. Pl. XLIV, No. 3. 13th–14th century. Found in Thames Street.

A 3679. Sheath decorated with a design of formal birds and foliage outlined with a blunt tool. Length 8·2 in. 14th century. Found in Temple Avenue.

A 3667. Part of sheath with fold projecting from upper part, decorated with criss-cross pattern and interlace outlined with a blunt tool. Length 5¾ in. Pl. XLIV, No. 1. 14th century. Found in Westminster.

A 3684. Sheath with fold projecting from upper part, decorated with interlace pattern outlined with a blunt tool. Length 8¼ in. Pl. XL, No. 1. 14th century. Found at Broken Wharf, Thames Street.

A 17714. Sheath in two parts decorated with an abstract design outlined with a blunt tool. Fold projecting from upper part. Length 8 in. 14th century. Found in London.

A 7924. Sheath, imperfect, decorated with formal animals in low relief on the front, and stamped fleurs-de-lis on back. Length 7½ in. Pl. XLI, No. 1. 14th century. Found in Westminster.

A 451. Sheath for round-handled knife with an incised design. Length 6½ in. Fig. 61, No. 1. Found in London.

38.315. Sheath decorated with an abstract design, outlined with a blunt tool. Length 8½ in. Early 13th century. Found in Thames Street.

A 22511. Sheath decorated with stamped and incised design. Length 9 in. Fig. 61, No. 2. 15th century. Found in Finsbury Circus.

A 3759. Part of sword-sheath, fleur-de-lis outlined against a stamped mille-fleur background. Length 8¼ in. 14th century. Found in Thames Street.

A 3678. Part of sword-sheath, decorated with a fleur-de-lis outlined against a stamped mille-fleur background. Length 12½ in. Pl. XLI, No. 2. 14th–15th century. Found in Bell Alley.

A 3663. Case for a circular object, decorated with an all-over stamped design of fleur-de-lis. Length 4½ in. 14th–15th century. Found on the site of the Royal Aquarium, Westminster.

A 3768. Part of sheath, stamped with a design of heraldic birds. Length 3¾ in. 15th century. Found in Westminster.

A 3683. Sheath for a knife, decorated with a stamped design of fleurs-de-lis. Length 9¼ in. Pl. XLII, No. 1. 15th century. Found at Broken Wharf, Thames Street.

A 3682. Sheath decorated with a stamped design of lions rampant. Length 7½ in. Pl. L, No. 3. 15th century. Found at Broken Wharf, Thames Street.

A 3666. Part of sheath, decorated with stamped lions and fleurs-de-lis. Length 7 in. Pl. L, No. 1. 15th century. Found at Westminster.

A 3662. Part of sheath, decorated with stamped eagles displayed. Length 7½ in. Pl. L, No. 2. 15th century. Found on the site of the Royal Aquarium, Westminster.

A 16755. Sheath of a rondel dagger, traces of an incised design against a punched background. Length 5½ in. 15th century. Found in London.

A 2351. Sheath for a rondel dagger and a knife, incised decoration. Length 9 in. Fig. 59. 15th century. Found in Finsbury Circus.

A 3677. Part of a sheath, design deeply incised. Length 9½ in. Pl. XLVI, No. 1. 15th century. Found in Bell Alley.

33.24. Sword-sheath, roughly decorated and punched. Length 23 in. 15th century. Found in Cross Street, Finsbury.

A 10635. Sheath decorated with a plant motif outlined with a blunt tool. Length 8¾ in. Fig. 61, No. 3. Late 15th century. Found in the Town Ditch, Old Bailey.

A 10634. Sheath for a knife, decorated with a crudely carved design against a pricked background. Length 6½ in. 15th century. Found in the Town Ditch, Old Bailey.

A 17436. Imperfect sheath for knife, with blade still in it, decorated with birds and oak-leaves outlined with a blunt tool. Length 5½ in. 14th–15th century. Found in Great Smith Street.

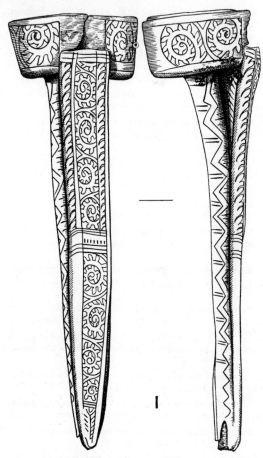

FIG. 59.—A 2351. Dagger-sheath, 15th century (⅓).

Leather sheaths.
1, A 3683, 15th-century, stamped with fleurs-de-lis; 2, A 10636,
13th-century, embossed.

PLATE XLIII.   [*To face p.* 193.

Part of a late 13th-century leather sword-sheath.   The back is engraved with
animals in acanthus roundels.   (In the British Museum.)

A 10633. Part of a sheath, decorated with an embossed design. Length 5¾ in. 15th–16th century. Found in the Town Ditch, Old Bailey.

A 24815. Plain sword-sheath. Length 27½ in. Fig. 62, No. 2. Late medieval. Found in the Town Ditch, Aldersgate.

A 24804. Plain sword-sheath. Length 27½. Late medieval.

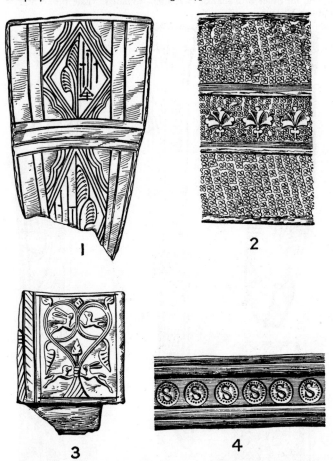

FIG. 60.—Ornamental leatherwork, illustrating different medieval techniques.

No. 1. 38.316. Sword-sheath, 14th century, engraved with a blunt tool (½).
No. 2. 38.314. Belt, 14th–15th century, punched and incised (¼).
No. 3. (In the British Museum.) Case moulded in relief (½).
No. 4. A 25476. Strap, early 15th century, stamped (¼).

193

38.319. Sheath for a big knife or sword and three smaller knives ; imperfect. Length 18 in. Fig. 62, No. 1. 15th–16th century.

Also illustrated :

Pl. XLIII. Part of a sword-sheath, engraved on the one face with coats of arms ; on the other with animals in acanthus-roundels. Late 13th century. In the British Museum.

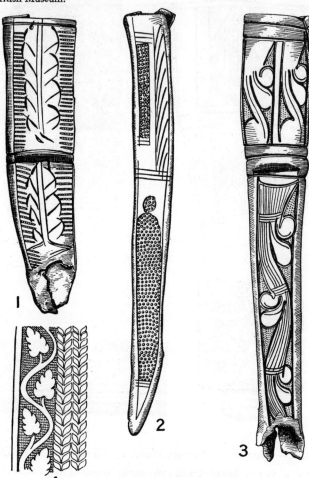

FIG. 61.—Late medieval leatherwork.
1, A 451 ; 2, A 22511 ; 3, A 10635 ; 4, A 3804 (½).

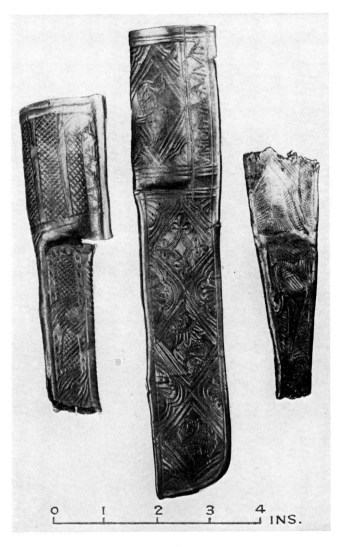

Leather sheaths.
1, A 3667, 14th century; 2, in the Guildhall Museum, 15th century;
3, A 3681, 13th–14th century.

PLATE XLV. [*To face p.* 195.

(*a*)

(*b*)

A 28570.   Inkwell in *cuir bouilli*, early 16th century ($\frac{1}{1}$).

Pl. XLIV, No. 2. Knife-sheath with engraved and pricked design. 15th century. In the Guildhall Museum.

(b) Costrels

A 10640. Small leather costrel, decorated on one side with panels of a scroll design divided by embossed ribs. Width 3½ in. Pl. XLIX 14th–15th century. Found in the Town Ditch, Old Bailey.

A 3804. Imperfect leather costrel, decorated on one side with an incised and punched design. Width 7½ in. Fig. 61, No. 4. 15th century. Found in the Town Ditch, Newgate.

(c) Belts and Straps

A 26221. Part of a belt with incised decoration and motto " Love me, bind fast. Love me truly (?) " repeated against a punched background. Length 36½ in. Pl. XLVI. 15th century. Found in Tenter Street, Moorfields.

A 25476. Part of a belt, decorated with a series of stamped S's in circles. Length 30 in. Fig. 60, No. 4. Early 15th century. Found in the Town Ditch, Aldersgate.

A 3771. Part of a strap, decorated with a small, stamped design. Length 15 in. 15th century. Found in Finsbury.

38.314. Part of a leather belt, decorated with incised fleurs-de-lis against a stamped mille-fleurs background. Length 14½ in. 14th or 15th century. Fig. 60, No. 2.

A 3765. Part of a belt, decorated with round metal studs. Length 7½ in. Found in Thames Street.

A 24971. Part of a belt decorated with circular metal plaques. Length 9½ in. Found in the Town Ditch, Aldersgate.

A 22506. Part of a belt, one brass stud in position, resembling a flower. Length 37½ in. 15th or 16th century. Found in Finsbury Circus.

A 3694. Part of a strap, decorated with metal studs. Length 13½ in. Fig. 63, No. 9. Found in Worship Street.

A 3779. Two pieces of strap, one decorated with circular studs and the other with applied pieces of metal. Length 9 in. and 10 in. Found in Worship Street.

A 3809. Part of a leather strap, decorated with circular metal studs. Length 6½ in. Found in Thames Street.

A 10639. Part of strap with copper tag and studs, engraved with boars' heads. Length 6¾ in. Fig. 63, No. 10. Found in the Town Ditch, Old Bailey.

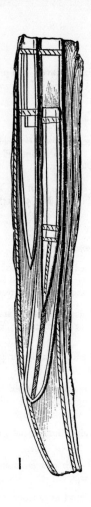

FIG. 62.

1, 38.319. Knife-sheath, with
smaller sheaths attached.
2, A 24815. Sword-sheath ($\frac{1}{4}$).

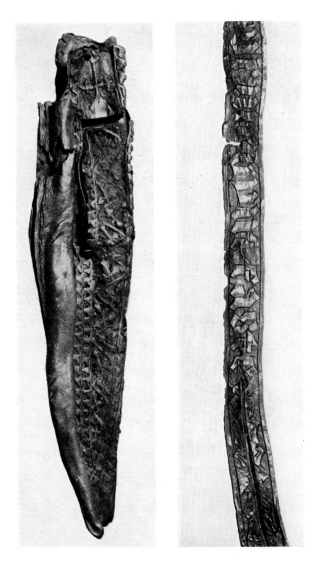

Left. A 3677. Sheath with incised ornament, 15th century ($\frac{1}{2}$).

Right. A 26221. Part of a leather belt inscribed "Love me, bind fast. Love me truly(?)" 15th century ($\frac{1}{3}$).

PLATE XLVII.

[*To face p.* 197.]

Part of a large leather object, possibly a saddle. Mid-14th century. (In the British Museum.)

A 3764. Part of leather strap, decorated with three rows of metal studs. Length 7½ in. Found in Thames Street.

A 2011. Part of leather strap, decorated with a double row of metal studs. Length 10½ in. Found in Worship Street.

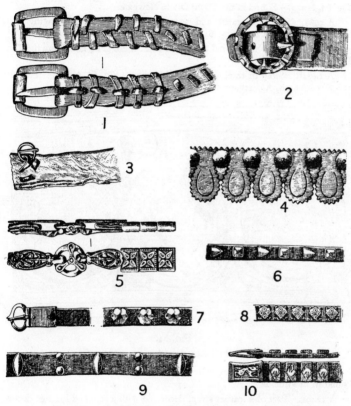

FIG. 63.—Leather straps.

1, A 3968; 2, A 24945; 3, 40.13; 4, A 3763; 5, A 17992; 6, A 26321; 7, A 3691; 8, A 26234; 9, A 3694; 10, A 10639 (½).

A 26234. Part of strap with five remaining metal studs. Length 7 in. Fig. 63, No. 8. Found in Moorfields.

A 3763. Part of a belt, decorated with studs, and applied leather, with serrated edge. Length 21 in. Fig. 63, No. 4. Found in Thames Street.

A 26321. Strap decorated with ten metal studs. Length 7 in. Fig. 63, No. 6. Found in Moorfields.

A 3770. Strap with a suspended knot and tassel decoration. Length 9½ in. 15th or 16th century. Found in Finsbury.

A 3691. Strap with flower-shaped studs and buckle. Length 22 in. Fig. 63, No. 7. Found in the Town Ditch, Newgate.

A 3968. Strap decorated and secured with leather and hanging metal buckle. Length 11 in. Fig. 63, No. 1. Found in Thames Street.

A 25265. Strap with metal tag at one end. Length 6⅜ in. From the Town Ditch, Aldersgate Street.

A 24945. Strap in three pieces with buckle. Fig. 63, No. 2. Found in the Town Ditch, Aldersgate.

FIG. 64.

A 27347. Book cover, 13th–14th century (¼).

A 3624. Part of a leather belt with perforated decoration. Length 4¾ in. Found in Moorfields.

A 22498. Part of a leather strap, decorated with a stamped lozenge decoration. Length 4 in. 15th or 16th century. Found in Finsbury Circus.

40.13. Piece of leather with a small circular pewter buckle attached by a thong. Fig. 63, No. 3.

(d) Miscellaneous Leatherwork

A 27347. Book cover, decorated with formal beasts in rondels against a pricked background. Fig. 64. 13th–14th century. Found in the City.

A 28570. Inkwell in *cuir-bouilli*, decorated with stamped figures of saints. Height 1·72 in. Pl. XLV. 15th–16th century.

198

PLATE XLVIII.

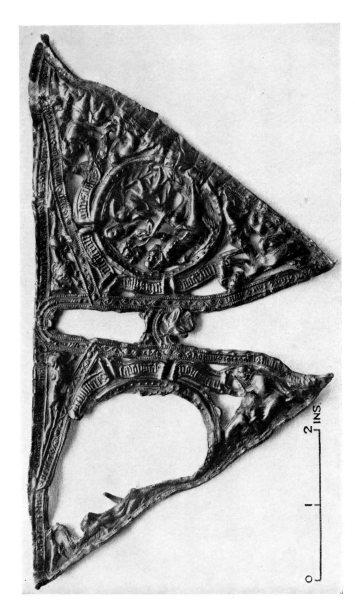

Leather object of uncertain use, finely decorated in relief against an openwork ground.   Late 15th century.
(In the British Museum.)

PLATE XLIX.

[*To face p.* 199.

A 10640.   Miniature leather costrel, 15th century ($\frac{1}{1}$).

A 17992. Leather strap, enclosed in metal links, with one big, metal link. Length 7½ in. Probably a lady's belt, c. 1520-40. Fig. 63, No. 5. Found in the Temple.

A 2456. Metal tag with a leather fringe. Length 5 in. Found in London.

A 22482. Strap with metal rings as links and fringed tag. Length 18¾ in. 15th or 16th century. Found in Finsbury Circus.

A 3702. Leather tassel with serrated strings. Found in Thames Street.

38.317. Damaged leather binding with two metal clasps ; traces of decoration. 8½ by 6¼ in. Found in London.

Also illustrated :

Pl. XLVII. Part of a large leather object, perhaps a saddle, elaborately decorated in relief moulded from the front against a punched, granulated ground. The ornament consists of vine-scrolls and grotesque monsters. Mid-14th century. In the British Museum.

Pl. XLVIII. Leather object of uncertain use, ornamented with figures and scrolls moulded in relief against an openwork ground. The technique is exceptional and the craftsmanship unusually fine. Late 15th century. In the British Museum.

BRONZE JUGS AND COOKING VESSELS

(i) *Jugs*

Several medieval bronze jugs can be dated by associated finds or by the decoration which they bear. One of the same general form as Pl. LI, but lacking the three projecting legs, was found near Dunfermline containing a hoard of 300 coins, deposited c. 1345 (*Numismatic Chronicle*, 5th series, XVI, 1936, 308 ; *Antiquaries Journal*, XVI, 1936, 323, Pl. LX). A slightly more elaborate version of the Dunfermline jug is the specimen bearing the arms of England and the badge of Richard II, now in the British Museum, that was recovered from the treasure of King Prempeh at the sacking of Kumassi (*Proc. Soc. Ant.*, 2, XVII, 1897-8, 82 ff. ; *British Museum Guide to Medieval Antiquities*, 1924, p. 241, Fig. 156). It bears a late 14th-century Lombardic inscription on the belly, and is in most respects identical with yet another jug in the Victoria and Albert Museum (*Proc. Soc. Ant.*, 2, XVII, 1897-8, 85). Both these vessels and the similar London Museum specimen can safely be regarded as the work of contemporary bell-founders.

A second jug in the Museum collections is smaller and has no legs. The fat-bellied, long-necked form of this vessel can be closely matched in contemporary pottery, and there can be little doubt that it belongs to the 14th century.

The later medieval and post-medieval development of the type is well illustrated in Scandinavia (S. Grieg, *Middelalderske Byfund fra Bergen og Oslo*, pp. 127–60, Figs. 76–101). In general the spout of these later vessels is restricted or non-existent, the lid is hinged, and the division of neck and body is more marked than in the 14th century.

A 4587. Pl. LI. Large cast bronze ewer with projecting spout and three short legs. Height 11·8 in. The handle has been broken and repaired in iron. Around the neck and body run three lines of Lombardic lettering :
    (i) Thomas E(l)yot
    (ii) Hi reco(m)mand me to eu
    (iii) Wylleam Elyot
The spout was inserted separately after the casting, but the founder failed to allow for this and the inscription consequently lacks several letters. These have been roughly added on the spout itself. *c.* 1400. From London.

A 16801. Pl. LII. Small bronze jug, height 6·0 in. 14th century. From London.

(ii) *Three-legged Ewers*

A common form of medieval vessel is the three-legged ewer with a tubular spout represented in Pl. LIII. It can be seen for example in the Luttrell Psalter, f. 157*b*, *c.* 1335–40 (Fig. 68, No. 6). A similar vessel contained the hoard of 754 coins, ranging from Edward I to Richard II, found in 1897 at Balcombe, Sussex (*Sussex Archæological Collections*, XLII, 1899, 209–13); and another held the Fortrose hoard of 1,100 coins of Robert III of Scotland (*Proceedings of the Society of Antiquaries of Scotland*, XIV, 1880, 182–219). Both of these hoards were buried in the closing years of the 14th century. Another vessel of identical form was found at Ashby Castle, Leicester, in a well, which had been filled up before 1476 (*Antiquaries Journal*, XVIII, 1938, 179). It would seem, therefore, to be of 14th- and early 15th-century

Decorated leather sheaths.
1, A 3666; 2, A 3662; 3, A 3682.

PLATE LI.

[*To face p.* 201.]

A 4587.   14th-century bronze jug from London.

date. The animal-head terminal is a consistent feature of these vessels. It appears in a less formalized guise on the spout of a pottery vessel, similar, but lacking the three legs, which was made for Charles III of Anjou, King of Sicily, *ob.* 1386 (engraving in the Bibliothèque Nationale, Paris, MS. franç. 20070), and also on a pottery jug from London in the Museum (see p. 227, Fig. 75, No. 2).

A 2752. Pl. LIII. Bronze three-legged ewer, with long tubular spout ending in a conventionalized animal's head. Height 9·2 in. From an old house in Battersea.

(iii) *Bronze Bowls*

Wood and, in the later Middle Ages, pewter were the ordinary materials for bowls and dishes, but bowls made of other metals or of metal and wood were also used for special purposes. Such, for example, were mazer bowls (*e.g. British Museum Guide to the Medieval Antiquities*, 1924, pp. 173-5) or bowls of Limoges enamel. Another well-defined group, which occurs both in England and abroad, consists of shallow copper bowls with a narrow, flat, everted rim and engraved on the inner surface. The engraved designs, which indicate a date in the 12th, or, in some cases, in the first half of the 13th century, fall usually into one of three groups : (i) biblical scenes, (ii) classical mythology, (iii) figures of virtues and vices. The relation between the members of each group is so close as to suggest a common centre of manufacture, probably on the Rhine. Besides the example in the museum, at least three others are recorded from London, one from the Bank of England (*Antiquaries Journal*, XIII, 1933, 170, Pl. XXVII) and two from Lothbury (*Archæologia*, XXIX, 368, Pl. XXXIX). All three carry figures of virtues and vices and belong probably to the early 13th century ; and the Bank of England specimen is additionally interesting in that it was shown on cleaning to retain slight traces of the gilding with which all these bowls were probably further adorned. The bowl in the Museum collection is unusual both in the simplicity of its design and in the technique of its execution. Instead of being incised with a fine point it is burnished with a blunt tool, and the bowl may probably be regarded as a local, provincial copy of an imported type. For a full discussion of these bowls, see *Archæologia*, LXXII, 1910, 133–60.

Another bowl, to which a medieval date may be tentatively ascribed, is illustrated in Fig. 66. The raised bosses on the border recall those found on late Roman and Dark Age bowls, but consist of separate studs, instead of being beaten out of the body of the rim. It has a handle for suspension.

The remaining medieval bowl in the Museum had originally three handles, of which the scars only remain, and it bears punched ornament, now almost obliterated, on the base. It does not fall within any distinctive category, but its ornament can be ascribed to a late medieval, perhaps even a post-medieval, date.

40.15. Copper bowl, decorated on the inner surface with a shallow burnished design consisting of wavy lines, arcs of circles, and conventional trees. The lay-out of the design is reminiscent of that illustrated in *Antiquaries Journal*, XIII, 1933, Pl. XXVII. Fig. 65. From London.

A 27350. Bronze bowl with studded rim. Diam. 6·9 in. Fig. 66. From the site of the Saracen's Head, Snow Hill.

A 10397. Thin bronze bowl, bearing the scars of three attached handles. The rim is roughly rolled over. On the bottom a lightly-punched design, now very worn. Diam. 7·7 in. Fig. 67. From Westminster.

(iv) *Cooking-vessels*

During the earlier part of the Middle Ages metal cooking-vessels were occasionally used, but earthenware was the ordinary material. During the 13th century, however, pottery began to give place to metal, and by the 14th century it seems to have been largely superseded.

Of the forms of metal cooking-pot to be seen in contemporary representations, three appear sufficiently often to justify consideration. The great round-bottomed cauldron can be seen in the Bayeux tapestry (*cf.* Fig. 68, No. 1), and it is very possibly directly descended from the similarly shaped cauldrons of Roman times. A fine, detailed representation of a similar cauldron can be seen in the Maciejowski Bible, *c.* 1250. It persists in this simple form certainly into the 14th century (*e.g.* in Bodleian MS. 264, D. Hartley and M. Elliot,

A 16801.   Bronze jug from London, 14th century.
(See p. 200.)

PLATE LIII.

[*To face p.* 203.

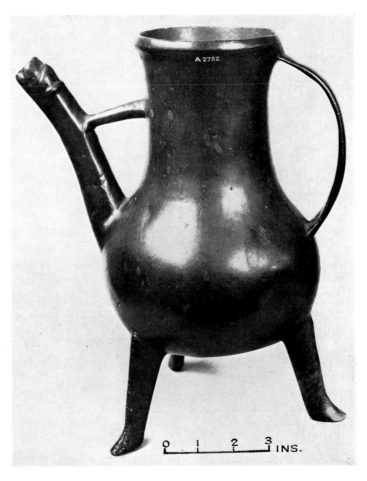

A 2752.   Bronze three-legged ewer, 14th–15th century, from Battersea.
(See p. 200.)

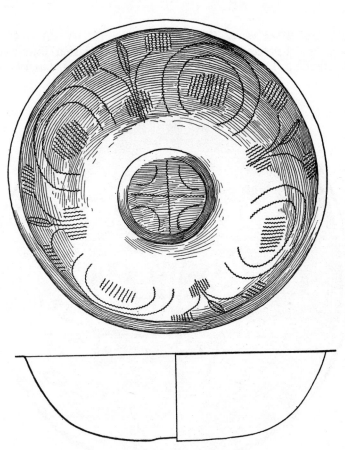

FIG. 65.—40.15. Copper bowl from London *c.* 1200 (⅓).

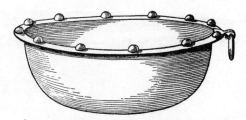

FIG. 66.—A 27350. Bronze bowl from the site of the Saracen's Head,
Snow Hill (⅓).

203

Life and Work of the People, 14th century, Pl. 7e). A smaller version, the handle of which appears to fasten into two upstanding "ears" (as on some Saxon bowls, *e.g. London and*

FIG. 67.—A 10397. Late medieval bronze bowl from Westminster (½).

A 9935.　Late medieval bronze vessel from Bride Lane ($\frac{1}{3}$).

PLATE LV.   [*To face p.* 205.

A 22649.   Bronze skillet, 14th century, from King William Street.

the Saxons (*London Museum Catalogue*), Fig. 25), is used in the mid-13th-century Maciejowski Bible for drawing water, f. 9*b*, *cf*. f. 27*b*; but in the 15th century it appears hung over the fire as a cauldron (D. Hartley and M. Elliot, *Life and Work of the People, 15th century*, Pl. 43 ; source not stated), and it is found occasionally, dated *c*. 1500, in Scandinavia (S. Grieg, *Middelalderske Byfund fra Bergen og Oslo*, pp. 208–9, Fig. 172). The great three-legged cauldrons without handles shown in the early 14th-century Queen Mary's Psalter (Fig. 68, No. 2) are an uncommon (perhaps fanciful ?) form, presumably a hybrid between the round-bottomed cauldron and the three-legged vessel next to be described.

More common is the shaped cauldron with three legs and an angular handle at either side of the neck. This could either be hung from a chain over the fire (Fig. 68, No. 7), or stood directly in the flames (Fig. 68, No. 8 ; *cf*. Fig. 68, No. 5). It can be seen already in a late 12th-century English Bestiary (Fig. 68, No. 3) ; and it is common in the later Middle Ages. A mid-13th-century specimen is figured in the Maciejowski Bible, f. 27*b*. With very little modification it has survived down to modern times ; and it may in passing be noted that the same is true of the toothed arrangement for their suspension shown in the Maciejowski Bible, *loc. cit.*

Three-legged skillets with a projecting strip-handle make their appearance in the 13th century (Fig. 68, No. 4). Examples of similar form can be seen in 14th-century manuscripts, *e.g.* in the Psalter of Robert de Lisle, *British Museum Reproductions of Illuminated MSS.*, series II, Pl. XXIV, early 14th century ; or in the 14th-century Romance of Alexander, Bodleian MS. 264, D. Hartley and M. Elliot, *Life and Work of the People, 14th century*, Pl. 6*c*. Another form, shaped like an open bowl on three low legs with a tubular handle projecting from the side, appears abroad in the 15th century (C. Glaser, *Les peintres primitifs allemands*, Pl. 21), but English representations seem to be lacking. In Scandinavia it appears sporadically in the 15th century (S. Grieg, *Middelalderske Byfund fra Bergen og Oslo*, p. 196 ff.).

205

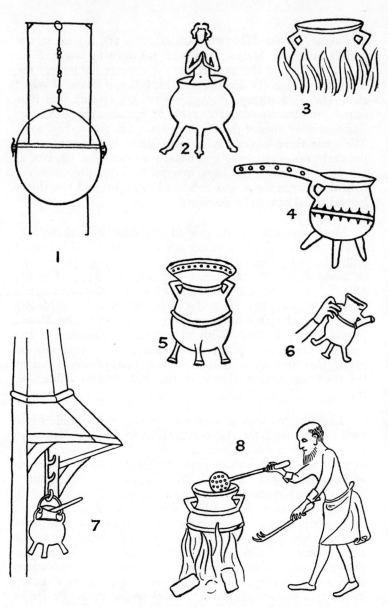

Fig. 68.—Metal vessels illustrated in contemporary paintings and manuscripts.

206

A 27445. Bronze cooking-vessel, 14th century, from Sumner Street,
Blackfriars.

PLATE LVII.   [*To face p.* 207.

A 17940.   Medieval bronze mortar from London.

A 9935. Pl. LIV. Bronze vessel with an iron chain for suspension. The body is formed of two sheets of metal, a circular, slightly sagging base and a long strip, the two ends of which are riveted together to form the sides. The rim is rolled over an iron hoop to give strength, and the attachments for the chain are riveted in position. From an old well in Bride Street.

A 22649. Pl. LV. Bronze, three-legged, strip-handled skillet. The ends of two of the legs are broken. 14th century. Height 6·2 in., maximum diameter 4·9 in. From King William Street.

A 27445. Pl. LVI. Bronze, three-legged cooking-vessel with angular handles. 14th century. Height 8·9 in., diameter at mouth 6·45 in. Found under the floor of an old house in Sumner Street, Blackfriars.

(v) *Mortar*

A 17940. Pl. LVII. Bronze mortar. The flanges, wider alternately at the top and at the bottom, unmistakably betray oriental influence (*cf.* Arthur U. Pope, *A Survey of Persian Art*, Vol. VI (1939), Pl. 1280 A, 10th–11th century; he illustrates also 12th–13th century engraved specimens), although it is not itself of oriental manufacture. It may well be centuries later in date than its prototype.

WOODEN VESSELS

Wooden implements of all sorts must have been extremely common in the Middle Ages, but it is only exceptionally that they have survived to the present day. It is therefore worth calling attention to the group of wooden bowls found in London in 1929 in the 14th century filling of a well on the site of the Bank of England (*Antiquaries Journal*, XVII, 1937, 414–8). The types are extremely simple, and they may safely be taken as typical of the domestic utensils in everyday use throughout the medieval period.

No. 1. Painted altar-frontal of SS. Julitta and Quiricius, 1150–1200, in Barcelona Museum (E. Harris, *Spanish Painting*, Pl. IV).

No. 2. Queen Mary's Psalter, f. 235. Early 14th century.

No. 3. An English Bestiary, *c.* 1200 (*British Museum Reproductions of Illuminated MSS.*, series III, Pl. XIII).

No. 4. Trin. Coll. Camb. MS., 0.9.34. 13th century (D. Hartley and M. Elliot, *Life and Work of the People, 11th–13th centuries*, Pl. XXXIX).

No. 5. Luttrell Psalter, f. 117, 1335–40.

No. 6. Luttrell Psalter, f. 157, 1335–40.

No. 7. An English Bible Picture Book, olkham MS. 666, f. 18*a*, early 14th century (*Walpole Society*, Vol. XI, Pl. X).

No. 8. Luttrell Psalter, f. 207, 1335–40.

PLATE

The quality rather than the quantity of English medieval goldsmiths' work can be judged from the few pieces which remain to us. In order to get an idea of the nature and variety of the articles made, it is better to go to the literary sources, especially wills and inventories, rather than to the museums. The paucity of surviving specimens gives an erroneous idea of the wealth and skill of the medieval craftsman. Secular plate in any case, owing to the changes of fashion and the varying fortunes of families, would hardly have survived in any quantity from so remote a period. But it is owing to the Reformation that so little medieval ecclesiastical plate has survived. Vast treasures of earlier plate completely disappeared from the monasteries at this time, while subsequent ecclesiastical regulations ensured the destruction of all articles in the churches, which had any connection with previous ceremonies. This was all the more disastrous, as the Church was probably the best client of the goldsmiths in the Middle Ages, being not only wealthy, but the recipient of many gifts, most of which were scrupulously preserved. But nothing like the treasure of Conques has survived in this country, where the churches' guardianship was so rudely broken.

The only piece of pre-Reformation church plate in the London Museum is the foot of a pyx which was subsequently turned into a chalice (Pl. LVIII). It is silver-gilt and the stem is Gothic in style, conforming to the last type of chalice made before the Reformation, according to C. J. Jackson (*History of English Plate*, I, p. 342). It is definitely described, however, as a pyx in Sir Stephen Pecocke's will, which is quoted by Jackson in his description of this unusual piece (*op. cit.*, p. 150).

The stem has been cut off just above the knot, and is hexagonal with a cable moulding on each angle. The knot is a flattened sphere with its upper and lower surfaces spirally gadrooned, encircled by a ribbed band to which six vertical pieces are affixed like short lengths of cable. The juncture of stem and foot is masked by open tracery work in the form of six two-light windows, with pierced buttresses set in the angles. The six lobes of the spreading hexagonal foot are slightly

B 783.　"The Peacock chalice."　Height 10¾ in.)

PLATE LIX.

[*To face p.* 209.

A 2719. Latten chalice, early 16th century, from London Wall (¼).

ridged in the middle, and each terminates in a point with an ogee curve on either side. The edge of the foot is vertical, enriched with a stamped band of roses and sprays of foliage, and resting on a flat base with a projecting margin. The following inscription is pounced round the foot : " Praye for the solle of Stewyn Pekoc and Marget hys wyff, which gave this in the worshippe of the Sacrement." It is stamped with the date letter for 1507. The large bell-shaped cup was added to adapt it for the use of the reformed church in 1559.

In addition, the Museum has a latten or brass chalice of the same period (Pl. LIX). It stands 7½ in. high, with a small bell-shaped bowl supported on a hexagonal stem, the join being masked by a bold scallop. The knot has six circular openings which in a silver model would probably have contained crystal, jewels, or enamel. The spread of the foot is at first hexagonal, but becomes circular, and rests on a sexfoil base 5¼ in. in diameter, with a vertically moulded edge. According to C. J. Jackson (*History of English Plate*, I, p. 341) and W. W. Watts (*Old English Silver*, p. 115) silver chalices of this description with a hexagonal stem and a sexfoil base belong to the beginning of the 16th century, being just prior to the type represented by the stem of the Peacock chalice. This brass chalice can probably be dated therefore to the early years of the 16th century, although the bowl is bell-shaped, instead of being rather shallow and flat at the bottom, as is generally the case with silver examples. It may have been made to bury in the coffin of a priest, a custom sometimes observed during the Middle Ages.

So little remains of the only piece of medieval secular plate in the Museum that it is difficult to tell to what type of bowl it originally belonged (Pl. LX). It may possibly be the base of a mazer, the most popular type of drinking vessel in the later Middle Ages, in which case the sides of the bowl would have been of maple wood, with a silver band round the top. On the other hand, the fragments of gadrooned edge which remain suggest that it was wholly of silver, perhaps a rose-water dish, whose use medieval table-manners necessitated between courses. It strongly resembles a parcel gilt silver bowl from the Church Plate of the City of Bristol, exhibited at the Burlington Fine Arts Club in July, 1939 (No. 57), the sides of which are spirally gadrooned. Either type of vessel might have had a print or boss at the bottom, but it is an almost invariable feature of the mazer. The costume worn by the female figure on the print, suggests a date round about 1400, although the moulded socket set on a rayed and fringed plate, is typical of mazers in the latter part of the 15th century (C. J. Jackson, *History of English Plate*, II, p. 599).

This fragment consists of a solid circular base moulding, 3¾ in. across, under a recessed band decorated with a delicately stamped flower pattern. The sides appear to have been spirally fluted. In the centre is a raised box, engraved with a kneeling woman, crowned and picking flowers, with the inscription " Apriel." Encircling this is a cabled moulding and fourteen wavy ridged waves radiating on a slightly domed matted ground.

B 783. Silver-gilt chalice and paten, " The Peacock Chalice." Height of cup 10¾ in. Foot hall-marked 1507–8, cup hall-marked 1559–60, paten hall-marked 1575–6. Pl. LVIII. C. J. Jackson, *History of English Plate*, Fig. 167. *Cf.* Freshfield, *The Communion Plate of the Churches of the City of London*. Lent by the Rector, Churchwardens, and Council of the United parishes of St. Martin Ludgate, St. Mary Magdalene, Old Fish Street, and St. Gregory by St. Paul's.

A 2719. Latten chalice. Early 16th century. Height 7½ in. Pl. LIX. Found London Wall.

29.201/7. Base of bowl, silver gilt. Diameter 3¾ in. Pl. LX. Early 15th century. Leadenhall, 1929.

POTTERY

The Museum collection of pottery is fully representative of the outstanding quality of the medieval wares found in London. It is seldom, however, that the haphazard methods in which the pottery has usually been salvaged from excavations in the City permit of observations that enable it to be accurately dated. Accordingly, a selection is here made of vessels to which dates may be given by analogy with dated material found elsewhere, as well as examples of the more decorative jugs that are particularly characteristic of medieval London.

PLATE LX.

29.201/7.   Base of silver-gilt bowl, early 15th century, from Leadenhall ($\frac{1}{1}$).

It should be pointed out that there is no evidence that any of the pottery in the collection was actually made in London. No pottery kilns of this period have been discovered, either in London or its immediate neighbourhood, although a kiln for tiles was found near Farringdon Street many years ago (see p. 235). It is indeed probable that much of London's medieval pottery was made in Surrey, where the primary materials, clay for the pots and wood for firing the kilns, are abundant. The actual kilns, or ' wasters ' (pottery spoilt in firing and thrown away) which indicate their presence, are known at several places in East Surrey, at Limpsfield (*Proceedings of the Society of Antiquaries*, 2nd series, IV, 358 and XV, 52), Earlswood (*Surrey Archæological Collections*, XXXVII, 245), Cheam (*Ibid.*, XXXV, 79), and Ashtead, all within 20 miles of London. In this region the pottery industry was concentrated and flourishing from the 13th century onwards, and its products far too great to supply only local needs. This London orientation of the Surrey pottery industry is confirmed by one piece of documentary evidence, for in 1260 the bailiffs of Kingston-on-Thames were ordered to send 1,000 pitchers to the King's butler at Westminster (L. Salzman, *Medieval English Industries*, p. 170).

The pottery itself supports the above suggestion. A jug (waster) from Earlswood, decorated with vertical rouletted strips and circular stamps, is very similar in shape and decoration to many examples found in London and, in particular, compares closely with two jugs in the London Museum (A 27262 and A 27218). Another vessel from Earlswood (*British Museum Catalogue of English Pottery*, p. 57, Fig. 36), with plastic ornament of a hunting-scene, has a display of human and animal forms probably derived from designs on paving-tiles, and the same source is suggested for the heraldic beasts on a jug found near London Bridge (*Ibid.*, p. 63, Fig. 49). The same connexion can also be shown by pottery of other types ; cooking-pots and flanged bowls of *c.* 1300 from the Bank of England (*Antiquaries Journal*, XVII, 414) are exactly matched at Guildford (*Surrey Archæological Collections*, XLV, 142), and both groups are, without much doubt, the products of a Surrey kiln. At the prolific 15th-century kiln at Cheam, jugs, bowls, pipkins, etc., were made in great variety, and

211

wares from this kiln have been found in London; but only the more distinctive jugs (p. 226) can certainly be identified as made at Cheam.

(i) 13th century

DECORATED JUGS

Until recently plain jugs of the types described below (p. 214) were almost the only pottery securely dated to the 13th century, and in consequence there has been a tendency to place the more highly decorated vessels at a later date. However, several discoveries at castles and other sites of known history have amply shown that decorated jugs in a great variety of shapes and ornamentation were in use throughout the 13th century. Indeed, it is becoming increasingly clear that the finest products of the medieval potter belong almost exclusively to this time.

The status of the medieval potter should be considered in any appreciation of his wares. He was a craftsman without a guild, and so the industry was largely without organization or cohesion. In consequence, although a general similarity is evident in pottery from different regions of England, it has a strong local and traditional character which gives it at once the charm of a peasant art, but is the despair of the archæologist with his concern for typology.

The most general type of jug is tall and ovoid (Frontispiece and Pl. LXII, No. 1) with a heavy sagging profile that is possibly influenced by the form of leather vessels, such as the ' black jack ' in common use then and later. Another leading type is broad and squat (Pl. LXII, No. 3), and was in use at the same time as the taller and more graceful jugs.

Often the foot is pressed down by thumb-marks round the edge to steady the vessel on its sagging base. The thumb-pressing is of varying emphasis, from a few marks spaced round the edge and quite inadequate to steady the pot (Fig. 69, No. 4) to a continuous series reaching to the lowest level (Frontispiece, and Fig. 69, No. 3). All stages appear to have been practised at the same time and occur throughout the 13th century. Although plain flat bases were usual in the 14th and 15th centuries, the thumb-pressed base again reappears in the latter period (p. 226).

The range of decorative motifs that give to medieval pottery its highly individual character, particularly in the 13th century, is illustrated by the jugs in the Frontispiece and Pls. LXI–LXII. The two jugs reproduced in colour give some idea of the richness of the coloured clays sometimes used to enhance the elements of the pattern. The main design is usually carried out in strips of clay applied to the surface or by incised lines, which form a framework for the subsidiary elements. These may consist of applied studs of clay, either worked into floral patterns by the potter's fingers or very commonly bear the impressions of baked clay or wooden stamps. Such stamps are known in great variety, and may be simple geometric patterns of rosettes, stars, or concentric rings, heraldic shields, fleurs-de-lis and scallop-shells, or the realistic figures of fabulous animals and birds, often with a strong resemblance to the designs on paving-tiles.

Less formal in treatment is decoration in free style, often consisting of conventionalized trees or foliage (Pl. LXII, No. 1). This appears to be more frequent in the late 13th century, and possibly is then inspired by the painted designs on polychrome pottery (p. 217).

The most realistic of all decoration on jugs are the human faces (Pl. LXII, No.2). These have a grotesque character bordering on caricature and are not without individual expression. The face is usually built up by several methods; the nose, chin, and ears are applied lumps of clay modelled to shape by hand, the eyes are made by a stamp or are incised, and the mouth is an incised line. The arms and hands are usually modelled in the round, and in one instance gloves are shown.

Glaze is usually present on decorated jugs and not only forms a uniform background for the colour harmonies of the decoration, but serves to make the vessel less porous. Glaze was introduced in the Norman period, and in the 12th century is sparingly used, thin, and usually green. In the 13th century the glaze is richer in quality and covers most of the

213

surface. It has a lead basis and various shades of yellow, green, or brown were obtained by the addition of copper, iron, or manganese salts.

A 11299. Jug with ovoid body and thumb-pressed base. Height 16¼ in. Applied decoration of green lattice-pattern and red pellets, with large red rosettes above, under a clear yellow glaze. The moulded neck is banded with red and yellow and an irregular overwash of green. Frontispiece. From Swan Street, Southwark.

A 2001. Jug with ovoid body and waisted foot. Height 12¾ in. Applied decoration of green rouletted strips and red pellets on the neck, and green rouletted chevron with red rosettes on green stalks on the body. Buff ware with yellowish green glaze. Pl. LXI. From the site of the Greyfriars' Monastery, Smithfield.

A 26449. Jug with ovoid body and bridge-spout. Height 12¼ in. Applied decoration of conventionalized trees with groups of scales. Between the lower series of trees are four large billets in high relief. Whitish ware with thick dark green glaze. Pl. LXII, No. 1. From the corner of Bishopsgate and Leadenhall Street.

31.45/2. Fragment of jug of buff ware with mottled dark green glaze. On the front is a large human face, with prominent nose, impressed pellets as eyes, incised mouth, and large pointed ears. The arms are modelled in the round, crossed at the wrists, with hands clasping the chin. The lower part has incised and rouletted lines, probably representing the dress, as carried out in colours on a similar jug in the Guildhall Museum (*Catalogue*, Pl. LXVI, No. 5). Pl. LXII, No. 2. From London.

A 16773. Squat jug of buff ware with light green glaze. Height 8 in., maximum diameter 9¼ in. The sagging base is closely thumb-pressed round the edge. Slip decoration of white lattice-pattern on neck and body. Pl. LXII, No. 3. From Mark Lane.

PLAIN JUGS

In addition to the more ornate jugs, vessels of simpler character were in general use, and several in the collection may be fairly closely dated. The small jug (Fig. 69, No. 1) is frequently found in London, and is securely dated to the latter part of the 13th century; a jug of this type was found with coins of Henry III and Edward I in Friday Street (*Archæological Journal*, LIX, 7), and again with a jetton of *c.* 1300 at Blossoms Inn (*Antiquaries Journal*, XII, 178). These jugs are about 6 in. to 9 in. high, biconical in form, with moulded rim, splayed flat base, and plain handle. Decoration is absent, but sometimes the neck is lightly grooved and a splash of pale green glaze may be present on the upper part.

PLATE LXI.

A 2001.   13th-century jug from London.
(Scale slightly over $\frac{1}{3}$.)   (See p. 213.)

Another type of small conical jug (Fig. 69, No. 2) is so similar in ware and technique to the above that it is certainly of the same date. Neither of these two types is provided with a lip for pouring, so they may have been used as mugs for drinking ale.

The small ovoid jug (Fig. 69, No. 3) is a simple version of the highly decorated vessels already described. The thumb-pressed base is typologically later than the stage shown in Pl. LXII, No. 3, and in Fig. 69, No. 4. The bridge-spout is found on jugs throughout the 13th century, but in this instance it imitates the ' parrot-beak ' spouts of imported polychrome jugs (p. 217) and serves to date the vessel to not earlier than the last quarter of the century.

Another basic form is the tall jug with cylindrical neck and ovoid body (Fig. 69, No. 4). The base is sagging and the edge is thumbed down at intervals, but not sufficiently to steady the vessel. The closest analogy is a jug dated by coins to not later than 1250, found at Eccles, Lancashire (L. Jewitt, *Reliquary*, V (1864–5), p. 89).

The large plain jug (Fig. 69, No. 5) is typical of London. The pots are constant in size, from 13 in. to 17 in. high ; the slender graceful shape, waisted above the base, and long handle are characteristic. A low cordon separates the neck from the body, and a thin green or yellow glaze is usually present. Tall jugs of similar ' baluster ' form have been found at Oxford (*Archæological Journal*, III, 62 ; *cf. Oxoniensia*, IV, 122) with a coin of Henry III, and there is slight evidence that in London these jugs are contemporary with polychrome ware.

A 25645. Biconical jug of light red ware with splashes of thin yellowish green glaze on upper part. Height 8·6 in. The neck is lightly grooved. Fig. 69, No. 1. From Threadneedle Street.

5–12. Small conical jug of buff ware with few spots of green glaze on base. Height 6·1 in. Fig. 69, No. 2. From London.

A 20383. Ovoid jug of buff ware with bridge-spout and thumb-pressed base. Yellow glaze on spout and body down to shoulder. Height 7 in. Fig. 69, No. 3. From the site of the Cloth Fair.

A 5056. Ovoid jug with cylindrical neck, of buff ware with speckled green glaze. Height 12 in. The neck is faintly striated and the sagging base has thumb-marks at four places. Fig. 69, No. 4. From London Wall.

A 15258. Baluster jug of buff ware with light yellowish green glaze. Height 16·2 in. Fig. 69, No. 5. From St. Martin's-le-Grand.

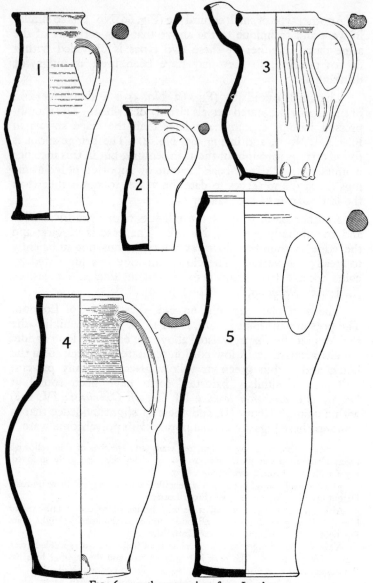

FIG. 69.—13th-century jugs from London.
1, A 25645 ; 2, 5-12 ; 3, A 20383 ; 4, A 5056 ; 5, A 15258 (¼).

POLYCHROME JUGS

This name is given to a class of pottery remarkable for the fineness and thinness of its almost white ware, and the delicacy of its painted decoration of leaf and scroll patterns, opposed birds and shields, and heraldic devices. The colours used are brilliant yellow and green, and the designs are outlined in dark brown. Occasionally human masks in relief are applied to the rim, and a vessel from Exeter has plastic ornament of the figures of musicians, and a long spout in the form of an animal's head and neck. Characteristic features of the jugs are the large bridge-spouts with ' parrot-beak ' outline, the sharply moulded rim, broad strap-like handle, and flat base. The surface is usually covered by a thin transparent lead glaze.

Polychrome pottery is found in London more frequently than at any other place in Britain ; nine jugs and fragments are known from the City, and as the finest pottery of the period it doubtless reached only the tables of the rich city merchants. Elsewhere the jugs have been found mainly at the sites of castles and towns on or near the south and west coasts of England and Wales, and once in south-west Scotland. Several of these sites are castles built by Edward I, or earlier sites re-occupied during his campaigns in Wales, and the available evidence suggests the period 1275–1300 for polychrome pottery. In quality it is too fine to be of local make, and was imported from south-west France, where it has been found near Bordeaux. In that region unornamented pottery of the same character is known in the 12th century. The painted decoration has close affinity with the contemporary maiolica of central Italy, but the reason for its transmission to Aquitaine is not yet clear (*Archæologia*, LXXXIII, 114–34). The most up-to-date distribution-map is in *Archæological Journal*, XCIV, 132, Fig. 2.

The excellence of polychrome ware inspired the local potters to imitate it. Green-glazed jugs showing its influence in ware, shape, and the bridge-spout are found not only at sites producing polychrome jugs, but at other places in southern England. The painted decoration, however, was

FIG. 70.—Polychrome jugs from London.
1, 40.16 ; 2, A 23356 (¼).

beyond the skill of the English potter, although its influence may be seen in the red-painted scroll designs on jugs found at Rye (*Sussex Archæological Collections*, LXXIV, 62, Pl. XIV, 5) and possibly in the applied leaf patterns on some jugs from London (Pl. LXII, No. 1).

40.16. Polychrome jug of whitish ware, upper part and handle missing. Painted decoration of two opposed green birds with long tails, and three yellow heater-shaped shields. Below the handle is a triple green leaf. Fig. 70, No. 1. From Doctors' Commons. Lent by Pitt-Rivers Museum, Farnham.

A 23356. Polychrome jug of whitish ware, with bridge-spout restored in plaster. Height 9·85 in. Painted decoration of a green leaf and yellow stem within a yellow shield-shaped border. Below the handle is a triple green leaf and beneath the spout a vertical wavy line between green bands. Fig. 70, No. 2. From Moorgate.

STORAGE-JARS

Medieval agriculture was most prosperous in the late 13th and early 14th centuries, and the abundance of wheat is reflected by a number of large vessels evidently used for storing grain. These jars, the largest pots yet known in the medieval period, are about 20 in. to 24 in. high and 20 in. shoulder diameter. All are elaborately decorated with the applied thumb-pressed strips that occasionally are found on the contemporary cooking-pots (*cf.* Fig. 72), and in addition some have subsidiary decoration of incised lines. The jars have been found at a dozen sites in the south-eastern counties centred on London (*Antiquaries Journal*, XIX, 303), and some were certainly made in pottery kilns in Essex and Hertfordshire. The available evidence is consistent in placing these vessels in the late 13th century. A jar found near Knebworth, Herts, contained the stirrup illustrated in Fig. 25, No. 1, and in character most of the other jars agree with this dating.

35.174. Storage-jar of sandy grey ware. Height 20¾ in., maximum diameter 18½ in. The mouth is narrow, and the broad, sagging base is steadied by a prominent collar marked by finger-tip fluting. Applied decoration of vertical thumb-pressed strips reaching from the neck nearly to the base. Fig. 71. Found in digging under West Yoke farm-house, near Fawkham, Kent. Given by Sir Thomas Hohler.

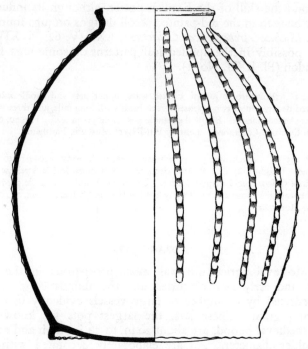

FIG. 71.—13th-century storage-jar from Fawkham, Kent. 35.174 (⅙).

COOKING-POTS

Pottery vessels were used extensively for cooking purposes throughout the medieval period, but were largely replaced by metal vessels in and after the 14th century. They are wheel-turned with varying skill. In the 12th century the ware is usually reddish or brown and tempered with stone grit or pounded shell, but in the 13th century grey wares are predominant, usually sandy in texture, and fired harder than previously. The rounded or sagging base is characteristic of cooking-pots, and appears first in the late Saxon period (*Proceedings of the Cambridge Antiquarian Society*, XXXIII, 148, Pl. II, Fig. 2); it is probably derived from metalwork (*e.g. London and the Saxons* (London Museum *Catalogue*), p. 147, Fig. 25). The increased surface of the pot exposed to the heat would

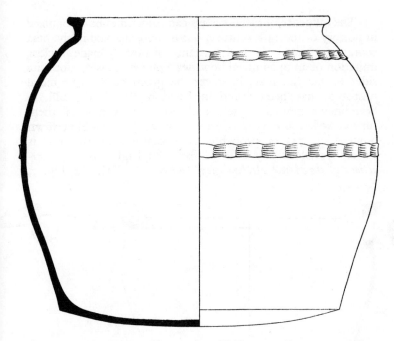

FIG. 72.—13th-century cooking-pot from Walthamstow, Essex. 30.21 (¼).

facilitate cooking, and it is likely that the more obtuse angle of the base made it less liable to fracture in use. Occasionally, but apparently not earlier than the mid-13th century, the inner surface of the pot is partially glazed to render it less porous.

Decoration is seldom present on vessels so liable to be broken and thrown away, and is restricted to simple motifs of incised lines, finger-tip marks, or applied thumb-pressed strips. Although early forms of rim lingered on, usually rims of the early 13th century are thickened and have a slight beading on the inner margin (*Antiquaries Journal*, XV, 330, Fig. 4). Towards the end of the century the rims become more angular and are either square in section or broad and flanged (*Proceedings of the Suffolk Institute of Archæology*, XXII, 334, Figs. 1–9). The Walthamstow cooking-pot (Fig. 72) is exceptionally large and probably not earlier than *c.* 1300.

The influence of metal vessels can sometimes be recognized in pottery of the 13th century, but is more marked in the next century (p. 224). An early instance of pottery made in close imitation of an open metal bowl with pierced lugs on opposite sides of the rim may, however, be given here. The metal prototype has been found in London (Pl. LIV), and in Scandinavia similar vessels and also clay copies of them survive as late as *c.* 1500 (see above, p. 205). The Silvertown bowl (Fig. 73) is probably 13th century, as the rim is closely paralleled by a bowl from Rayleigh Castle (*Transactions of the Essex Archæological Society*, n.s., XII, 182, Fig. 7, No. 13).

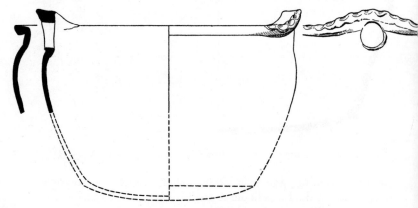

FIG. 73.—13th-century bowl from Silvertown. C 952 (¼).

30.21. Complete cooking-pot of hard, gritty grey ware. Height 13 in. maximum diameter 15½ in. Broad angular rim with internal beading, and sagging base. Applied decoration of thumb-pressed strips on the upper part. Fig. 72. From Walthamstow, Essex.

C 952. Fragment of bowl of grey ware with white grit, light red surface caked with soot. Diameter 11 in. The broad rim is pulled upwards to form a handle above the large hole piercing the neck, and has finger-tip decoration. Fig. 73. From the Thames, Silvertown.

(ii) 14*th century*

JUGS

The scarcity of dated 14th-century jugs, and these consisting mainly of plain vessels, makes the attribution of pottery in the

13th-century jugs from London.
1, A 26449; 2, 31.45/2; 3, A 16773 (¼).

collection to this period very tentative. Whilst on general grounds it is reasonably certain that finely-decorated jugs continued to be made, there has been in the past a tendency to ascribe too late a date to many medieval vessels. The development of pottery in the north of England and Scotland, where the bulk of the dated material has been found, is not necessarily applicable to London. The increasing and more general use of metal vessels no doubt resulted in the partial replacement of pottery jugs at the table, and conversely vessels which show quite clearly the influence of metallic forms may be referred to this century. In the absence of comparative material it is not possible to gauge the extent of this influence, but in any case it is likely to be more apparent in the towns and trading centres where metalwork was plentiful. In remote and country districts the persistence of earlier forms is to be expected. A jug dated about 1324, found at Boyton Manor, Wilts (*Numismatic Chronicle*, 1936, p. 155) is remarkably similar to Pl. LXII, No. 3, and has many analogies in the preceding century.

The influence of metalwork is seen in the types simulating metal jugs and ewers. The body has a tendency to angularity of profile, and the divisions between neck, body, and base are more carefully defined and sometimes emphasized by grooves or cordons. The base is usually spreading and flat, thus dispensing with thumb-pressing of the edge (Pl. LXIII Nos. 1–2). A jug of the same general character (Pl. LXIII, No. 3) has a long gutter-like spout and the base is supported on three short feet, both features being derived from metal ewers.

The decoration of these jugs shows a lack of freedom, partly as a result of the more regular wheel technique now employed, but mainly due to the influence of metalwork. A zonal effect is apparent and often is emphasized by incised lines or raised cordons, which restrict the stamped or applied patterns to formal horizontal bands.

In shape the small jug (Pl. LXIII, No. 4) belongs to the above class, but is remarkable for the carefully modelled human face, apparently crowned, applied to the front. The mask was made in a mould, as a second and identical example is known from London (Burlington Fine Arts Club, *Catalogue of Early*

223

English Earthenware, p. 4, Pl. IV). The realistic treatment of the face has led to the suggestion (*Journal of the British Archæological Association*, III, 63) that it represents Edward II ; the reversed curls of the beard were the fashion in his reign and are shown on his effigy in Gloucester Cathedral.

A 27515. Jug of light red ware, with angular shoulder and spreading base. Height 10 in. Partially covered with light green glaze. Applied decoration of strips and pellets, combined with coloured slips of yellow and dark brown. On the neck are two rows of pellets and bands of yellow and brown, and on the body is a chevron of yellow bands and brown triangles with yellow pellets. Pl. LXIII, No. 1. From Lime Street.

A 22540. Jug of buff ware with over-all speckled green glaze. Neck above cordon and handle restored in plaster. Height about 13 in. Prominent angular cordons on neck, body, and above the spreading base. Stamped decoration of two birds pecking at a tree. Pl. LXIII, No. 2. From Coleman Street.

C 676. Jug of light red ware with thick yellow glaze on neck and upper part of body. Height 10¾ in. Long bridge-spout, neck grooved, body angular at shoulder, and base supported by three small feet. Zonal decoration of trellis-patern in green slip and two rows of conical bosses. Pl. LXIII, No. 3. From London.

A 20145. Small jug of buff ware with poor light green glaze. Height 4¼ in. Applied decoration of a human face with moustache and beard, and apparently wearing a crown. The face is realistically and carefully modelled, but the arms of applied strips and incised lines for fingers are clumsy and poorly made. Pl. LXIII, No. 4. From London Wall.

COOKING-POT

In the 14th century metal vessels, such as cauldrons (p. 202), largely replaced pottery for cooking purposes. At London this replacement may have started earlier than elsewhere. At Bodiam Castle, for instance, clay cooking-pots were still in use in the late 14th and 15th centuries. Pottery imitations of cauldrons have been found at several sites. The earliest dated example was recently found at Leicester in association with late 13th-century cooking-pots, but the majority, including the fragment from London (Fig. 74), are probably not earlier than the following century.

A 23654. Fragment of cooking-pot of buff ware with thick greenish yellow glaze inside rim and on handle. Rim diameter 10½ in. The angular handle and everted rim imitate metal cauldrons, and the drawing is restored in accordance with these indications (*cf.* Pl. LVI). Decorated on handle with incised lines and stab-marks. Fig. 74. From Leadenhall Market.

224

PLATE LXIII.

14th-century jugs from London.

1, A 27515; 2, A 22540; 3, C 676; 4, A 20145 (1–3, ¼; 4, ⅜).

PLATE LXIV. [*To face p.* 225.

15th-century jugs from London.
1, A 22817; 2, A 24924; 3, A 15285 (¼).

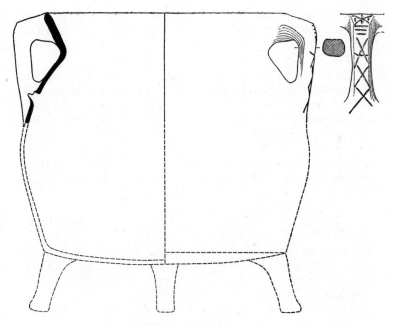

Fig. 74.—14th-century cooking-pot from London. A 23654 (¼).

(iii) *15th century*

Jugs

In the 15th century the decline of the medieval tradition is carried a stage farther, and in some respects the pottery anticipates the wares of the Tudor period.

As in the previous century, the influence of metal forms is frequently apparent and is well shown by two jugs. The first (Pl. LXIV, No. 1, and Fig. 75, No. 1) has an obvious similarity to earlier vessels of the same character (*cf.* Pl. LXIII, No. 2), but its main interest lies in the mask and arms on the front, stylized almost to the point of extinction, but retaining in the thumb-pressed strips forming the arms a decorative motif of great frequency in the earlier centuries. The other jug (Fig. 75, No. 2) imitates the shape of a common type of metal vessel (p. 200) and has a tubular spout ending in the conventionalized animal-head that is peculiar to metal ewers (Pl. LIII).

Apart from these examples of plastic ornament, decoration is usually restricted to zones of incised lines and cordons derived from metalwork (Fig. 75, No. 2), and not uncommonly red-painted designs of scrolls or groups of lines faintly reflect the curvilinear patterns of the 13th century. The mass-production of pottery at this period was a large factor in the collapse of the medieval tradition, and further resulted in the manufacture of jugs of the same form graded into several sizes.

The type site for 15th-century pottery is Bodiam Castle (*Sussex Archæological Collections*, LXXVI, 223). The close similarity of many of the types found there to the products of the kiln at Cheam (*Surrey Archæological Collections*, XXXV, 79), facilitates the identification of 15th-century pottery from London. The Cheam kiln had an enormous output of jugs, pipkins, bowls, etc., and its wares were sent to London. Pl. LXIV, No. 2, is a jug of Cheam ware found in London, and two others with red-painted designs, also found in the City, are in the British Museum (*Catalogue of English Pottery*, p. 65, No. 58) and the Guildhall Museum (*Catalogue*, p. 187, No. 158). It is very probable that many of the smaller plain jugs from London were also made at Cheam, but they are less distinctive than the vessels mentioned above.

The other vessels illustrated are represented at both Bodiam and Cheam. The large pitcher (Pl. LXIV, No. 3) has a bung-hole for a tap above the base, and so probably held liquor with a sediment. The sagging base with thumb-pressed edge is a remarkable survival of an early feature, but is paralleled at Cheam. The plain jugs in Fig. 75, Nos. 3–5, are of simple ovoid form or with biconical body and cylindrical neck. The bifid rim (Nos. 3 and 5), plain handles of round or oval section, and flat bases are characteristic. Glaze is usually restricted to the upper part and often forms a large patch or ' bib ' on the front only.

226

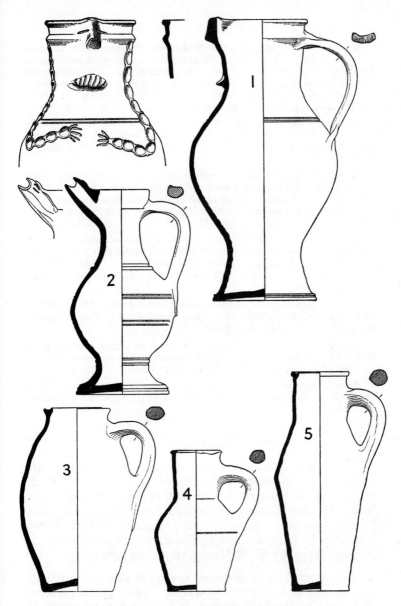

FIG. 75.—15th-century jugs from London.

1, A 22817 ; 2, A 27544 ; 3, A 26130 ; 4, A 5062 ; 5, A 1767 ($\frac{1}{4}$).

A 22817. Jug of buff ware with thick, glossy dark green glaze on upper part and handle. Height 11¾ in. Moulded rim on cylindrical neck, slightly angular shoulder, and waisted foot with moulded base. Degenerate mask decoration on front; ridged nose, incisions for eyes and incised beard on chin. Arms of applied thumb-pressed strips and incised lines as fingers. Pl. LXIV, No. 1, and Fig. 75, No. 1. From Aldwych.

A 24924. Jug of buff ware with large patch of dark brown glaze on front. Cheam ware. Height 9¾ in. Biconical body with narrow girth-grooves on shoulder. Pl. LXIV, No. 2. From the site of Christ's Hospital, Smithfield.

A 15285. Pitcher of buff ware with thick, dark green glaze on upper part. Height 11½ in. On opposite sides above the shoulder is a group of vertical bands of dark red paint. Broad handle with incised lines and stab-marks. Above the base is a projecting bung-hole with finger-tip decoration. Sagging base thumb-pressed all round edge. Pl. LXIV, No. 3. From Bell Alley.

A 27544. Jug of whitish ware with over-all thick yellowish green glaze. Height 8·6 in. Narrow neck, globular body, and waisted foot with spreading base. Zones of girth-grooves on body and foot. Tubular spout ending in a conventionalized animal-head with open mouth. Fig. 75, No. 2. From Whitefriars Street.

A 26130. Ovoid jug of buff ware with splash of greenish brown glaze on front. Height 7¾ in. Bifid rim. Long thumb-mark at base of handle. Fig. 75, No. 3. From Gresham Street.

A 5062. Small jug of buff ware with splash of yellow glaze on front. Height 6 in. Cylindrical neck, angular shoulder with girth-groove, and wide flat base. Fig. 75, No. 4. From Chamberlain's Wharf.

A 1767. Slender jug of buff ware with speckled green glaze on front. Height 9¼ in. Shape similar to last. Bifid rim. Fig. 75, No. 5. From Lombard Street.

Bibliography

The most useful accounts of medieval pottery, with references to the older literature, are still those by R. L. Hobson in *Archæological Journal*, LIX (1902), 1–16, and in the British Museum *Catalogue of English Pottery* (1903). For more general treatment and artistic appreciation, *English Pottery* (1924) by B. Rackham and H. Read, and *English Pottery and Porcelain* (1933) by W. B. Honey, should be consulted.

Recent work is to be found mainly in excavation reports and can only be briefly indicated here. The regional character of pottery in the 12th century is well shown by papers in *Antiquaries Journal*, on Old Sarum (XV, 174), Lydney Castle,

Glos. (XI, 240), and Alstoe Mount, Rutland (XVI, 396). The finest series of 13th-century pottery is from Grosmont Castle and White Castle, Monmouthshire (*ibid.*, XV, 320), also material from Clarendon Palace (*ibid.*, XVI, 55, and forthcoming report) and from Winchester (Winchester City Museum). Long series of unstratified 12th- and 13th-century pottery types are published from Rayleigh Castle (*Transactions of the Essex Archæological Society*, n.s., XII, 147) and Old Sarum (*Wiltshire Archæological Magazine*, XLVI, 259). The wide range of the products of the kilns at Rye (late 13th century) is particularly instructive (*Sussex Archæological Collections*, LXXIII, 83; LXXIV, 45; LXXVII, 107). Pottery covering the whole of the 13th century from Oxford (*Oxoniensia*, IV, 89) should be compared and contrasted with the material from London. The 14th century is best represented by pottery from kilns at Nottingham (*Transactions of the Thoroton Society*, XXXVI, 79) and at Ashton, near Chester (*Annals of Archæology and Anthropology*, XXI, 5). References to other material are given in the text.

FLOOR-TILES

From the early 13th century onwards decorative earthenware pavements were a regular feature of English ecclesiastical and, less commonly, civil architecture. The varieties of tile in use were many, but practically they may be reduced to five headings—tile-mosaic, inlaid, printed, relief, and line-impressed. Other types such as the free-hand incised gospel tiles from Tring (A. Lane, *Victoria and Albert Museum : Guide to the Collection of Tiles*, Pl. 19, Nos. L and M), or occasional specimens bearing slip-painted designs (*e.g.* two from Witham, Essex, in the British Museum), are exceptional. Plain glazed tiles were also regularly employed in combination with inlaid, stamped, or line-impressed tiles. Used alone they were less common, although in the 15th century, in East Anglia, large glazed tiles, 10 or 11 in. square and coloured brown, yellow, or dark green, enjoyed a considerable popularity (*Archæological Journal*, XC (1933), pp. 265-75, Butley Priory).

For a general account of medieval floor tiles, see A. Lane, *Victoria and Albert Museum : Guide to the Collection of Tiles,* 1939, and Loyd Haberly, *Medieval Paving-tiles,* 1937, both of which have good bibliographies ; also R. Forrer, *Geschichte der europäischen Fliesenkeramik,* 1901 ; and, for French tiles, E. Amé, *Les carrelages émaillés du moyen âge et de la Renaissance,* 1859.

(i) *Tile-mosaic*

In classical antiquity two main types of decorative mosaic paving were employed, one the tessellated pavement familiar to Romano-British archæology, the other, *opus sectile* (which was only exceptionally used in Roman Britain, *Sussex Arch. Colls.,* 79, 15–17, Fig. 8) consisting of larger, interlocking pieces of coloured stone or marble. Tessellated pavements were not unknown during the late 11th and 12th centuries in France (R. de Lasteyrie, *L'architecture réligieuse en France à l'époque romane,* pp. 566–8). Some, *e.g.* fragments from St. Denis now in the Musée de Cluny, Paris (R. de Lasteyrie, *op. cit.,* Fig. 570), are in the Byzantine tradition and may have been derived from Italy. Others, *e.g.* the pavements at St. Paul-trois-châteaux (Drôme) and Lescar (Haute Garonne) are evidently direct imitations of Gallo-Roman models. Of the latter type there are half a dozen dated examples, ranging from 1090 (a destroyed pavement at Reims) to the second quarter of the following century (the pavement at Lescar, laid down by Bishop Guy, 1115–41), but they were never common and in this country they are unknown.

Opus sectile was widely employed in medieval Italy, but in France and England, where marble and coloured stone are not readily available, its occurrence is exceptional. Its place was taken by tile-mosaic, which is simply an adaptation of the classical form of pavement to a new and more convenient material. Variety of colouring was obtained by the use of a pipeclay slip or by staining the lead glaze with manganese or copper oxide ; and designs of considerable complexity were sometimes attempted, *e.g.* a fleur-de-lis design at New-bottle Abbey (*Proceedings of the Society of Antiquaries of Scotland,* lxiii (1928–9), 292, Figs. 7 and 8). Mosaic pavements are peculiarly associated with the Cistercian foundations in the North Country. Elsewhere mosaic played only a subsidiary part and was used chiefly to elaborate pavements of inlaid tiles. A late, and in many ways unusual, specimen is the pavement in Prior Cranden's Chapel at Ely (1321–41), and by the middle of the 14th century tile-mosaic was generally obsolete.

Fig. 82, No. 77. A 10408. Fragment of tile-mosaic, glazed yellow. From Garlick Hill.

(ii) *Inlaid Tiles*

The majority of decorated English medieval floor tiles are either inlaid or printed. The distinction is based on methods of manufacture, for, to a casual glance, the finished tile looks much the same in either case. The design appears in yellow against a red ground (very occasionally in red against yellow), but whereas inlaying involved two distinct processes, printing combined the two in a single operation. The inlaid tile was first impressed with a wooden stamp upon a suitable prepared square of clay, and pipeclay was then spread into the resulting hollows. The two stages were quite distinct, as may be seen from the not uncommon omission of the pipeclay filling (*e.g.* Pl. LXV). In printing, on the other hand, the pipeclay was apparently spread straight on to the raised portions of the wooden stamp and so impressed directly upon the clay—a process closely analogous to the printing of designs on paper with an inked wood-block. The differences between the resulting products are only apparent on a close inspection. In the former the pipeclay is always fairly thick and the edges of the design are clearly defined. Printed tiles, on the other hand, are rarely clear-cut. If the stamp has been too heavily " inked " or clumsily applied, the pipeclay spreads and smudges the design. Consequently the impressions resulting from a single stamp may vary considerably from tile to tile, and in extreme instances the design may be quite unrecognizable.

Inlaid tiles are believed to have been first manufactured in Northern France. It has been suggested that, like tile-mosaic, they were immediately derived from a type of stone pavement

231

(A. Lane, *Victoria and Albert Museum : Guide to the Collection of Tiles*, p. 23), the design of which is cut in shallow counter-relief on a slab of free-stone and appears in outline against a background of dark resinous composition. The decorative roundels of this type in the retro-choir of Canterbury Cathedral appear to be unique in England (*Archæologia Cantiana*, xlii (1930), Pl. 189), but in France they were not uncommon. There does not, however, seem to be any clear evidence of the use of inlaid tiles much, if at all, before the end of the 12th century. By that date, relief-tiles, made with wooden stamps, and mosaic, in which pipeclay was freely used as a colouring slip, were both well established; and it is probably true to say that all three techniques played their part in giving rise to the inlaid tiles of the 13th century. The 12th century was an age of experiment, and though many types of decorative pavement were in use, all were closely related. The mosaic roundels of St. Denis and of Reims, the stone roundels of Canterbury and of St. Omer, the inlaid roundels of Chertsey are all part of a single tradition.

Although the inlay-technique may have originated in France, it was in this country that it found its finest expression. It is only in Anjou and Poitou that French tiles of a comparable quality can be found; and the close similarity between the designs on these tiles and those on the earliest English inlaid tiles suggests that it was from this region that the craft was first introduced into England. The earliest tiles in this country are found in Wessex, in an area of which the most notable surviving sites are Salisbury Cathedral (begun in 1223), Winchester Cathedral, and Romsey Abbey (a related group of tiles, showing an even stronger affinity with Anjou, was found in the last century at Jervaulx Abbey, Yorkshire; many of the designs are in red on yellow, a peculiarly French characteristic. H. Shaw, *Specimens of Tile-pavements*, London, 1858, Pls. vii–xii). These Wessex tiles were also used to pave the royal palace of Clarendon, near Salisbury (*Antiquaries Journal*, XVI (1936), Pl. XIV), and the kiln for their manufacture has recently been excavated within the precincts of the Palace itself. This kiln was in use for a few years only, between 1234 and 1236; and although other sites, such as Romsey and Winchester, were almost certainly supplied from other kilns using the same stamps, the whole series belongs without doubt to the second quarter of the 13th century. The high quality and technical accomplishment of these tiles suggests a deliberate importation of tile-wrights, presumably under royal patronage. Their craft, however, quickly took root, and the celebrated pavement in the Chapter House at Westminster (laid between 1253 and 1259) and the remains of a similar pavement from Chertsey Abbey (some ten years later) are the high-watermark of medieval tile manufacture. It is suggestive that these pavements, too, and the fragments of yet another of the same class, from Hailes Abbey, Glos, can probably be associated with the royal house (A. Lane, *Victoria and Albert Museum : Guide to the Collection of Tiles*, p. 24).

From these beginnings the manufacture of inlaid tiles rapidly assumed a more pedestrian level, and in some parts of the country they were in common use by the close of the 13th century. The distinction between inlaid and printed tiles has not yet been generally applied, and it is impossible therefore to be certain of the exact incidence of either type. It seems, however, that the former belong in the main to the south, chiefly in Wessex, where designs derivative from the Clarendon series continued to exercise an effect as late as the 15th century, and in the upper Thames basin. Outside these regions the majority of red and yellow tiles belong to the later Middle Ages, when inlaying had in many districts been already largely superseded by printing.

It may be added that although the technical distinction between inlaying and printing is clear and rigid, it is not always easy to distinguish in the case of individual specimens which process has been employed. The majority of London tiles are printed. Tiles of the 13th century are not common in London, and, when used, they were imported from elsewhere. It was not until the 14th century that tiles came into general use in London, and by that time the deeply-cut stamps of the earlier tiles were being replaced everywhere by a shallower type, which gave a less clear design, but was more economical in pipeclay. This development led directly to the invention of tile-printing. The earliest printed tiles were deeply stamped, so that the pipeclay design was, if anything, slightly below the reserved surface of the tile, and so preserved from wear. The stamps from which London Museum Types 1–10 were made could well have been used for inlaying (see Pl. LX), and these may be regarded as some of the earliest printed tiles made in this country.

Fig. 81, No. 63. A 25310. Deep, clear-cut inlay. Originally glazed green and yellow. This tile belongs to the Clarendon series (*Antiquaries Journal*, XVI, 1936, Pl. XIV) although unlike most of these tiles it is not " keyed " on the back. Mid-13th century. From St. Stephen's Chapel, Westminster.

Fig. 81, No. 64. A 11131. Deep, clear-cut inlay, glaze entirely gone. Four shallow keys at the back. This design is also found at Exeter and Dunchideock (Devon). From Tabard Street.

Fig. 82, No. 73. 35.118/19M. Deep, clear-cut inlay, brown and yellow, crackled glaze. The design (two birds flanking a formal tree) and the technique are typical of a number of Wessex tiles. From St. Mary's Hospital, Spital Square, Bishopsgate.

Fig. 83, No. 81. Inlaid tile of a style approximating to that of the Chertsey pavement. Second half of the 13th century. From the site of Christ's Hospital, Newgate (in Taunton Museum).

Not illustrated. A 20265. A border tile, 5·0 in. by 2·5 in., deep inlay, three complete and two half-circles, between two bands running length-ways. The design is found also at Salisbury, Keynsham, Muchelney, and other Wessex and Somerset sites. From Bucklersbury.

(iii) *Printed Tiles*

Printed tiles were far less durable than the inlaid tiles from which they were derived, and even when new the design was generally coarser. On the other hand, they were cheaper and easier to produce. In consequence, although they undoubtedly represent an artistic and technical decline, they achieved a popularity that their predecessors had never known. Despite the activities of time and of churchwardens, there remain examples in hundreds of churches all over the country, wherever there were materials to hand, often, indeed, at a surprising distance from the nearest possible kiln.

Unlike the men who made the pavements for Clarendon and for Westminster, the later medieval tile-wright was a humble craftsman, and his products reflect a traditionalism of design that often bears little relation to contemporary artistic currents. An exception must be made of the tiles that were manufactured at Great Malvern, in the mid-15th century. These were of a technical excellence unequalled elsewhere, save perhaps in contemporary France, and the products of this kiln were used throughout the Severn basin, and as far afield as St. David's Cathedral and St. Mary's Abbey, York. Outside this region there was, however, no such renaissance of craftsmanship. The late 15th- and early 16th-century printed tiles of the upper Thames basin have neither technical nor artistic merit (see Loyd Haberly, *Mediæval Paving Tiles*, Oxford, 1937); and it may well be that in south-eastern England the craft was by then already dead. That at least seems to be a reasonable explanation for the importation of Flemish printed tiles, mainly to sites in and around London, in the late 15th and early 16th century (*Antiquaries Journal*, XVIII (1938), 442–3, Pl. XCV); to the sites there listed add Edmonton parish church (in the Victoria and Albert Museum) and Gloucester (F. Renaud, *Tiles*, MS. in the library of the Society of Antiquaries); also perhaps St. Albans, Poynings, and Horsted Keynes; see below, *s.v.* No. 66. In Wessex, on the other hand, printed tiles of good quality were being made as late as the 16th century (F. Stevens, "The Inlaid Paving Tiles of Wilts," *Wiltshire Archæological Magazine*, XLVII).

Some at least of the printed tiles that were used in London were made locally, for the remains of a tile-kiln were found in Farringdon Street (*Transactions of the London and Middlesex Archæological Society*, iii, 31–6). Unfortunately there is no record of the tiles that it contained. Others came from Penn in Buckinghamshire. In Edward III's reign there are records of the transport of tilers from Penn to London and of tiles themselves to Windsor, and other records confirm the existence of a flourishing local industry. The recent discovery at Penn of tiles, some of them kiln-wasters, gives substance to the documentary evidence. These include London Museum Types 4, 9, 14, 16, 18–20, 24 (?), 53, and 79; and there can be little doubt that other types await identification. Many of the designs which are most commonly found in London are widely distributed in the Thames basin, sporadically in North Kent, but chiefly in South Oxfordshire, South Buckinghamshire, East Berkshire, and Hertfordshire (*cf.* the distribution of Hurley Types 1 and 2, *Berkshire Archæological Journal*, xlii (1938), 119, Fig. 1). Their distribution leaves little doubt that they were manufactured either at Penn, or at other kilns in the Chilterns. These tiles are all printed, but they include the earliest and best specimens; and it is therefore interesting to observe that there is documentary evidence of tile-manufacture at Penn at least as early as 1332.

One other group deserves mention. A number of tiles that occur in association on several sites in the London area, *e.g.* on the site of St. Mary's Hospital, Spital Square, Bishopsgate, in St. Faith's Chapel, Westminster Abbey, at Lesnes Abbey (Kent) and at Bengeo (Herts) are also recorded from several sites round Coventry, notably at Baginton Priory and Kenilworth . Castle (P. B. Chatwin, "The Medieval Patterned Tiles of Warwickshire," *Transactions and Proceedings of the Birmingham Archæological Society*, LX, 1936, Fig. 10, Nos. 6, 8, 9, 11, 17, 19 and 21 = London Museum Nos. 37, 56, 85, 55, 41, 51 and 25). There is some reason for regarding the Warwickshire specimens as the product of a local kiln, and as the London specimens were evidently also made locally, some potter must presumably have migrated with his stamps from one area to the other.

The following lists, which have been prepared in collaboration with Mr. E. C. Hohler and with the help of Mr. P. D. R. Williams-Hunt, do not claim to have isolated all the minor varieties through which a design might pass owing to the recutting or the replacement of worn stamps. Reference is made in abbreviated form to the following works:

Loyd Haberly, *Medieval Paving Tiles*, Oxford, 1937.

J. B. Ward Perkins and P. D. R. Williams-Hunt, "The Medieval Floor Tiles at St. Mary's Priory, Hurley, Berks," *Berkshire Archæological Journal*, XLII, 1938.

P. B. Chatwin, "The Medieval Patterned Tiles of Warwickshire," *Transactions and Proceedings of the Birmingham Archæological Society*, LX, 1936.

Several reference to tiles, since vanished, are drawn from a volume of tracings compiled by Lord Alwyne Compton, now in the library of the Society of Antiquaries of London,

Burlington House. The tiles of Buckinghamshire, and in particular the recent finds at Penn, will shortly be published by Mr. E. C. Hohler in the *Records of the Bucks Archæological Society*, XIV, 1941.

Fig. 76.

No. 1. 27.27/1. From London.

Also found at Windsor Castle (from Penn) and at St. Giles', Cripplegate. A slightly larger variant, with additional dots, also appears at St. Giles', Cripplegate; at St. Bartholomew-the-Great, Smithfield; at Oxford Cathedral, Notley Abbey, Steventon Church and Marston Church (Oxon); at Hurley (Berks); at St. Mary's Church, Horsham (Sussex); and at Southfleet (Kent). Haberly, Nos. CXVI and CXVII; Hurley, No. 10.

No. 2. A 4655. From London.

36.10. (Probably from a different stamp.) From London.

Also found in "an old church on London Wall" (British Museum); at All Hallows, Lombard Street; at Cookham (Berks); at Pitstone (Bucks); at Chesterford (Essex); and Dunstable Friary (Beds). Probably the same as Haberly, No. CLIV, from Merton College, Oxford.

No. 3. A 4617. From London.

Also found at St. Albans; and at Windsor Castle (from Penn).

No. 4. A 4611. From London.

A 4613. From London.

36.144/1. From Fetter Lane.

Also found at Penn (Bucks), where it was made; at Little Marlow, Missenden Abbey, Bledlow, Ditton Park Chapel (Stoke Poges), and Pitstone (Bucks); at Chertsey Abbey (Surrey: for another Penn tile at Chertsey see H. Shaw, *Specimens of Tile-pavements*, London, 1858, Pl. xxi); and at Barham (Kent). Probably not all from the same stamp.

No. 5. A 4654. From London.

No. 6. A 4652. From London. (Pipeclay omitted, yellow glaze.) Pl. LXV.

A 24779. From Nuns' Chapel, St. Helen's Place, Bishopsgate.

33.104/35, b. and c. "From the site of Baynard's Castle." Pl. LXV.

Also found at All Hallows, Lombard Street; at Pitstone, Whitchurch, and Iver (Bucks); at Reading (Berks); and at Somerton (Bucks). Haberly, No. CLXXIV.

No. 7. A 16882. From London.

A 26227. From the corner of Wood Street and Gresham Street.

A 28078. From St. Christopher-le-Stocks, Bank of England.

Also found at All Hallows, Lombard Street; at St. Botolph's, Thames Street; at St. Bartholomew-the-Great, Smithfield; at Thame Abbey (Oxon); at Ludgershall, Saunderton and Great Hampden (Bucks): and at Hurley Priory and Binfield (Berks). Hurley, No. 9.

No. 8.　35.118/19L.　From St. Mary's Hospital, Spital Square, Bishopsgate.
　　　　36.9.　From London.
　　　　38.230/2.　From London (3 specimens).
　　　　Also found in St. Faith's Chapel, Westminster Abbey; at Notley
　　　　Abbey, Marston, Chinnor, Marsworth, Little Marlow, Great
　　　　Kimble, Great Hampden, and Saunderton (Bucks); at Hurley
　　　　Priory, where it is associated with No. 14, Windsor, and Maple-
　　　　durham (Berks); at Bosham and Appledrum (Sussex); and at
　　　　St. Cross, Winchester (Hants).　Haberly, No. CIX; Hurley,
　　　　No. 23.　A smaller version has been found at Penn (Bucks),
　　　　where it was made.

No. 9.　A 27801.　From Blomfield Street, E.C.2.
　　　　Also found at Penn (Bucks), where no doubt it was made;
　　　　at Whitchurch (Bucks); and at St. Cross, Winchester (Hants).

No. 10.　A 9374.　From Bermondsey Street.
　　　　Also found at Osney Abbey, Dorchester Abbey, Oxford Cathedral,
　　　　and Braughton Castle, near Banbury (Oxon); at Bierton,
　　　　Amersham, Haddenham, and Notley Abbey (Bucks); at East
　　　　Hagbourne (Berks) and at St. Albans (Herts).　Haberly, No. CXV;
　　　　Hurley, *s.v.*, No. 7.

No. 11.　A 4622.　From St. Bartholomew-the-Less, Smithfield.
　　　　Also found at St. Bartholomew-the-Great, Smithfield; at Little
　　　　Marlow, Pitstone, Whitchurch, Newton Longville, Great Kimble,
　　　　Radnage, and perhaps at Thame Abbey (Bucks); and at Hurley.
　　　　Priory (Berks).　Haberly, No. CXXVII; Hurley, No. 15.

No. 12.　A 24628.　From site of Nuns' Chapel, St. Helen's Place, Bishopsgate.
　　　　A 24762.　From same find-spot.
　　　　A 24813.　From same find-spot.
　　　　Also found at St. Bartholomew-the-Great, Smithfield; at Hurley
　　　　(Berks); at Milton Keynes, Marsworth, and Little Marlow
　　　　(Bucks); and at St. Cross, Winchester.　Hurley, No. 7.

FIG. 77.

No. 13.　A 24626–7.　From site of Nuns' Chapel, St. Helen's Place, Bishops-
　　　　gate.
　　　　A 24870.　From London.
　　　　Patterns differing only in size and in proportions are found at
　　　　Penn (Bucks), where some at least of them were made; at
　　　　St. Bartholomew-the-Great, Smithfield; at Bierton, Monks
　　　　Risborough, Great Kimble, Chalfont St. Giles, Saunderton,
　　　　Chesham Bois, Amersham, Missenden Abbey, Milton Keynes,
　　　　Marsworth, Little Marlow, Horsenden, Great Hampden, Notley
　　　　Abbey, Aylesbury, Stone, and Wyrardisbury (Bucks); at Windsor
　　　　Castle, Hurley Priory and Steventon (Berks); at Warborough
　　　　(Oxon); at Kings Langley and St. Albans (Herts); and at
　　　　Elstow (Beds).

238

No. 14. A 4658. From London.

No. 15. A 20387-8. From Cloth Fair, E.C.1.
35.118/19K. From St. Mary's Hospital, Spital Square, Bishopsgate.
Also found in St. Faith's Chapel, Westminster Abbey; at
Saunderton and Horsenden (Bucks); and at Hurley Priory
(Berks). Hurley, No. 25.

No. 16. 38.230/4. From London.
Also found in Edward the Confessor's Chapel, Westminster
Abbey; at St. Albans (Herts); at Merton Priory (Surrey); and
at Penn (Bucks), where it was made. *Surrey Archæological Collections*, XXXVIII, 57. Probably the same as Haberly, No. C.

No. 17. A 20386. From Cloth Fair, E.C.1.
Also found at Oxford Cathedral and Dorchester Abbey (Oxon);
at West Hendred (Berks); and at St. Cross, Winchester (Hants).

No. 18. 38.230/5. From London.
Also found at Penn (Bucks), where it was made; and at Great
Hampden, Whitchurch, and Saunderton (Bucks). Probably the
same as Haberly, No. LXXIX. The petals in two of the corners
should perhaps rather be the half of a four-lobed motif.

No. 19. A 27124-5. From the site of the Savoy Palace.
38.263. (A kiln-waster.) From Penn (Bucks).
Made at Penn; also found at Iver and Pitstone (Bucks); a
Reading (Berks); and at Northchurch (Herts).

No. 20. A 24811-2. From site of Nun's Chapel, St. Helen's Place, Bishopsgate.
A 24814. From same find-spot.
A 24958. From Crosby Square.
Also found on the site of East India House, Leadenhall Stree
(in the British Museum); at Penn (Bucks), where it was made
and at Muchelney (Somerset). *Cf.* No. 82.

No. 21. B 59. From Cannon Street.

No. 22. 35.118/19T. From St. Mary's Hospital, Spital Square, Bishopsgate
See below, No. 24.

No. 23. A 4605. From London.
A 4662. From Crosby Square.
38.230/1. From London.
36.144/2. From Fetter Lane.
Also found at St. Albans (Herts); and at Barham (Kent). *Cf.* also
Hurley, No. 45.

No. 24. A 27115. From the site of the Savoy Palace.
A 27117. From the same find-spot.
This confusing design (*cf.* No. 22) was manufactured in a number
of slightly different forms, which are widely distributed in Oxfordshire, Buckinghamshire, and Hertfordshire. See Hurley, No. 36;
to the sites there listed add St. Bartholomew-the-Great, Smithfield.

FIG. 76.—Stamped tiles from London (¼).

Above, left: 33.104/35.   Stamped tile.
Above, right: A 4652.   Stamped tile, with pipeclay omitted.   (See p. 231.)
Below: A 7954.   Relief tile, manufactured at Bawsey, Norfolk.   (See p. 253.)

FIG. 77.—Stamped tiles from London (¼).

FIG. 78.

No. 25. A 28076. From St. Christopher-le-Stocks, Bank of England.

35.118/19J. From St. Mary's Hospital, Spital Square, Bishopsgate.
Also found in St. Faith's Chapel, Westminster Abbey; and at
Kenilworth Castle (Warwick), Chatwin, Fig. 10, No. 21.

No. 26. A 12324. From Crutched Friars.
Also found at Kilburn Priory; at Penn (Bucks), where it was
made; and at Wexham (Berks).

No. 27. A 20794. From Kinghorn Street.
The corners probably contained a plain, straight-sided white
triangle, on the analogy of a design found at St. Albans (Herts).
and Weston Turville (Bucks); or possibly a dot, as at Moulsoe
(Bucks).

No. 28. A 27818. From Wilson Street, E.C.2.
Also found at St. Bartholomew-the-Great, Smithfield; at Bierton,
Pitstone and Wyrardisbury (Bucks); and at St. Albans (Herts).
This design occurs in a number of variant forms in the Thames
basin and Eastern Wessex. See *Sussex Arch. Coll.*, lxxv, Pl. vii,
cf. No. 30.

No. 29. A 27122–3. From the site of the Savoy Palace.
Also found at Hitcham and Whitchurch (Bucks); at Reading
(Berks) and at Thame Abbey (Oxon). Haberly, No. CXVIII.

No. 30. A 13516. From London Wall.
See No. 28. Also found at Langley Marish and Hitcham (Bucks);
Titsey (Surrey); and at St. Cross, Winchester.

No. 31. A 24810. From site of Nuns' Chapel, St. Helen's Place, Bishopsgate.
Also found in Cannon Street (in the British Museum), at All
Hallows, Lombard Street, and at Kilburn Priory; at Windsor
Castle (from Penn); at Pitstone, Horsenden, and Saunderton
(Bucks); at Dunstable (Beds); and at Northchurch, Sandridge,
and St. Albans (Herts). There are several slightly different
stamps of this design.

No. 32. A 27724. From Clements Lane, W.C.2.
Also found at Blackfriars (in the Victoria and Albert Museum).

No. 33. A 28067. From Little Trinity Lane.
Also found at Canterbury Cathedral; at Pitstone and Ludgershall (Bucks); and at St. Albans (Herts). Haberly, No. CLXXV.

No. 34. A 27862. From Blomfield Street, E.C.2.
Also found at All Hallows, Lombard Street; at Cannon Street
(in the British Museum); and at Pitstone (Bucks).

No. 35. A 9517. From Westminster.
Also found at St. Saviour, Southwark; at Whitchurch, Little
Missenden, Great Missenden, Amersham, Pitstone, Little Marlow
and Hitcham (Bucks); and at Hurley Priory and Binfield (Berks).
Haberly, No. XCII; Hurley, No. 14. There are several closely
related variants from other sites.

242

No. 36. A 27863. From Blomfield Street, E.C.2.
Also found (?) at St. Bartholomew-the-Great, Smithfield.

FIG. 79.
No. 37. A 20264. From Basinghall Street.
35.118/19C. From St. Mary's Hospital, Spital Square, Bishopsgate. Also found in St. Faith's Chapel, Westminster Abbey; at St. Bartholomew-the-Great, Smithfield; at Canterbury and at Lesnes Abbey (Kent); at Baginton Priory (Warwick); and at Bengeo (Herts). Chatwin, Fig. 10, No. 6.

No. 38. A 16883. From London.
Also found at Flaunden (Herts).

No. 39. A 26184. From Gresham Street, E.C.2.

No. 40. A 4619. From Temple Church.
33.104/35a. "From the site of Baynard's Castle." Also found in St. Faith's Chapel, Westminster Abbey; and at Cannon Street (in the British Museum).

No. 41. A 4668. From Temple Church.
A 13736. (Perhaps from a different stamp.) From London Wall. Also found in St. Faith's Chapel, Westminster Abbey; at Lesnes Abbey (Kent); and at Baginton Priory (Warwick). Chatwin, Fig. 10, No. 17; there are also several closely related examples from other sites.

No. 42. A 15269. From Basinghall Street.

No. 43. A 4607. From London.

A 4659. From London.
A 26226. From the corner of Wood Street and Gresham Street.
A 27116. From the site of the Savoy Palace.
This design, Heraldic gyronny, is extremely common and appears in a number of slightly differing varieties. *Cf.* Hurley, No. 22; *Sussex Arch. Coll.*, lxxv (quoting several other London sites).

No. 44. A 15270. From Basinghall Street.
Also found in St. Faith's Chapel, Westminster Abbey; and at Bengeo (Herts).

No. 45. 35.118/190. From St. Mary's Hospital, Spital Square, Bishopsgate. Also found at St. Bartholomew-the-Less, Smithfield; and at Canterbury Cathedral and Langdon Abbey, Dover (Kent).

No. 46. A 302. From Westminster.
Also found at Langdon Abbey, Dover (Kent); and at Poynings (Sussex).

No. 47. B 60. From Cannon Street.

No. 48. A 17146. From Leadenhall Street.

25 26 27

28 29 30

31 32 33

34 35 36

FIG. 78.—Stamped tiles from London (¼).

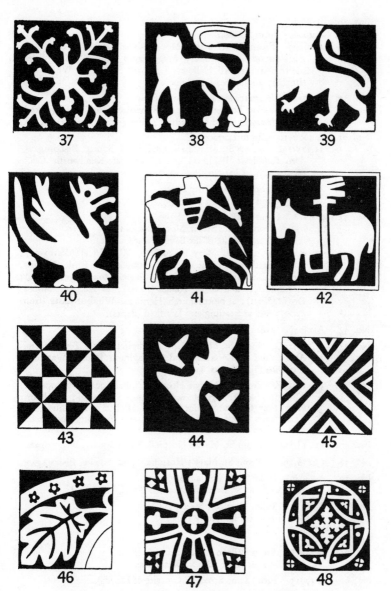

37 38 39
40 41 42
43 44 45
46 47 48

FIG. 79.—Stamped tiles from London (¼).

Fig. 80.

No. 49. A 4608. From London.

A 26269. From Tenter Street, Moorfields, E.C.2.

Also found at St. Mary Magdalene's Church, Milk Street (destroyed); at All Hallows, Lombard Street; at Whitchurch (Bucks); and at Reading Abbey.

No. 50. A 27121. From the site of the Savoy Palace.

Also found at Thame Abbey and Somerton (Oxon); at Shulbrede Priory (Sussex); and at Reading Abbey. Haberly, No. CXXX.

No. 51. A 4609–10. From London.

35.118/19B. From St. Mary's Hospital, Spital Square, Bishopsgate.

Also found at Baginton Priory and at Kenilworth Castle (Warwick). Chatwin, Fig. 10, No. 19.

No. 52. A 28038. From Little Trinity Lane.

Also found at Kilburn Priory.

No. 53. A 4618. From Christ's Hospital.

A 26186. From Tenter Street, Moorfields, E.C.2.

A 27118. From the site of the Savoy Palace.

Also found at St. Mary Magdalene, Milk Street (destroyed); at St. Bartholomew-the-Great, Smithfield; at Little Marlow, Pitstone, Bledlow, and Ditton Park Chapel, Stoke Poges (Bucks); at Sandridge, and at St. Albans (Herts); at Langdon Abbey, Dover (Kent); at Northchurch (Herts); at Windsor Castle (from Penn); and at Reading and Warfield (Berks).

No. 54. A 28037. From Little Trinity Lane.

No. 55. 35.118/19D. From St. Mary's Hospital, Spital Square, Bishopsgate.

Also found at Cookham and at Baginton Priory (Warwick). Chatwin, Fig. 10, No. 11.

No. 56. 35.118/19F. From St. Mary's Hospital, Spital Square, Bishopsgate.

Also found at St. Bartholomew-the-Less, Smithfield; at Kilburn Priory; at Baginton Priory; at St. Michael's, Coventry; and Kenilworth Castle (Warwick); and at Canterbury and Lesnes Abbey (Kent). Chatwin, Fig. 10, No. 8.

No. 57. 35.118/19E. From St. Mary's Hospital, Spital Square, Bishopsgate.

No. 58. 35.118/19G. From St. Mary's Hospital, Spital Square, Bishopsgate.

No. 59. A 14649. From King William Street.

Also found at St. Bartholomew-the-Great, Smithfield.

No. 60. A 26185. From Gresham Street, E.C.2.

A 2836. From Little Trinity Lane.

Fig. 81.

No. 61. A 27698. From Wilson Street, E.C.2.

Also found at Hyde Abbey, Winchester.

No. 62. A 27915. From Lime Street, E.C.3 (site of Lloyds).

(Nos. 63–4. Inlaid tiles.)

246

No. 65.   (In the Guildhall Museum.)   From London.
An imported Flemish tile of the late 15th or early 16th century. The same stamp appears on a larger tile at Leenwarden. See above, p. 235.

No. 66.   A 13737.   From Crutched Friars.
Possibly, but not certainly, Flemish.   *Cf.* No. 65.   Also found at St. Albans (Herts), and at Poynings and Horsted Keynes (Sussex).

Fig. 82.
No. 67.   35.118/19U.   From St. Mary's Hospital, Spital Square, Bishopsgate.

No. 68.   A 2011.   From Westminster.
Also found at Kilburn Priory.

No. 68.   A 2011.   From Westminster.

No. 69.   B 62.   From Cannon Street.
Also found at Canterbury and Folkestone.

No. 70.   35.118/19A.   From St. Mary's Hospital, Spital Square, Bishopsgate.
Also found at Canterbury and at Bengeo (Herts).

No. 71.   35.118/19S.   From St. Mary's Hospital, Spital Square, Bishopsgate.

No. 72.   A 26297.   From the corner of Wood Street and Gresham Street, E.C.2.
Also found in the Guildhall Museum, from London.

(No. 73.   Inlaid tile.)

No. 74.   A 4623.   From London.
Also found at Canterbury; and at Reading Abbey.

No. 75.   A 28013.   From Little Trinity Lane.
Also found at Lesnes Abbey (Kent).   *Cf.* Haberly, No. CXLIV, from Thame Abbey=Hurley, No. 57.

No. 76.   A 28039.   From Little Trinity Lane.

(No. 77.   Tile-mosaic.)

Fig. 83.
No. 78.   A 25709.   From the site of St. Anthony's Hospital, Threadneedle Street.

No. 79.   35.118/19R.   From St. Mary's Hospital, Spital Square, Bishopsgate.
Also found at All Hallows, Lombard Street; at Penn (Bucks), where it was made; at Thame Abbey and Rycote (Oxon); at Hurley Priory and Wallingford (Berks); at Stone (Bucks); and at Cobham (Kent).   Haberly, No. CXLII.

No. 80.   35.118/19H.   From St. Mary's Hospital, Spital Square, Bishopsgate.

(No. 81.   Inlaid tile.)

FIG. 80.—Stamped tiles from London (¼).

FIG. 81.—No. 61, stamped tile from Wilson Street; No. 62, stamped tile from Lime Street; No. 63, inlaid tile from St. Stephen's Chapel, Westminster; No. 64, inlaid tile from Tabard Street; No. 65, stamped tile, Flemish, early 16th century; No. 66, stamped tile, possibly Flemish, early 16th century. (No. 65 is in the Guildhall Museum.) (⅓).

Not illustrated :

No. 82.   As No. 20, but the spaces between the inner and outer circles each
          contain two white spots. There are several variant stamps of
          this design.
          A 27120. From the site of the Savoy Palace.
          38.230/3. Two examples from London.
          Also found at Pitstone, Slapton, Horsenden, Whitchurch, Iver,
          and Amersham (Bucks).

No. 83.   As No. 82, but with only one white spot.
          A 28014. From the site of St. Katherine Colman, Fenchurch
          Street.
          Also found at Wallingford (Berks) ; at Pitstone, Edlesborough,
          and Missenden Abbey (Bucks) ; and at Dunstable (Beds).

No. 84.   Small tile, 4 in. square, three leopards of England facing to the right.
          35.118/19N. From St. Mary's Hospital, Spital Square, Bishopsgate.

No. 85.   Battered tile, same set as No. 45, four concentric quarter-circles, designs
          at inner and outer corners illegible.
          35.118/19P. From St. Mary's Hospital, Spital Square, Bishopsgate.
          Also found at Kenilworth Castle (Warwick). Chatwin, Fig. 10,
          No. 9.

No. 86.   Battered tile, a quarter-design, the outermost circle of which contains
          six quatrefoils, the inner linked fleurs-de-lis.
          35.118/19Q. From St. Mary's Hospital, Spital Square, Bishopsgate.

No. 87.   Battered tile, a quarter design, consisting of oak leaves and rosettes,
          found also at Barham (Kent) and Binfield (Berks) ; similar to
          Hurley, No. 51.
          A 27119. From the site of the Savoy Palace.

No. 88.   Battered tile, a quarter-design, of the same type as No. 36, the main
          segment occupied by three six-lobed flowers.
          A 27103. From the site of the Savoy Palace.

No. 89.   A fleur-de-lis ; similar to No. 70, but the ends of the subsidiary shoots
          do not curl.
          A 4614. From London.

No. 90.   Heraldic gyronny, a variant of No. 43.
          A 13721. From London Wall.

(iv) *Relief-tiles*

Though far less common than inlaid and printed tiles,
relief-tiles enjoyed a considerable local popularity in East
Anglia throughout the Middle Ages, and occurred sporadically
elsewhere in the 13th century. This form of paving appears
to have been invented in Alsace in the mid-12th century. From

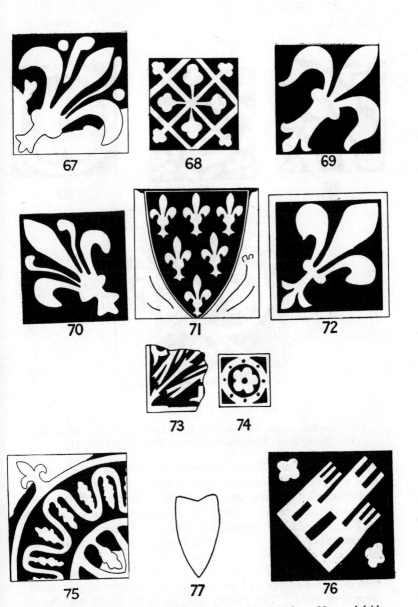

FIG. 82.—Nos. 67–72 and 74–76, stamped tiles from London ; No. 73, inlaid tile from St. Mary's Hospital, Spital Square, Bishopsgate ; No. 77, mosaic tile from Garlick Hill (¼).

251

FIG. 83.—Nos. 78–80, stamped tiles from London; No. 81, inlaid tile
from Christ's Hospital, Newgate (in Taunton Museum) (¼).

the Rhineland and North Switzerland, where it rapidly took
root and long remained popular, it travelled to this country,
and relief-tiles of 13th-century date are found at a number of
scattered sites, ranging from North Berwick (East Lothian)
to Buckfast Abbey (South Devon), and Whitelands Abbey
(Caermarthenshire). The wide distribution and varied character
of these 13th-century tiles alike suggest that they were in
part at least the work of immigrant craftsmen; and it is certain
that nowhere except in East Anglia did this type of pavement
take firm root. The raised designs wore badly and were
uncomfortable underfoot. They were better suited to wall-
decoration, a use to which they were commonly put abroad,

but very rarely in England. Large numbers of these tiles were manufactured at Bawsey, near Castle Rising, Norfolk, in the 14th century, and widely used in the Fenland and the northern part of East Anglia. The products of this kiln occasionally went farther afield, and three specimens are recorded from London, one in the London Museum (Pl. LXV), another in the Guildhall Museum, and a third illustrated by Forrer, *Geschichte der europaïschen Fliesenkeramik*, p. 57, Fig. 123. For relief-tiles in general, see J. B. Ward Perkins, " English Mediæval Embossed Tiles," *Archæological Journal*, XCIV, 1938, 128 ff.

A 7954.   Relief-tile, manufactured at Bawsey, near Castle Rising, Norfolk. 14th century.   Pl. LXV., No. 3.   From London.

(v) *Line-impressed Tiles*

Another group of tiles to which a 14th-century date may be assigned are those which bear an impressed linear design. These designs often have the superficial appearance of free-hand incision with a pointed tool, but on closer inspection they are in fact invariably found to have been impressed with a stamp. Technically they are closely akin to the line-impressed tiles of the Rhineland, although the latter are rarely glazed (A. Lane, *Victoria and Albert Museum : Guide to the Collection of Tiles*, pp. 33–4), and there can be little doubt that it was from Germany that they were introduced into England. In this country they enjoyed considerable local popularity in two districts, in Cheshire, Shropshire, and Staffordshire, whence they were occasionally introduced into Ireland, and in the Fenland and parts of East Anglia. In both cases the uniformity of the designs employed seems to point to centralized manufacture. At Ely, in Prior Cranden's Chapel (1321–41) line-impressed tiles were used in conjunction with a late form of tile-mosaic, but the designs are identical with those recorded from Elstow (Beds), from Cambridge, from Icklingham (Suffolk), and from a number of sites in that region.

PILGRIM-SIGNS AND OTHER PEWTER BADGES

The pilgrimage was a medieval institution whose intimate connection with the everyday life of people of all classes it is not now easy to appreciate. To many these organized expéditions to some holy shrine afforded the only means of travel in an age when transport was bad and the hazards of the road many. The pages of Chaucer bear abundant testimony to the peculiarly medieval union of religious and secular elements which the pilgrimage involved. Occasionally a critic, such as Thomas Thorpe, the Wyclifite priest, in his examination before Bishop Arundel in 1407, would complain that " such fonde people waste blamefully Goddes goods in ther veyne pilgrimagis." But to the ordinary person there was nothing curious in the features which attracted people such as the Miller and the Wife of Bath side by side with the Poor Parson and the Ploughman. The pilgrimage was accepted both as an occasion for pious devotion and as an opportunity for cheerful travel and for novelty, and there can be little doubt that both these aspects contributed to the enormous popularity which it enjoyed in the 13th, 14th, and 15th centuries.

The objects of pilgrimage were various. Some, such as the shrine of St. Thomas of Canterbury or that of Our Lady of Walsingham, enjoyed an international reputation. At the other end of the scale were a multitude of minor shrines such as that of St. Kenelm at Winchcombe, Gloucestershire, or the Rood of Grace, at Boxley, Kent; and some even, such as the shrine of Sir John Schorn, Vicar of North Marston, Bucks ("Sir John Schorn, gentleman born, conjured the devil into a boot "), or the tomb of Henry VI, at Windsor (Grosjean, *Henrici VI Angliae Regis Miracula Postuma*, Société des Bollandistes, 1935), the patron saints of which had never received the benefit of official canonization. And, between the two extremes, there were the great abbeys such as Winchester, Bury, and York, to which came pilgrims from all over the country.

Pewter badges of St. Thomas of Canterbury from the Thames at London $(\frac{1}{1})$.

PLATE LXVII.

[To face p. 255.

Pewter badges of St. Thomas of Canterbury from the Thames at London ($\frac{1}{1}$).

The pilgrim was not restricted to England. The more pious and the more adventurous could visit the great continental shrines such as St. James of Compostella or St. Peter at Rome, or he might go yet farther afield to the cities of the East and to the Holy Land.

> " And thries hadde she been at Jerusalem;
> At Rome she hadde been, and at Bouloigne,
> In Galice at Seint Jame, and at Coloigne."
>
> (The Wife of Bath ; Chaucer, *Prologue to the Canterbury Tales*)

The pilgrim in Langland's *Vision of Piers Plowman* (*c.* 1360–1400) was even more widely travelled :

> " And hundred of ampulles
> On his hat seten
> Signes of Synay   *St. Catherine, Mt. Sinai*
> And shelles of Galice   *St. James of Compostella*
> And many a crouche on his cloke   *St. Antoine de Viennois*
> And keyes of Rome   *St. Peter, Rome*
> And the vernicle before   *St. Veronica, Genoa*
> For men shulde know
> And se bi hise signes
> Whom he sought hadde."

In the east he claimed to have visited " our Lordes Sepulcre ; in Bethlem and Babiloyne, I have been in both, In Armonye and Alisaundre," and he adds :

> " Ye may se by my signes
> That sitten on myn hatte."

The signs of which he speaks were usually made of lead or pewter, sometimes of brass, and they were sold at the various shrines as talismans and as visible tokens of pilgrimage.

> " Then, as manere and custom is, signes there they bought
> For men of contré should know whom they had sought."
>
> (*Supplement to the Canterbury Tales*)

Sometimes they were worn round the neck, more often they were pinned on to the hat. Philip de Commines (vol. ii, 8) records that Louis XI used to wear " an old hat and an image of lead upon it."

The signs were made in stone or iron moulds, of which several are extant, *e.g.* one of St. Thomas in the British Museum, one in the Guildhall Museum, one of Our Lady of Walsingham in King's Lynn Museum, and several in the Musée de Cluny, Paris. The manufacture was in the hands of the monks, and the regulations issued by Louis and Johanna of Sicily in 1354 to control their manufacture at St. Maximin, in Provence, show that it could be a source of considerable profit (M. Hucher, *Bulletin Monumental*, XIX; T. Hugo, *Archæologia*, XXXVIII, 1860, 132). The Archbishops of Compostella had on several occasions to acquire authority to excommunicate persons selling scallop shell badges elsewhere than in that city.

Most of the badges belong to the 14th and 15th centuries. That they were used at a much earlier date is however clear from a passage in which Giraldus Cambrensis (*De rebus a se gestis ap. Angl. Sacr.*, ii, p. 481), writing before 1223, speaks of a company of pilgrims as recognizable by the signs hung about their necks. From their fragile nature they are very easily destroyed, and the largest collections are those that have been dredged from the Thames, now in the British Museum, the London Museum, and the Guildhall Museum, and those from the Seine in the Musée de Cluny, Paris. The identification of the individual signs rests upon the often ambiguous symbolism of the objects portrayed. It is noticeable that, with a few well-known exceptions, the signs in French collections differ from those found in England, and there can be no doubt that the majority of those listed below are of English derivation. Besides the pilgrim signs there are a certain number of secular badges, worn, it would seem, by the retainers of noble families, perhaps by members of certain guilds. It is possible also that, as in the 16th century (Sir John Evans, *Proceedings of the Society of Antiquaries*, 2, xxii, 106), some of the badges may have been personal amulets unconnected with any formal pilgrimage.

For pilgrim signs, see further *Archæologia*, XXXVIII, 1860, 128–34; LXXIX, 1929, 33; *Archæological Journal*, XIII, 1856, p. 133; *Journal of the British Archæological Association*, XXI (1865), 192–6; XXIV (1868), 219–30; C. Roach-Smith, *Collectanea Antiqua*, I (1848), 81–91; II (1852), 43–50; and Tancred Borenius, *Medieval Pilgrim Badges* ("*Sette of Odd Volumes*," 1930), with bibliography. For French specimens see Fourgeais, *Collection de plombs historiés trouvés dans la Seine*, Vol. II, *Enseignes de Pélerinages* (Paris, 1862–6).

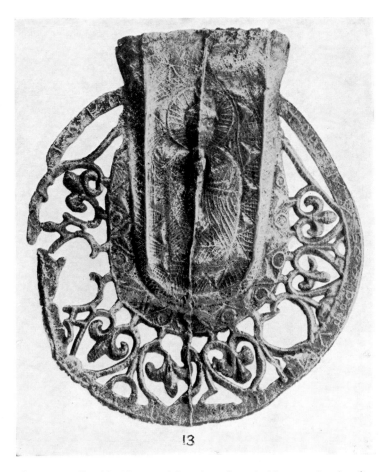

Pewter ampulla of St. Thomas of Canterbury from the Thames at London ($\frac{1}{1}$).

PLATE LXIX. [To face p. 257.

Pewter badges from the Thames at London (½).

St. Thomas of Canterbury

Thomas à Becket was murdered at Canterbury in 1171 and canonized in 1173, and the scene of his martyrdom rapidly became a centre of pilgrimage.

> " And specially, from every shires ende
> Of Engelond, to Caunterbury they wende,
> The holy blisful martir for to seke."
>
> (Chaucer, *Prologue to the Canterbury Tales*)

The shrine had an international reputation, and several pewter badges of St. Thomas are preserved in continental collections. The Saint's London connections, however, naturally made his relics an object of special veneration to Londoners. His chapel on London Bridge must have been the starting-place of innumerable pilgrimages ; and of the many pilgrim signs recovered from the Thames nearby it is notable how many are those of St. Thomas.

The signs usually take the form of a mitred head, sometimes, as in the Guildhall Museum, within a canopied shrine, or of a mitred figure mounted on a horse. Of the curios displayed to attract the pilgrim Canterbury bells were evidently popular :

> " What with the noise of their syngyng and with the sound of their piping and with the jangeling of their Canterbury bellis and with the barking out of doggis after them. . . ."
>
> (The examination of Thomas Thorpe before Archbishop Arundel in 1407.)

and pewter reproductions of these bells are not uncommon. More complicated signs are also found.

A 15307. A figure in bishop's robes without mitre, within a small shrine. Pl. LXVI, No. 5. From Fresh Wharf.

A 24766/1. Mitred figure mounted on a horse. Pl. LXVII, No. 12. See *Archæologia*, LXXIX, 1929, 33, Fig. 5. From the Thames at Dowgate.

A 24766/2. Mitred bust. Pl. LXVI, No. 1. See *Archæologia*, LXXIX, 1929, 33, Fig. 6. From the Thames at Dowgate.

A 24766/3. Mitred head. Pl. LXVI, No. 6. From the Thames at Dowgate.

A 24766/4. Mitred head within a circular frame set with circles and diamonds. See *Twenty-five Years of the London Museum* (1937), Pl. XXV, 1 ; *Archæologia*, XXXVIII, 1860, Pl. IV, 4. Pl. LXVII, No. 11. From the Thames at Dowgate.

A 24766/5. Small mitred head. See *Twenty-five Years of the London Museum* (1937), Pl. XXV, 4. Pl. LXVI, No. 2. From the Thames at London.

A 24766/6. Small mitred bust. Pl. LXVI, No. 3. From the Thames at London.

A 24766/7. Small disc bearing a mitred head. *Cf.* C. Roach Smith, *Collectanea Antiqua*, I, Pl. XXXI. Pl. LXVII, No. 9. From the Thames at London.

A 24766/8. Small mitred head with traces of a surrounding shrine. Pl. LXVI, No. 4. From the Thames at London.

A 24766/22. Head of a horse, presumably from a sign similar to A 24766/1. Pl. LXVI, No. 8. From the Thames at London.

A 24766/41. Part of a Canterbury bell, inscribed C]AMPAN[A THOMAE. *Cf. Archæologia*, XXXVIII, 1860, Pl. V, 9–10. From the Thames at Dowgate.

53.1/1. Pewter Canterbury bell. Lent by the Guildhall Museum. Pl. LXVI, No. 7.

A 26156. An elaborate Lombardic T depicting the flagellation of Henry II at Canterbury on July 12th, 1174, in penance for the murder of Becket. See *Twenty-five Years of the London Museum* (1937), Pl. XXV, 6. Pl. LXVII, No. 10. From the Thames at London.

A 27323. A large ampulla depicting on the one side St. Thomas beatified, on the other his murder. The elaborate border bears the jingling hexameter: *Optimus egrorum medicus fit Thoma bonorum* (" Thomas is the best healer of the holy sick "). This inscription is also found on a similar ampulla in the Guildhall Museum, and other ampullæ of the same form are preserved in the British Museum (*Archæologia*, LXXIX, 1929, 33, Fig. 7) and in York Museum (C. Roach Smith, *Collectanea Antiqua*, Vol. II, Pl. XVIII). See *Twenty-five Years of the London Museum* (1937), Pl. XXV, 10. Given by P. A. S. Phillips, Esq. Pl. LXVIII, No. 13.

Our Lady of Boulogne

This shrine, conveniently situated on the French coast, was especially popular with English pilgrims, and its signs are as common here as they are abroad. Of the Wife of Bath, who had done all the right pilgrimages, we learn that " at Rome she hadde been and at Bouloigne " (Chaucer, *Prologue*). The sacred image was supposed to have arrived miraculously by sea in a crewless ship, and this is symbolized by the ordinary form of the token, an image of the Virgin and Child standing upon a crescent-shaped vessel.

A 24766/15–18. Four pewter signs of stock type. *Cf.* Roach Smith, *Collectanea Antiqua*, I (1848), Pl. XXXIII, 11, 14; II (1852), Pl. XVI, 7. Pl. LXXI, No. 41. Found in the Thames at London.

A 14606 and 14609. Two pewter signs of stock type. Pl. LXXI, No. 40. Found in the Thames at London Bridge.

Our Lady of Walsingham

This pilgrimage ranked second only to that of St. Thomas of Canterbury, and like it had an international reputation. Erasmus, in his dialogue *Perigrinatio Religionis Erga,* gives a picture of the returning pilgrim :

Menedemus. " What kind of attire is this that thou wearest ? Thou art bedizened with semicircular shells, art full of images of tin and lead, and adorned with straw chains, and thy arm is girt with bracelets of beads ? "

Ogygius. " I visited S. James of Compostella, and as I came back I visited the Virgin beyond the sea who is very famous among the English."

It is clear that the pewter sign was only one of the many knick-knacks which the pilgrim was expected to purchase.

Signs which may with certainty be ascribed to the Walsingham pilgrimage are not common, but to it probably belong many of the unidentifiable figures of the Virgin and Child. An ampulla found at Cirencester bears the crowned W of Walsingham, and another is recorded from Dunwich (*Archæological Journal,* XIII, 1856, 132–3). A mould for the making of Walsingham signs is preserved in the King's Lynn Museum, and it is possible, but by no means certain, that the workshop ascribed by Richard Southwell, one of Cromwell's visitors, to the practice of alchemy was in fact the seat of the manufacture of pilgrim signs (*Archæological Journal,* XIII, 1856, 133).

A 17216. An elaborate sign portraying the Annunciation, inscribed ECCE : ANC(I)L AVE : MARIA. A sign, almost identical but with the word WALSYNGHAM added below, makes the ascription certain (*Archæological Journal,* XIII, 1856, 133). See *Twenty-five Years of the London Museum,* Pl. XXV, 2. Pl. LXIX, No. 14. From London.

Unidentified Shrines of the Virgin

A number of badges bear simply figures of the Virgin and Child without further mark of identification. Many of these no doubt come from Walsingham.

A 14612. Portion of a badge depicting the Virgin, sceptred, and Child. Pl. LXIX, No. 15. From the Thames, London Bridge.

A 14613. The Virgin and Child, with a dove at her feet. Pl. LXIX, No. 16. From the Thames, London Bridge.

A 20828. Crude badge of the Virgin and Child. Pl. LXIX, No. 21. From Swan Pier.

A 24766/23. The Virgin within a vesica-shaped surround. Pl. LXIX, No. 19. From the Thames, London.

A 24766/24. The Virgin and Child in an open-work oval frame with censers and flowers. Pl. LXIX, No. 20. From the Thames, London.

A 24766/26. The Virgin and Child on a small ridged button. Pl. LXIX, No. 18. From the Thames, London.

St. James of Compostella

The shrine of St. James of Compostella in Galicia was the foremost centre of pilgrimage in western Europe. It was popular as far afield even as Denmark, where it is noticeable that the majority of the signs preserved in the National Museum at Copenhagen belong to this pilgrimage; and examples are not uncommon in this country. The signs take the form either of an actual scallop-shell pierced for suspension or of a representation of a scallop-shell in some other material.

A 14610. Pewter sign in the form of a scallop-shell bearing a representation of a pilgrim in a characteristic, wide-brimmed pilgrim's hat. Pl. LXX, No. 28. From the Thames at London Bridge.

A 25357. Bronze badge in the form of a scallop-shell with a projecting stud on the back. A similar badge was found near the 14th-century pottery-kiln at Rye. Fig. 89. From St. Mary Axe.

St. Antoine de Viennois

A 24766/9. Pl. LXX, No. 31. Pewter tau-cross of the Order of Hospitallers of St. Antoine-de-Viennois. Inscribed P SIVE TAU (Potence sive Tau) the motto of the order. The broken loop at the base was probably intended for suspension of a bell. The tau-cross and suspended bell are portrayed on an ampulla from the moat at Canterbury, and the loop is again found on a cross from the Thames, now in the Guildhall Museum. The latter sign and one from the Thames at Dowgate (*Archæologia*, XXXVIII, 1860, Pl. IV, 1) bear a crucifixion in place of an inscription, but otherwise they are similar to the present example.

The Abbey of St. Antoine in the Dauphiné, the mother-house of the order, was a famous place of pilgrimage on account of its cures for the epidemic disease known as St. Anthony's fire, and distinguished Englishmen, *e.g.* St. Hugh of Lincoln, in 1200, Earl Talbot, and others, in 1459, are known to have visited it. But pilgrim-signs similar to the present are rarely found outside England, and they must therefore be attributed to St. Anthony's Hospital in Threadneedle Street, the daughter-house established in 1243 (see, further, Dr. Rose Graham

260

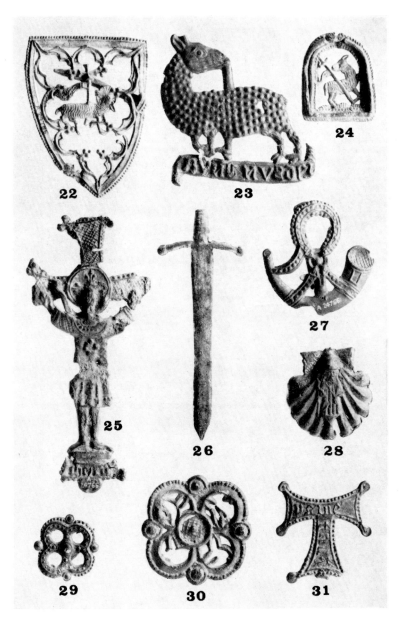

Pewter badges from the Thames at London ($\frac{1}{1}$).

PLATE LXXI. [*To face p.* 261.

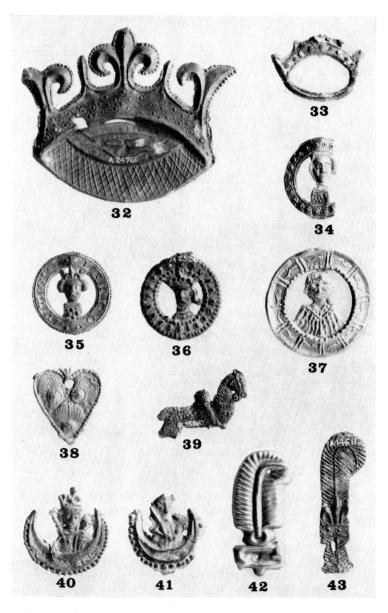

Pewter badges from the Thames at London. No. 42 is made of brass ($\frac{1}{1}$).

in *Archæological Journal*, LXXXIV, 341–406). An exception is a fine pewter tau-cross inscribed STI ANTHONII DE PRESTO (the abbey of Praestø, another provincial shrine of St. Anthony) in the National Museum at Copenhagen (*Danmarks Kirke, Praestø*, Amt. I, p. 51, Fig. 21).

The tau-cross is occasionally to be found with another significance. The Vulgate rendering of Ezekiel lx. 4, " signa thau super frontes virorum gementium et dolentium super cunctis abominationibus," inspired its use on several medieval works of art, and it is probably in this connection that it is to be found on two tombstones at Southwell Minster (R. Graham, *loc. cit.*, p. 367), and upon certain brasses, *e.g.* of Elizabeth, wife of Sir Edward Tame, at Fairford, Gloucestershire, 1534 ; and of Sir John Touchet, Lord Audley, at Shere, Surrey, *c.* 1525. Found in the Thames at London.

Ampullæ

The use of ampullæ, or small flasks, goes back to early Christian times, *e.g.* the celebrated 6th-century ampullæ in the cathedral treasury at Monza, and in the Middle Ages they were common to many shrines : " and hundred of ampulles on his hat seten " (the pilgrim in the Vision of Piers Ploughman). At Canterbury they were filled with water from Becket's well, the water of which was, it was said, tinged with the martyr's blood, and elsewhere they might be used to contain holy water or consecrated oil. A fine example from Canterbury is listed above.

A 3817. Pl. LXXIII, No. 53. From the site of the Aquarium at Westminster.

A 8866. Pl. LXXIII, No. 57. From London.

A 2016. Pl. LXXIII, No. 56. From Thames Street. Other ampullæ of this form are known to have come from Canterbury (*Archæologia*, LXXIX, 1929, 33, Figs. 1–2).

A 20811. Pl. LXXIII, No. 54. From Swan Pier.

Royal Saints

Badges bearing either a crowned head or a simple crown are common, but in the absence of any further identifying mark an exact ascription is rarely possible. The two chief English shrines of Royal Saints were those of St. Edward, at Westminster, and of St. Edmund, at Bury, but there were others of a minor character, *e.g.* that of St. Kenelm, at Winchcombe (*Archæologia*, XXXVIII, 1860, Pl. V, 11). For other signs of St. Edward, see *Journal of the British Archæological Association*, XXI (1865), Pl. 9, No. 4, and *Archæologia*,

XXXVIII, 1860, Pl. IV, 7 ; of St. Edmund, *Journal of the British Archæological Association*, XXIV (1868), Pl. 17, No. 12.

A 2520. A crowned head within a circular frame. Pl. LXXI, No. 36. From London.

A 20810. A crowned head within a circular frame which bears a garbled inscription : IANCOVLMAS (?). Pl. LXXI, No. 35. From Steelyard.

A 24766/20. A similar badge, but crownless. Pl. LXXI, No. 34. From the Thames at London.

A 24766/28. A large crown. Pl. LXXI, No. 32. From the Thames at London.

A 24766/29. A small crown. Pl. LXXI, No. 33. From the Thames at London.

The Knights Templars

The signs of this order seem invariably to bear in some form or other the badge of the Templars, the Paschal Lamb.

A 8872. Pl. LXX, No. 24. From London.

A 24766/13. Pl. LXX, No. 23. From the Thames at London. The inscription is a garbled version of AGNUS DEI.

A 24766/14. Pl. LXX, No. 22. From the Thames at Dowgate. An almost identical example from the Thames is in the British Museum (see *Archæologia*, XXXVIII, 1860, Pl. V, 1).

St. Hubert

The sign of St. Hubert, the patron saint of hunting, is the hunting-horn. The location of the shrine, or shrines, for which these signs were made is by no means clear.

A 24766/10. Pl. LXX, No. 27. From the Thames, London.

A 24766/11. The identification of this sign is rather dubious. From the Thames, London.

A 24766/12. Fragmentary. From the Thames, London.

The Five Wounds

Signs representing the five Wounds of Christ are not uncommon, although it is hard to identify the shrine from which they were purchased.

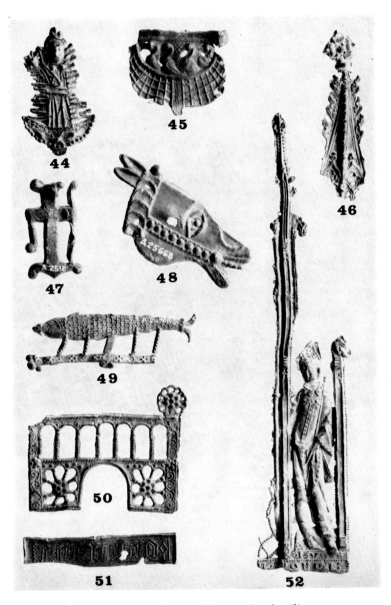

Pewter badges from the Thames at London ($\frac{1}{1}$).

PLATE LXXIII.　　　　　　　　　　　　　　　　　　[*To face p.* 263.

Pewter ampullæ from the Thames at London (⅓).

A 1379. A straight-sided cross within a circle, with circles at the five intersections. There is an identical sign in the Guildhall Museum. From London Wall.

A 2017. Pl. LXX, No. 30. From Thames Street.

A 20814. Pl. LXX, No. 29. This sign retains the pin by which it was attached to the clothing. From Swan Pier.

St. Paul

The sword, symbolizing the execution of St. Paul, is not a common sign. It was presumably purchasable in London, at St. Paul's Cathedral.

A 14608. Pl. LXX, No. 26. From the Thames at London Bridge.

Miscellaneous Badges, some of civil character

A 295. A collar of SS, 15th century. Pl. LXXIV, No. 62. From Brook's Wharf, Thames Street.

A 2518. Cruciform badge of uncertain significance. Pl. LXXII, No. 47. From Cloth Fair.

A 2540. Small pewter pin with a circular head. From the Thames at London Bridge.

A 2569. A figure standing upon a crescent. Possibly a version of Our Lady of Boulogne. Pl. LXXII, No. 44. From Westminster.

A 14581/1. The right-hand panel of an elaborate shrine, containing the figure of a bishop, and at his feet the inscription SATV..S (?). Beneath the whole the inscription . . . ·NA.MONDI :. Pl. LXXII, No. 52. From the Thames at London Bridge.

A 14581/2. Probably part of the canopy and mitre of a sign depicting St. Thomas within a shrine. From the Thames at London Bridge.

A 14581/3. Part of an elaborately canopied shrine. Pl. LXXII, No. 46. From the Thames at London Bridge.

A 14581/4. Part of the foot of a shrine. From the Thames at London Bridge.

A 14607. Small leaf-like sign with a stud behind. From the Thames at London Bridge.

A 20250. Fragmentary badge probably inscribed FID IN DEO. From the Thames at London.

A 20809. A shrine with central opening and Romanesque arcading above Pl. LXXII, No. 50. From Steelyard.

A 20812. A chained swan. This was the personal device of the Bohun family and this may be a retainer's badge. See *Twenty-five Years of the London Museum*, Pl. XXV, 11. Pl. LXXIV, No. 63. From Swan Pier.

A 24766/19. A bust within a circular frame. Pl. LXXI, No. 37. From the Thames at London.

A 24766/21. A bird's wing. From the Thames at London.

A 24766/25. A figure in long-sleeved costume, c. 1450, holding a child. Possibly for St. Christopher. Pl. LXIX, No. 17. From the Thames at London.

A 24766/27. A much-battered kneeling figure. From the Thames at London.

A 24766/30. A fish. Pl. LXXII, No. 49. From the Thames at London.

A 24766/31. A small badge with an illegible central device. From the Thames at London.

A 24766/32. A human-headed bird. Pl. LXXIV, No. 58. From the Thames at London.

A 24766/33. A bagpipe-player. The costume belongs to the latter part of the 15th century. Pl. LXXIV, No. 59. From the Thames at London.

A 24766/34. Probably part of a badge, the Pelican in her Piety; or possibly geese in a boat, St. Werburgh (?). Pl. LXXII, No. 45. From the Thames at London.

A 24766/35. A wodewose. Pl. LXXIV, No. 60. From the Thames at London.

A 24766/36. A centaur armed with a bow. Pl. LXXIV, No. 65. From the Thames at London.

A 24766/37. A small heart, on one side a rod flowering into a hawthorn bush, (?) for St. Joseph, Glastonbury. Pl. LXXI, No. 38. From the Thames at London.

A 24766/38. The upper part of a quiver? Pl. LXXIII, No. 55. From the Thames at London.

A 24766/39. A crucifix. Pl. LXX, No. 25. Two similar signs are preserved in the Guildhall Museum, and they may perhaps be ascribed to the Holy Rood at Boxley which was much visited in the Middle Ages. See also *Archæologia*, XXXVIII, 1860, Pl. IV. From the Thames at London.

A 25611. A loop with simple scroll-work on both faces. Pl. LXXIV, No. 64. From the Thames at London.

A 25667. An armed, mounted figure, perhaps St. George. The sword-belt is of early 15th-century type. Pl. LXXI, No. 39. From London.

36.146/2. Bronze badge, a kneeling figure. From Fetter Lane, on a site where the medieval material belonged almost exclusively to the 15th century. Given by H. S. Gordon, Esq.

SMALL ARTICLES OF DRESS
(i) *Belt-chapes*

The variety of forms of belt-chape in use during the Middle Ages is so large that an exhaustive account is impossible within the scope of this catalogue. It is, however, possible

264

to trace a more or less orderly development of general type at any rate up to the early 15th century; and one or two of the commoner forms can be fairly closely dated.

It was apparently during the 12th century that the knotted belt gave place in fashionable costume to the belt with metal buckle and pendent tag. These can be seen, for instance, on the effigies of King John, at Worcester, and of Queen Berengaria, at Espan, on both of which the tag ends in a metal chape of plain, roughly rectangular form. This, and the broader version that can be seen on such 13th-century military effigies as that of Robert de Vere, Earl of Oxford, d. 1221, at Hatfield Broad Oak, Essex (C. A. Stothard, *Monumental Effigies*, Pl. 36), are evidently the simple prototypes from which the later chapes evolved. This evolution is complicated by two factors. The one is the distinction between civil and military costume, although at least up to 1400 there are sufficient points of contact to show that the forms of belt-chape developed on more or less parallel lines. The other is the intermittent use of this form of belt. Thus there was a considerable period in the late 14th century, when the buckled sword-belt was replaced by a heavily ornamented belt passing round the hips and joined in front merely by a clasp. Similarly, in the 13th century a long pendent tag was a regular feature of feminine costume; but with the advent of shaped dresses, the belt, if any, disappeared from sight; and it was not until the close of the 15th century that pendent tags and ornamental chapes became once more a feature of woman's costume.

The evolution of the belt-chape in the 13th and 14th centuries is illustrated in Fig. 84, Nos. 1–17. Most of these are inevitably from military brasses and effigies, but Nos. 9, 16, and 17 indicate a parallel evolution of type in civil dress at any rate during the latter part of the period. Nos. 1–3 illustrate the survival of the original plain form. In No. 4, however, 1289, this has been developed by the addition of a terminal knob (which can be seen even earlier on the brass of Sir John D'Abernon, d. 1277, at Stoke d'Abernon, Surrey) and by the elaboration of an ogival opening at the top. The subsequent development of both these features does not call for detailed comment. Already by the middle

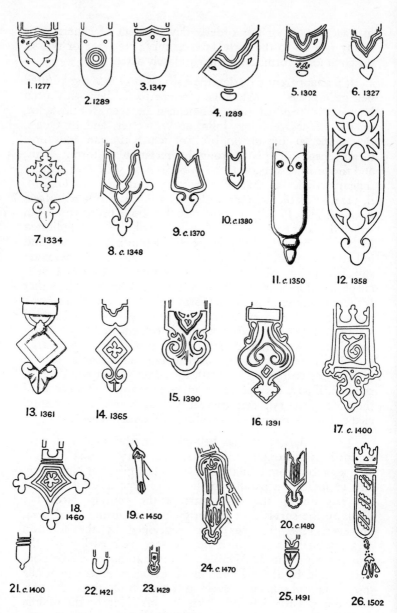

FIG. 84.—Representations of belt-chapes from contemporary effigies and brasses (see opposite page).

of the 14th century the terminal knob has become a leaf; and a good fixed point is provided by Nos. 13 and 14. These may be compared with the chape on the effigy of Sir John Wingfield, d. 1362, at Wingfield, Suffolk (C. A. Stothard, *Monumental Effigies*, Pl. 92), and with an actual specimen preserved in the Guildhall Museum, London (Fig. 85, No. 4).

Fig. 84, No. 11, from the mid-14th-century effigy of a lady, at Clehonger, Hereford, is important in that it provides a clue to the dating of a common type of medieval chape which has been the subject of some rather needless controversy (see *Antiquaries Journal*, XIII, 1933, 169; also XIV, 1934,

No. 1.   Brass of Sir John D'Abernon, d. 1277, at Stoke d'Abernon, Surrey.   (Chape of baldrick-strap.)

No. 2.   Brass of Sir Roger de Trumpington, d. 1289, at Trumpington, Cambs.   (Chape of baldrick-strap.)

No. 3.   Brass of Sir Hugh Hastings, d. 1347, at Elsingham, Norfolk. (Belt-chape.)

No. 4.   Brass of Sir Roger de Trumpington, d. 1289, at Trumpington, Cambs.   (Belt-chape.)

No. 5.   Brass of Sir Robert de Bures, d. 1302, at Acton, Suffolk.

No. 6.   Brass of Sir John D'Abernon, junior, d. 1327, at Stoke d'Abernon, Surrey.

No. 7.   Effigy of John of Eltham, d. 1334, in Westminster Abbey.

No. 8.   Brass of Sir John Gifford, c. 1348, at Bowers Gifford, Essex.

No. 9.   Brass of John Diggis (civilian), c. 1370, at Barham, Kent.

No. 10.   Brass of Symon de Felbrigg (civilian), c. 1380, at Felbrigg, Norfolk.

No. 11.   Effigy of a lady, c. 1350, at Clehonger, Herefordshire.

No. 12.   Effigy of Peter de Grandison, d. 1358, in Hereford Cathedral.

No. 13.   Effigy of Lord Cobham, d. 1361, at Lingfield, Surrey.

No. 14.   Brass of William de Audeley, d. 1365, at Horsheath, Cambs.

No. 15.   Brass of Sir Andrew Louterell, d. 1390, at Irnham, Lincs.

No. 16.   Brass of John Cory (civilian), d. 1391, at Stoke Fleming, Devonshire.

No. 17.   Brass of a wool-merchant, c. 1400, at Northleach, Glos.

No. 18.   Brass of John Browne (civilian), d. 1460, in All Saints' Church, Stamford, Lincs.

No. 19.   Brass of John Fastolff (military), c. 1450, at Oulton, Suffolk.

No. 20.   Brass of a civilian, c. 1480, at Cirencester, Glos.

No. 21.   Brass of a Dalison (military), c. 1400, at Laughton, Lincs.

No. 22.   Brass of John Lydwode (civilian), d. 1421, at Linwood, Lincs.

No. 23.   Brass of Robert Hayton (military), d. 1429, in All Saints' Church, Theddlethorpe, Lincs.

No. 24.   Brass of Ralph Cromwell, d. 1455, at Tattershall, Lancs.

No. 25.   Brass of Roger Salusbury (military), d. 1491, at Horton, Northants.

No. 26.   Brass of Robert Russell and wife, d. 1502, at Strensham, Worcs. (Lady's belt.)

183, and XV, 1935, 204). The chapes, and the corresponding buckles (Pl. LXXV), consist of three separate pieces, two flat outer plates covering a fork-shaped central-piece, between the prongs of which the end of the strap was fixed. This arrangement seems curiously insecure; but the use of these objects is put beyond all doubt by the survival of examples in the London and Guildhall Museums (*cf.* Fig. 63, No. 7), of which the leather strap is still in position. Comparisons with the superficially somewhat similar " Jew's harps " discovered in Saxon and Jutish graves are therefore neither necessary nor relevant. They undoubtedly belong to civil costume; and as the chapes visible on the pendent tags of a number of 13th-century French and English sculpture (*e.g.* the mid-13th-century statue of Childebert I from St. Germain-des-Près, now in the Louvre; and many statues of the Virgin. *Cf.* a Matthew Paris drawing in B.M. Royal MS. 2A, XXII, *Walpole Society*, XI, Pl. XXVII) do not show the ogival opening which is so marked a feature of these objects, they may presumably be referred to the 14th century.

Another group which calls for brief special notice is here illustrated by Fig. 84, Nos. 15–17. These large chapes, often with an elaborate leaf-terminal, belong to the period *c.* 1390–1410, when they are found on a number of brasses, both civil and military. A subsidiary feature, the small side-scrolls visible on No. 16, recurs on several representations, and also on surviving specimens, as A 2565. (For this group, see, further, *Antiquaries Journal*, XIX, 1939, 197–9.)

This group represents the final elaboration of the 13th–14th-century belt-chape. Soon after 1400 a new form of narrow sword belt came into use; and civilian belts with pendent tags went temporarily out of fashion. Representations of 15th-century chapes are extremely varied, and it is very hard to recognize any consistent development. They are on the whole small; and a common feature is the addition of a small ring or tassel pendant from a loop at the bottom of the chape. It is not until the close of the century that an easily recognizable form emerges. This is the very long, narrow chape (Fig. 85, No. 3), usually with a terminal projection that was worn in conjunction with a transverse buckle

268

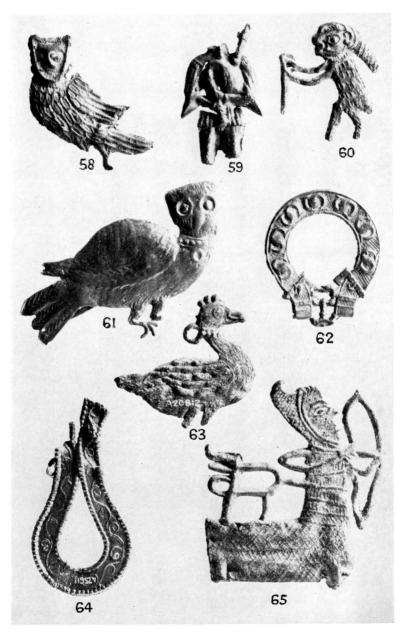

Pewter badges from the Thames at London ($\frac{1}{1}$).

PLATE LXXV.   [*To face p.* 269.

Medieval belt-chapes and buckles from London.

by ladies, *c.* 1485–1530, until it was replaced by the elaborate pendant of mid-16th-century fashion.

(*a*) " Forked " Type.

C 979. Pl. LXXV, No. 11. Bronze, 14th century. From London.

A 3156. Pl. LXXV, No. 10. Bronze, central " forked " portion missing. 14th century. From London.

(*b*) Other Forms.

A 11887. Pl. LXXV, No. 12. Bronze, the two plates at front and back welded together at the bottom. 14th century. From the Old Bailey.

A 21792. Pl. LXXV, No. 9. Two bronze plates, riveted together at the top. 14th century. From the Thames, Hammersmith.

A 2559. Pl. LXXV, No. 14. Bronze, with a loop for a pendant. The front and back are ornamented with a typical 15th century zig-zag roulette. From Worship Street.

A 2553. Pl. LXXV, No. 13. Bronze, with a loop for a pendant. Probably 15th or 16th century. From Broken Wharf, Thames Street.

A 2565. Fig. 85, No. 1. Bronze, with a figure of St. Christopher and a large leaf-terminal. A.D. 1390–1410. (See above, p. 268 ; and for fuller discussion, *Antiquaries Journal*, XIX, 1939, 303.) From Broken Wharf, Thames Street.

A 2554. Fig. 85, No. 6. Bronze, roughly inscribed IHC. From Broken Wharf, Thames Street.

C 164. Fig. 85, No. 7. Bronze, inscribed with the arms of King René of Provence. Late 15th century. From London.

37.227/2. Fig. 85, No. 3. Bronze, late 15th or early 16th century. Human mask on finial. From the Thames.

Also illustrated :

Fig. 85, No. 4. Bronze, *c.* 1360–70. In the Guildhall Museum. From London.

Fig. 85, No. 8. Bronze, 14th century. In the Guildhall Museum. From London.

(ii) *Belt-mounts for Scabbards*

The sword-belts of the earlier Middle Ages were fastened directly on the scabbard without the medium of metal mounts. Quite early in the 14th century, however, the elaborate arrangement then current, which can be seen, for example, very clearly on the brass of Sir Robert de Bures,

FIG. 85.—Medieval belt-fittings from London.

1, A 2565 ; 2, 30.17 ; 3, 37.227/2 ; 4, in the Guildhall Museum ; 5, A 24855 ;
6, A 2554 ; 7, C 164 ; 8, in the Guildhall Museum (⅔).

d. 1302, at Acton, Suffolk (see also G. Laking, *European Armour and Arms*, I, p. 87, Fig. 110), gave place to the use of metal mounts on the scabbard (see, for example, Pl. V) which were attached by loops to similar mounts on the ends of the belt. The number of mounts and exact arrangement of the straps varied considerably from time to time, but the form of the mounts themselves developed consistently for the greater part of the 14th century.

The late 14th century fashion of a heavy sword belt fastened direct on to the bottom of the surcoat did not involve their use, but during the first thirty years or so of the following century they were once more necessary, and it was only with the reversion to leather or cloth fittings towards the middle of the century that they finally went out of use. In almost all cases the belt-mounts are the exact counterpart of the belt-chape, with the addition at the end of a ring by which they were fastened to the scabbard-mounts. They need, therefore, no separate discussion.

30.17. Bronze belt-mount with elaborate moulded and incised ornament inscribed on the plate. There is a very similar specimen, found at Colchester, in the Ashmolean Museum. Fig. 85, No. 2. From London.

(iii) *Strap-end Buckles*

These hardly admit of useful generalization. The larger and more elaborate specimens may be classed as belt-buckles; and it may be noted that although broad belts with buckles had a certain vogue in civilian costume in the early 13th century (*e.g.* on the posthumous effigy of Henri le Jeune, and on the heart-tomb of Richard Cœur de Lion, both in Rouen Cathedral) and again *c.* 1390–1410 (*e.g.* on the brasses of a vintner at Cirencester, Glos, and of a wool-merchant at Northleach, Glos, both *c.* 1400), in general the broad belt seems to have been used rather with armour, and even then not after the early years of the 15th century. The smaller strap-end buckles had more varied uses. Some may have belonged to 15th-century sword-belts; others to belts worn by civilians over a much wider period. Many were, however, used for such purposes as the fastening of plate-armour (*cf.* the effigy of Thomas Beauchamp, Earl of Warwick, d. 1439,

271

in St. Mary's Church, Warwick; also a silver statuette of St. George, at Barcelona, *c.* 1435–45, F. M. Kelly and R. Schwabe, *A Short History of Costume and Armour*, 1066–1800, Pls. XXX–XXXI) or of the richer forms of horse-harness, and the forms were so universal that little generalization is possible. An exception is the pronged " Jew's harp " type of buckle (*e.g.* Pl. LXXV, Nos. 1–2) which is obviously contemporary with the similarly pronged belt-chape (p. 267).

A 1378. Bronze strap-end buckle. Pl. LXXV, No. 4. From Smithfield.

A 2496. Bronze strap-end buckle, decorated with rough roulette-ornament. The pin is of iron. Pl. LXXVI, No. 1. From Broken Wharf.

A 2513. Bronze strap-end buckle, similar to A 2496, but bearing the inscription, SALVE (?) in Gothic lettering on the plate. From the Town Ditch, Newgate.

A 2550. Bronze strap-end buckle, bearing some crudely incised letters on the plate. Pl. LXXV, No. 3. From the Town Ditch, Newgate.

A 2564. Bronze strap-end buckle with an iron pin. Pl. LXXV, No. 8. From Thames Street.

A 2632. Bronze strap-end buckle. Pl. LXXV, No. 5. From the Thames at Queenhithe.

A 2694. Plate of a bronze strap-end buckle, in the form of a scallop-shell. Pl. LXXVI, No. 8. From London.

A 2685. Narrow base-bronze strap-end buckle. Pl. LXXVII, No. 16. From Horseshoe Wharf.

A 3150. Bronze strap-end buckle of pronged type (plates missing). Pl. LXXV, No. 2. From London.

A 3600. Base-bronze strap-end buckle of pronged type (plates missing). From Angel Court.

A 3691. Bronze strap-end buckle of pronged type. The strap, of leather with ornamental studs, is still attached. Fig. 63, No. 7. From the Town Ditch, Newgate.

A 10068. Bronze strap-end buckle of pronged type. Pl. LXXV, No. 1. From London.

A 12257. Bronze strap-end buckle, similar to A 2550. From Crutched Friars.

A 16110. Bronze strap-end buckle, the plate of which is obviously reused; it bears punched spiral ornament. Pl. LXXVI, No. 2. From London.

A 20689. Bronze strap-end buckle. Pl. LXXV, No. 6. From Leadenhall Street.

A 20885. Bronze strap-end buckle of pronged type (plates missing). From Bankside.

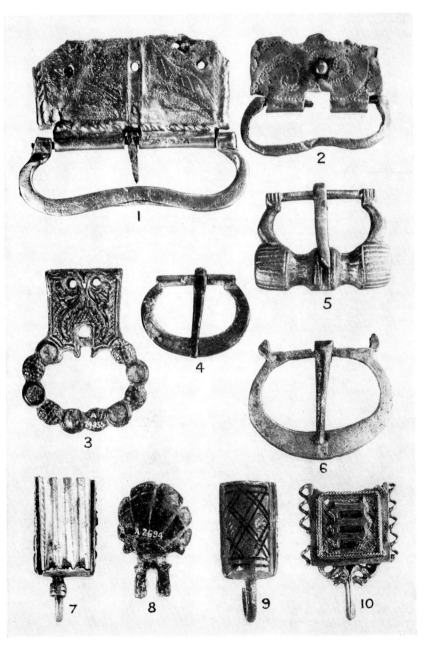

Medieval buckles and hooks from London ($\frac{1}{1}$).

PLATE LXXVII. [*To face p.* 273.

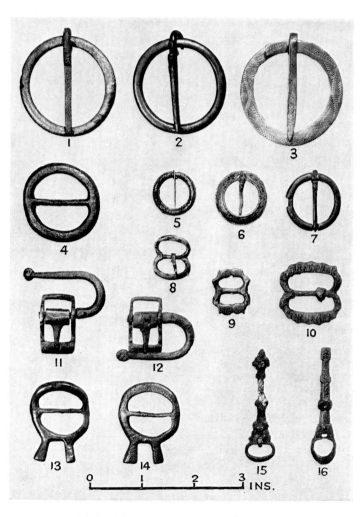

Medieval brooches and buckles from London.

A 21085.   Bronze strap-end buckle, similar to A 1378.   From Wormwood Street.

A 22902.   Narrow bronze strap-end buckle.   Pl. LXXVII, No. 15.   From Gate Street, Kingsway.

A 24855.   Pewter strap-end buckle, with elaborate cast ornament. Pl. LXXVI, No. 3 ; Fig. 85, No. 5.   From Westminster, site of Victoria Tower.

A 24857-8.   Two bronze strap-end buckles, similar to A 2564.   From Westminster, site of Victoria Tower.

A 24859.   Bronze strap-end buckle of pronged type (fragmentary).   From Westminster, site of Victoria Tower.

A 26179.   Bronze strap-end buckle of pronged type (plates missing).   From the Thames, London.

(iv) *Circular Brooches*

The circular brooches of the Middle Ages fall into two categories, those which were more or less elaborately decorated and those which were solely, or primarily, utilitarian.   The distinction is not of course rigid, but it is useful.   The majority of literary references and of contemporary representations are naturally concerned with the more elaborate forms, whereas it is the simpler types which were in everyday domestic use.

The use of heavily decorated circular brooches dates back to the migration period, and specimens reminiscent of the fine Jutish and Frankish brooches of the 6th and 7th centuries remained in fashion for many centuries (see F. Krüger, in *Germania*, 19, 1935, 53–7).   Jewelled circular brooches, consisting of a ring and transverse pin and worn at the throat or on the shoulder, are a common feature of 12th- and 13th-century costume.

At first they are very massive, reminiscent of the earlier forms with a solid disc (*e.g.* on the statue of the Queen of Sheba, *c.* 1175, from Notre Dame de Corbeil, now in the Louvre ; *cf. Proceedings of the Society of Antiquaries*, 2, XXIX, 13) ; but later they become increasingly light (*e.g.* on the effigy of Queen Berengaria, *c.* 1225, at Espan, C. A. Stothard, *Monumental Effigies*, Pl. 16 ; *cf.* the brass of King Eric Menved and Queen Ingeborg, 1319, at Ringstead, Denmark, W. F. Creeny, *Monumental Brasses on the Continent*, p. 3).

The Nun, in Chaucer's *Prologue*, wore :

> " A broch of gold ful shene
> On which was first i-writ a crowned A,
> And after, *amor vincit omnia.*"

Inscribed brooches are not uncommon, and there is an example bearing this actual inscription in the British Museum (for another, dated to the 14th century, see F. Parenteau, *Inventaire Archéologique*, Pls. 30 and 45). The inscriptions are normally religious or talismanic tags, similar to those which appear on the late 15th-century purse-bars (pp. 163–5). For a mould used in the manufacture of a brooch inscribed AVE MARIA GRATIA PLENA, see *Archæologia*, XIV, 272, Fig. 2.

The decorated brooches of the later Middle Ages are too various for detailed treatment in this context. For a good cross-section of early 14th-century usage, see J. G. Callander, " Fourteenth Century Brooches in the National Museum of Antiquities of Scotland," *Proceedings of the Society of Antiquaries of Scotland*, LVIII (1924), 160–84. The precise types there represented seem to have had only a local currency in Scotland and North Britain ; but the general style and decorative technique may be compared with that of many brooches found in England, which are no doubt roughly contemporary.

The plainer forms of circular brooch, consisting simply of a ring of metal and a transverse pin, had a more varied use. They are most frequently represented as worn at the throat, where the blunt pin passed through two prepared slits and fastened the opening of the undergarment, a usage identical with that of the more elaborate decorated brooches. Plain circular brooches worn in this way can be seen on the sculptured figures of the 12th-century doorway at Valcabrère (Haute Garonne), and in the 13th-century representations are very common, *e.g.* on the sculptures of Wells Cathedral, *c.* 1235–40 ; in the Maciejowski Bible, *c.* 1250, *passim* ; on effigy No. 10 in the Temple Church, London, 1250–75 (*Royal Commission on Historical Monuments, London, The City*, pp. 140–1). In the 14th century the undergarment is not ordinarily visible at the neck, but the use of these brooches continued as before. Two were found in Oxford associated with burials of White Friars, whose house was founded in 1318 (*Oxoniensia*, III, 1938, Fig. 21, b and c; *cf.* Fig. 21a, from Seacourt village, abandoned in the 14th century). A very late example of a plain, circular, blunt-ended brooch, worn at the throat in the medieval manner, can be seen on a wooden altar-front, dated 1687, at Oslo (Bugdøy Museum, No. 1043); but this instance is clearly exceptional.

Plain circular brooches were also used as fastenings elsewhere on the clothing. Many of the bodies found in the Mass-Graves at Visby, Gotland (1361), had a brooch on either thigh, either the fastenings of a cod-piece worn beneath the outer clothing, or possibly an attachment for hose. Some of the brooches were of iron, but in other respects they were identical with the common English type (*e.g.* Pl. LXXVII, Nos. 1–2). Such a usage obviously finds no place in contemporary representations. They could also be used for the fastening of such objects as leather boot-straps (*Archæologia*, LXXI, 101, Fig. 24, a late 15th-century boot from Moorfields). See also Fig. 63, No. 3.

Of the plain bronze brooches the common form is that illustrated in Pl. LXXVII, Nos. 1–2, with a blunt end and a projecting ridge near the head of the pin. An example of this distinctive type was found in association with a pottery kiln, *c.* 1280–1380, at Rye; another, from Stanley Abbey, can hardly be earlier than 1200 (*Archæologia*, LX, 1908, 516, Fig. 9). A third, in the National Museum at Copenhagen, was found with a hoard of coins, *c.* 1400, in Flødstrop Churchyard; and a few of the brooches from the Visby Mass-Graves (1361) were of the same form. There is in fact good archæological evidence for their use at any rate in the 13th and 14th centuries.

A 628. Tiny pewter circular brooch with an iron pin. Diam. 0·6 in. From Westminster.

A 2450. Bronze circular brooch, as Pl. LXXVII, Nos. 1–2. Diam. 1·7 in. From Long Lane, Bermondsey.

A 2451–2. Two bronze circular brooches, as Pl. LXXVII, Nos. 1–2. Diam. 1·75 in. and 1·85 in. From Aldgate.

A 2542.   Bronze circular brooch, decorated with bosses in relief and (?) set originally with coloured glass in imitation of jewelry.   Diam. 1·1 in.   Pl. LXXVIII, No. 1.   From Noble Street.

A 2543.   Bronze circular brooch, ornamented with applied shields and crescents.   Diam. 1·5 in.   Pl. LXXVIII, No. 2.   From Broken Wharf.

A 2666.   Bronze circular brooch, of flattened section, decorated with characteristic 15th-century zig-zag roulette ornament.   Diam. 2·0 in.   Pl. LXXVII, No. 3.   From Thames Street.

A 2667.   Bronze circular brooch.   Diam. 1·5 in.   Pl. LXXVII, No. 2.   From Horseshoe Wharf.

A 2668.   Bronze circular brooch, as Pl. LXXVII, Nos. 1–2.   Diam. 1·1 in.   From Thames Street.

A 3136.   Base-metal circular brooch with a bronze pin.   Diam. 1·3 in.   Pl. LXXVII, No. 6.   From London.

A 3545.   Bronze circular brooch.   Diam. 1·7 in.   Pl. LXXVII, No. 1.   From London.

A 10221.   Bronze circular brooch, as Pl. LXXVII, Nos. 1–2.   Diam. 1·6 in.   From London.

A 12277.   Small bronze circular brooch with remains of moulded ornament.   Diam. 0·8 in.   From Smithfield.

A 13826.   Bronze circular brooch, as Pl. LXXVII, Nos. 1–2.   Diam. 1·75 in.   From London Wall.

A 13827.   Bronze brooch, grooved opposite the middle of the pin.   Diam. 1·2 in.   Pl. LXXVII, No. 7.   From the Guildhall, beneath the Council Chamber.

A 13829.   Bronze brooch, with a raised moulding round the base of the pin.   Diam. 1·25 in.   From Carpenters' Hall.

A 14648.   Bronze brooch, as Pl. LXXVII, Nos. 1–2.   Diam. 1·5 in.   From Thames Street.

A 22901.   Bronze brooch, as Pl. LXXVII, Nos. 1–2.   Diam. 1·8 in. (broken).   From Tower Hill.

A 24853.   Small brooch (pin missing), with incised ornament imitating a wreath.   Diam. 0·95 in.   Perhaps post-medieval.   From Westminster, site of the Victoria Tower.

A 24860.   Small pewter brooch with a bronze pin.   Diam. 0·8 in.   From Westminster, site of the Victoria Tower.

C 983.   Tiny bronze circular brooch.   Diam. 0·5 in.   From London.

C 961.   Tiny bronze circular brooch.   Diam. 0·6 in.   From London.

36.146/3.   Tiny, bronze-gilt, moulded circular brooch.   Diam. 0·6 in.   From Fetter Lane.   Given by H. S. Gordon, Esq., F.S.A.

C 962.   Bronze circular brooch (broken) bearing a crudely incised inscription : " I : ORVSDV OLV [. . ."   Diam. 1·2–1·4 in.   Pl. LXXVIII, No. 4.   From London.

Medieval brooches and buckles from London ($\frac{1}{1}$).

PLATE LXXIX.   [*To face p.* 277.

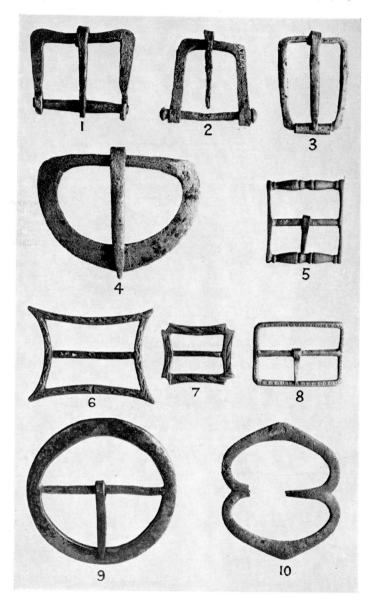

Medieval buckles from London ($\frac{1}{2}$).

(v) *Single Buckles*

The plain buckle, consisting of a single loop and pin, is an obvious and universal object, about which little can profitably be said. A certain number of forms can, however, be dated to the Middle Ages on the evidence of archæologically dated specimens or of contemporary representations. A few of these are noted below.

A 309. Large iron buckle. Maximum breadth 3·5 in. An identical buckle, in the Guildhall Museum, comes from the 15th-century deposits at Moorfields. Pl. LXXIX, No. 4. From Westminster.

A 559. Large iron buckle, similar to A 309, but more elongated. Maximum breadth 1·75 in. For a similar buckle from Cæsar's Camp, Folkestone (12th century), see *Archæologia*, XLVII, Pl. XVIII, 9. From Copthall Court.

A 597. Iron harness-buckle, similar to A 2630. Maximum length 1·9 in. From Westminster.

A 677. Large iron harness-buckle, similar to A 7654. Maximum length 3·2 in. From Westminster.

A 1371. Bronze buckle. Maximum breadth 1·3 in. Pl. LXXVI, No. 4. From Finsbury Circus.

A 1376. Brass rectangular buckle, slightly pointed at the end. Maximum length 1·3 in. From Finsbury Circus.

A 2630. White-metal harness-buckle. Maximum length 2·1 in. Pl. LXXIX, No. 3. From Thames Street.

A 2633. Ornamental bronze buckle. Maximum length 1·5 in. Pl. LXXVI, No. 5. From Thames Street.

A 2634. Brass buckle, in the shape of a Lombardic C. Maximum breadth 1·7 in. Pl. LXXVI, No. 6. From London.

A 2664. Iron harness-buckle. Maximum length 2·2 in. Pl. LXXIX, No. 2. From Town Ditch, Newgate.

A buckle of this form, found at the base of the bank of Bramber Castle (mentioned in Domesday), must date back at least to the mid-11th century (*Sussex Archæological Collections*, LXVIII, 241, Pl. I, No. 1); and others are recorded from Castle Neroche, 12th century (*Proceedings of the Somerset Archæological Society*, XLIX, ii, 25–53), and Dyserth Castle, 1241–63. This form belongs therefore to the earlier Middle Ages.

A 11273. Bronze buckle, similar in shape to A 1371, but decorated with a rosette and a beaded border. Maximum breadth 1·4 in. From Southwark.

A 22561. White-metal harness-buckle, similar to A 2664. Maximum breadth 2·3 in. From Finsbury Circus.

(vi) *Double Buckles*

The double buckle, consisting of two loops, one on either side of the central bar, and a pin, is another common object about which little of a general nature can be said. To the forms here illustrated by specimens in the Museum collections may be added a figure-of-eight shaped type of buckle, the two halves of which are usually set each slightly above the axis of the central bar. This form of brooch may be seen on the brass of a lady, *c.* 1490, at Orford, Suffolk, and it is represented in a 15th-century hoard of metalwork from Bury St. Edmunds, now in the Herts County Museum, St. Albans. The majority of buckles of this form appear to be of post-medieval date, but it was evidently already current in the closing years of the 15th century.

A 1391. Large bronze circular buckle. Diam. 3·4 in. From London Wall.

A 2507. Bronze circular buckle, decorated with transverse lines and two shallow recesses in the outer circumference. Diam. 1·5 in. Pl. LXXVIII, No. 5. An identical brooch in the Herts County Museum at St. Albans comes from a 15th-century deposit found at Bury St. Edmunds, Suffolk. From Mitre Street, Aldgate.

A 2562. Bronze rectangular buckle with incised decoration. Maximum breadth 1·7 in. Pl. LXXIX, No. 7. A similar buckle, found in association with pottery-kilns at Rye, can be dated between 1280 and 1380. From Thames Street.

A 2624. Square bronze buckle with moulded bars. Maximum length 1·9 in. Pl. LXXIX, No. 5. From London.

A 2625. Rectangular brass buckle with stamped decoration. Maximum breadth 2·1 in. Pl. LXXIX, No. 8. From Thames Street.

A 2629. Small bronze " spectacle " buckle. Maximum length 1·0 in. Pl. LXXVII, No. 8. From London.

A 3138. Large bronze " spectacle " buckle with incised zig-zag ornament. Maximum length 3·2 in. Pl. LXXIX, No. 10. A similar buckle is represented on an effigy, *c.* 1350, at Clehonger, Hereford; another belongs to a 15th-century hoard from Bury St. Edmunds, now in the Herts County Museum, St. Albans.

A 8864. Bronze circular buckle (bar broken), bearing in relief the inscription ORA † O MATER DEI MEMENTOR MEI. There is a closely similar buckle in the Guildhall Museum. Diam. 1·6 in. Pl. LXXVIII, No. 3. From London.

A 11270. Bronze circular buckle with two projecting wings, *cf.* A 18797. Diam. 1·3 in. Pl. LXXVII, No. 13. From Southwark.

A 12258.　Bronze "spectacle" buckle.　Maximum length 1·2 in. Pl. LXXVII, No. 10.　From Crutched Friars.

A 16435.　Bronze circular buckle (pin missing).　Diam. 1·6 in. Pl. LXXVII, No. 4.　From Dartmouth Street.

A 18797.　Bronze circular buckle with two projecting wings, cf. A 11270. Diam. 1·3 in.　Pl. LXXVII, No. 14.　From Thames Street.

A 20690.　Bronze circular buckle (pin missing).　Diam. 1·0 in.　From the Thames, Hammersmith.

A 22640.　Bronze buckle with roughly incised ornament.　Maximum breadth 2·9 in.　Pl. LXXIX, No. 6.

A 23638.　Bronze "spectacle" buckle.　Maximum length 1·5 in.　From the Thames, London.

A 23640.　Ornate bronze buckle (iron bar and pin missing).　Maximum length 1·8 in.　Pl. CXXVII, No. 6.　From the Thames, London.

A 23641.　Bronze "spectacle" buckle.　Maximum length 1·0 in. Pl. LXXVIII, No. 9.　From the Thames, London.

A 24945.　Bronze buckle, still attached to a leather strap.　It bears roughly recessed ornament alternately inside and outside the ring.　Fig. 63, No. 2.　Cf, Fig. 89, No. 5.　From the Town Ditch, Aldersgate.

36.91/2.　Bronze circular buckle (pin missing).　Diam. 1·9 in.　From London.

36.146/10.　Bronze circular buckle with roughly recessed ornament alternately inside and outside the ring.　Cf. Fig. 63, No. 2.　Diam. 2·3 in. Fig. 89, No. 5.　From Fetter Lane.　Given by H. S. Gordon, Esq.

(vii) *Strap-end Hooks*

A 2672.　Brass strap-end hook.　Pl. LXXVI, No. 7.　From Butler's Wharf.

A 15686.　Bronze strap-end hook, decorated with niello lines and zig-zag roulette, both characteristic of the late 15th century, e.g. on purse-bars of Type A1 (p. 165).　Pl. LXXVI, No. 9.　From London.

A 16870.　Elaborate silver strap-end hook, bearing the initial M. Pl. LXXVI, No. 10.　From London.　Given by F. Ransom, Esq.

(viii) *Locking Buckles*

A not uncommon form of buckle, of doubtful, but possibly late-medieval, date, is illustrated on Pl. LXXVII, Nos. 11–12. On the axis of the buckle rotates a curved arm, and this arm can be snapped into a groove at one end of the body of the buckle, which locks it in position.　The exact function of this device is obscure.

A 10642.   Pl. LXXVII, No. 11.   Form the Town Ditch, Old Bailey.
A 11974.   From St. Martins-le-Grand.
A 14916.   Pl. LXXVII, No. 12.   From Eldon Street, City.
A 16117.   (Arm broken.)   From Eldon Street, City.
A 18353.   (Arm only.)   From Old Queen Street.
A 23529.   (Arm broken.)   From Pall Mall.

SWORD-CHAPES AND DAGGER-CHAPES

(i) *Sword-chapes*

The ordinary sword-chape current in this country in the early part of the Middle Ages derives directly from its Saxon predecessor.   The chape shown on the effigy of Henry II, d. 1189, at Fontevrault (Fig. 86, No. 1), differs in no essential from those found in pagan Saxon graves (*e.g.* J. M. Kemble, *Horæ Ferales*, Pl. xxvi), and consists simply of a small strip of metal edging round the bottom of the leather scabbard. Metal chapes do not seem, however, to have been by any means universal in the 12th century, and surviving examples datable to the Norman period are virtually unknown.

Until the middle of the 14th century the sword-chape seems to have developed fairly consistently by the increasing elaboration of the simple U-shaped binding.   This is sufficiently illustrated by the examples in Fig. 86, Nos. 1–7.   A certain number of isolated examples must represent intrusive elements, *e.g.* that on the posthumous effigy of Robert of Normandy, *c.* 1290, in Gloucester Cathedral (C. A. Stothard, *Monumental Effigies*, Pl. 22).   In particular, it is perhaps possible to identify Scandinavian types.   Sword-chapes of the Viking period are nowhere common, but there is a fine 10th-century example from York (*Proceedings of the Society of Antiquaries*, 2, xxii (1907), 5 ff.).   The later medieval Scandinavian examples developed on similar lines, with an elaborate openwork metal framework (S. Grieg, *Middelalderske Byfund fra Bergen og Oslo*, p. 197), and although actual specimens of the type found in Scandinavia do not appear to have been recorded from this country, it is apparently represented several times in the Maciejowski Bible (*e.g.* f. 10*b*) and had therefore presumably at least a limited currency outside its place of origin.

280

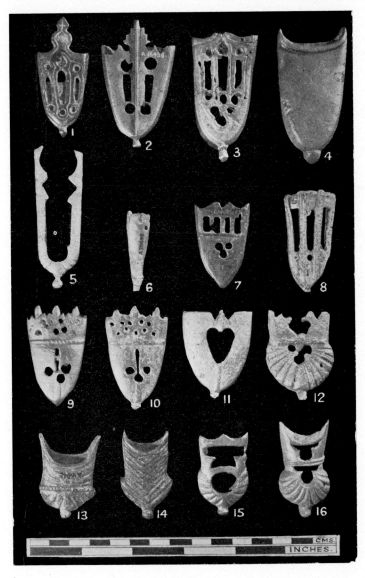

Medieval sword-chapes and dagger-chapes from London.

PLATE LXXXI.

[To face p. 281.

Enamelled figures from London.
1, A 24736; 2, C 137; 3, A 2508.
(See p. 288.)

A well-defined development of the early U-shaped binding is illustrated in Fig. 86, No. 8. The sword-chape on the effigy of the Black Prince, d. 1376, at Canterbury, is of this form, and it appears also on a number of brasses, of which the earliest and latest examples are apparently those of Sir Miles Stapleton, d. 1364, at Ingham, Norfolk, and of Sir William Bagot, d. 1407, at Baginton, Warwick (*cf.* also Fig. 88, Nos. 2–4). The type is therefore securely dated to the latter part of the 14th century.

To the closing years of the same century and to the first quarter of the 15th century belong also two other types of chape. The first of these, which is particularly adapted to the slender pointed form of sword-blade which had by then become current, appeared first as a plain terminal sheath (Fig. 86, No. 12), but rapidly assimilated the U-shaped opening of the preceding types, and in this form is represented, with great consistency, on a large series of brasses ranging from 1388 (Sir William de Echingham, at Etchingham, Sussex) to 1438 (Sir Brian de Stapilton, at Ingham, Norfolk— an exceptionally late example). The second type, which is characterized by an indented upper edge and usually by one or more longitudinal opening on the body (Fig. 86, Nos. 15–18) is also apparently developed from the same plain terminal sheath. Intermediate examples, with an indented upper edge, but otherwise plain, are portrayed on the brasses of Robert Russell, *c.* 1390, at Strensham, Worcs, and of Sir Edward Cerne, d. 1393–4, at Draycot Cerne, Wilts. The fully-developed type had only a brief currency and does not seem to be represented after 1410.

The 15th and 16th centuries are marked chiefly by the retention of old types, which appear in a bewildering number of minor varieties, but lacking any very clear characteristics by which they can be distinguished from earlier specimens. The basic U-shaped form remained common (Fig. 86, Nos. 9–11; for a striking example of the difficulties of distinguishing early and late examples, compare those depicted on the effigy of William Longspee, Earl of Salisbury, d. 1226, Fig. 86, No. 2, and on the brass of Robert Whyte, Esq., d. 1512, at South Warnborough, Hants); and the plain

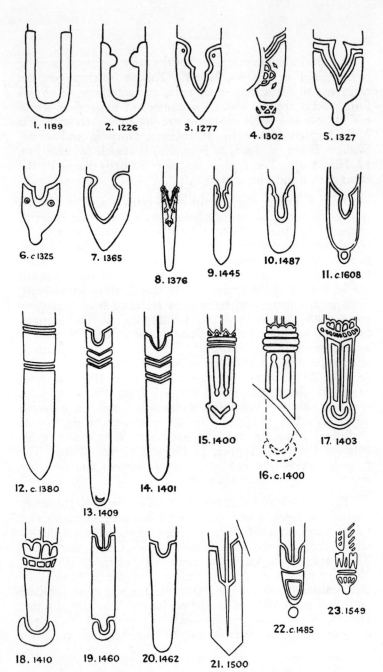

FIG. 86.—Representations of sword-chapes and dagger-chapes from contemporary effigies and brasses (see opposite page).

terminal-sheath with a small U-shaped opening at the top (Fig. 86, No. 20) also continued in use. It was only towards the close of the 15th century that a new type was evolved (Fig. 86, Nos. 22-3). It is found in a variety of sub-forms ; but all are distinguished from the earlier types by their generally squatter proportions and by their use of new modes of decoration. As in the case of so many of the smaller objects in use

No. 1.   Effigy of King Henry II, d. 1189, at Fontevraud (sword).

No. 2.   Effigy of William Longspee, Earl of Salisbury, d. 1226, in Salisbury Cathedral (sword).

No. 3.   Brass of Sir John D'Abernon, senior, d. 1277, at Stoke d'Abernon, Surrey (sword).

No. 4.   Brass of Sir Robert Bures, d. 1302, at Acton, Suffolk (sword).

No. 5.   Brass of Sir John D'Abernon, junior, d. 1327, at Stoke d'Abernon, Surrey (sword).

No. 6.   Brass of Sir John de Creke, c. 1325, at Westley Waterless, Cambs (sword).

No. 7.   Brass of William de Audeley, d. 1365, at Horseheath, Cambs (sword).

No. 8.   Effigy of the Black Prince, d. 1376, in Canterbury Cathedral (sword).

No. 9.   Brass of John Throckmorton, d. 1445, at Fladbury, Worcs (sword).

No. 10.   Brass of Sir Walter Mauntell, d. 1487, at Heyford, Northants (sword).

No. 11.   Brass of Thomas Windham, Esq., c. 1608, at Felbrigg, Norfolk (sword).

No. 12.   Brass, c. 1380, at Cliffe Pypard, Wilts (sword).

No. 13.   Brass of William Snayth, d. 1409, at Addington, Kent (sword).

No. 14.   Brass of William Grevel, d. 1401, at Chipping Campden, Glos (baselard).

No. 15.   Brass of a Dalison, c. 1400, at Laughton, Lincs (dagger).

No. 16.   Brass of William Willoughby, c. 1400, at Spilsby, Lincs (sword).

No. 17.   Brass of Sir Reginald Cobham, d. 1403, at Lingfield, Surrey (dagger).

No. 18.   Brass of Richard Hansard, d. 1401, at St. Kelsey, Lincs (sword).

No. 19.   Brass of John Ansty, d. 1460, at Stow-cum-Quy, Cambs (sword).

No. 20.   Brass of Sir Thomas Grene, d. 1462, at Green's Norton, Northants (sword).

No. 21.   Brass of John Tame, Esq., d. 1500, at Fairford, Glos (sword).

No. 22.   Brass, c. 1485, at Heacham, Norfolk (sword).

No. 23.   Brass of Thomas Shuckburgh, d. 1549, at Upper Shuckburgh, Warwick (sword).

in the Middle Ages, it is not always easy to square the evidence of contemporary representations with that of surviving examples. The latter, however, fall into a number of fairly well-defined and consistent groups (see Fig. 87), all of which appear to be datable to the late 15th or 16th century, both on the grounds of their general similarity to each other (specimens combining the characteristics of two of these groups are not uncommon) and to contemporary representations, and on the evidence of their discovery in association with pottery and other rubbish of the period at a site in Fetter Lane, all the objects from which are now in the Museum collections. Without the discovery of other datable deposits it is hardly possible to be more precise. It is, however, worth while to call attention to the form of sword-chape characteristic of the later 16th and early 17th centuries. It consists of a long, narrow, plain sheath, with one or more transverse ridges and an upward-projecting, triangular tongue (*e.g.* on the brass of Hercules Raynsford, Esq., d. 1583, at Clifford Chambers, Glos). The upward projection may be more elaborate in later specimens, and there is often a terminal knob (*e.g.* on the brass of Thomas Stoughton, d. 1591, in St. Martin's Church, Canterbury). Generally speaking, however, the form represented on early 16th century monumental effigies is remarkably consistent ; and by exclusion it may be fairly assumed to have limited the range of the forms which preceded it.

Of the individual sub-types (Fig. 87, Nos. I–VI) little need be said. All are quite common in this country ; and Types I, II, IV, and VI are also to be found in a number of French collections, Type IV being especially common. The types are not mutually exclusive, but they may serve as a convenient basis of classification.

(ii) *Dagger-chapes*

Metal dagger-chapes were only used on the sheaths of military daggers or of the more elaborate forms of civilian dagger. The great majority of surviving leather sheaths belonged to ordinary knives or knife-daggers and these have no metal terminal. Apart from a tendency towards simplifica-

Objects of bronze from London.
1, A 21084; 2, A 17773; 3, A 2510; 4, A 3099 ($\frac{1}{1}$).

PLATE LXXXIII.

[*To face p.* 285.

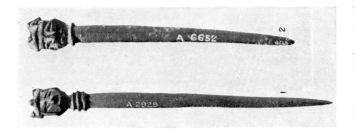

Medieval bronze pins from London ($\frac{1}{1}$).
1, A 2929; 2, A 6652. (See p. 288.)

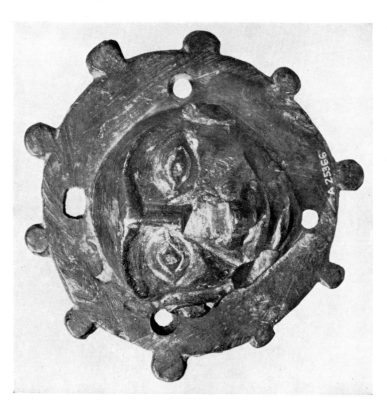

A 25366.   Bronze door-knocker, 15th century.   (See p. 290) (Slightly less than ($\frac{1}{4}$).)

tion, dagger-chapes seem, as might be expected, to have followed closely the contemporary fashion of sword-chapes. Examples of this practice may be seen on the brass of a Dalison, *c.* 1400, at Laughton, Lincs, and of William Grevel,

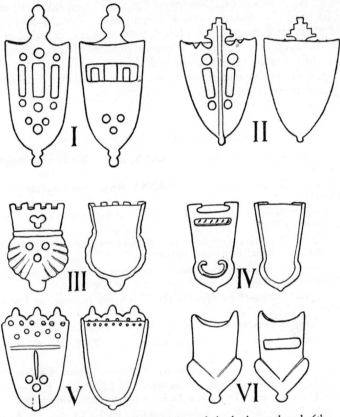

FIG. 87.—Types of chape current apparently in the late 15th and 16th centuries.

d. 1401, at Chipping Camden, Glos ; *cf.* also Fig. 88, Nos. 3 and 4. An alternative form of chape consisted of a slender, tubular cap, a simple form well adapted for use with a finely-pointed blade. Specimens of this type, which was current both in the 14th and in the 15th century, have been found

285

in association with rondel-daggers, with kidney-daggers, and with the more elaborate forms of knife-dagger, and it appears on a number of brasses and effigies, *e.g.* on the effigy of Sir Richard Blanchfront, mid-14th century, at Alvechurch, Worcs (C. A. Stothard, *Monumental Effigies*, Pl. 72); on the brass of Richard Hansard, d. 1410, at South Kelsey, Lincs; and on the effigy of Robert, Lord Hungerford, d. 1419, at Salisbury (Stothard, *op. cit.*, Pl. 129). A certain number of late-medieval and 16th-century chapes described above (p. 284, *s.v.* sword-chapes) are perhaps dagger-chapes, but the evidence does not seem to be sufficiently detailed for certainty.

SWORD- AND DAGGER-CHAPES

A 2447. Bronze chape, Type V. Pl. LXXX, No. 10. From Broken Wharf, Thames Street.

A 2481. Bronze chape, Type V. Pl. LXXX, No. 9. Found near the Tower of London.

A 2482. Bronze chape, Type V, similar to A 2447 and A 2481. From Chamberlain's Wharf.

A 2514. Bronze chape, of plain form with two transverse ridges, doubtfully medieval. From the Town Ditch, Newgate.

A 11886/2. Small, bronze, bullet-shaped chape, found with a late 15th-century quillon dagger, A 11886/1, in the Wandle, at Wandsworth.

A 15438. Bronze chape, Type IV. Pl. LXXX, No. 2. From the Thames at London.

A 20678. Bronze chape. Pl. LXXX, No. 11. From Cornhill.

A 20688. Small bronze tubular chape. Pl. LXXX, No. 6. From Leadenhall Street.

C 782. Base metal chape (fragmentary). From the Thames, Wandsworth.

36.116/1. 14 bronze chapes, various types. Pl. LXXX, Nos. 8, 12, and 16, and Fig. 88, Nos. 5–9. From Fetter Lane. Given by H. S. Gordon, Esq.

36.152/1. Bronze chape, modified Type III. Pl. LXXX, No. 15. From London.

36.152/3. Bronze chape, Type I (back only). Pl. LXXX, No. 7. From London.

36.152/4. Bronze chape, Type VI. Pl. LXXX, No. 14. From London.

36.152/5. Bronze chape, Type I. Pl. LXXX, No. 1. From London.

36.152/6. Base metal chape. Pl. LXXX, No. 5. From London.

36.152/7. Bronze chape, Type I. From London.

A 7395. 15th-century wrought-iron alms-box (½).
(See p. 288.)

B 211. Two fragments of a Syrian glass vessel. Found in the Pyx
Chapel, Westminster (¼).
(See p. 293.)

PLATE LXXXV. [*To face p.* 287.

Wooden doorway from the church of St. Ethelburga the Virgin within Bishopsgate.
(See p. 290.)

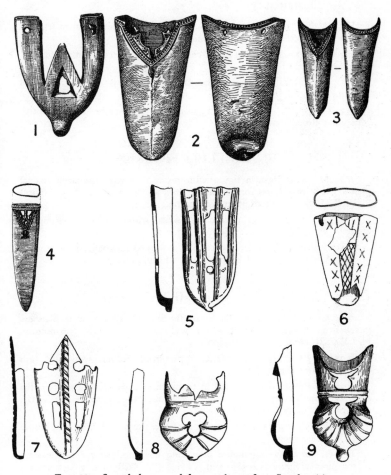

Fig. 88.—Sword-chapes and dagger-chapes from London ($\frac{2}{3}$).

1–4. Base-metal (1 and 3 in the Guildhall Museum; 2 and 4 in the British Museum).

5–9. 36.116/1. Five bronze chapes from Fetter Lane.

36.152/8.   Bronze chape.   Pl. LXXX, No. 4.   From London.
36.152/9.   Bronze chape, Type I.   Pl. LXXX, No. 3.   From London.
36.152/10.   Bronze chape, Type VI.   Pl. LXXX, No. 13.   From London.

Also illustrated :

Fig. 88, No. 1. Base-metal sword-chape. Early 14th century (?). In the Guildhall Museum. From London.

Fig. 88, No. 2. Base-metal sword-chape. c. 1375. In the British Museum. From London.

Fig. 88, No. 3. Base-metal dagger-chape, c. 1375. In the Guildhall Museum. From London.

Fig. 88, No. 4. Base-metal dagger-chape. 1375–1400. In the British Museum. From London.

ENAMELLED FIGURES

A 2508. Small bronze figure with remains of red champlevé enamel pierced with two holes for attachment to a shrine or some similar object Pl. LXXXI, No. 3. From Stoke Newington.

A 24736. Fragment of a crucifix, bronze with remains of champlevé enamel. Pl. LXXXI, No. 1. From Richmond.

C 137. Bronze figure from a crucifix, hollowed internally, with remains of champlevé enamel. Pl. LXXXI, No. 2. From London.

MISCELLANEOUS METAL OBJECTS

A 2510. Gilt bronze medallion : on the front the symbol of St. Matthew in relief, on the back an engraved rose-and-star pattern. Late 15th century. Pl. LXXXII, No. 3. From London.

A 2546. Bronze Lombardic letter A, presumably from a grave-slab. 14th century. From Thames Street.

A 2929. Bronze pin, the head in the form of a crowned head. Cf. the elaborate pins often depicted on medieval ecclesiastical vestments. Pl. LXXXIII, right, No. 1. From Austin Friars.

A 3099. Openwork brass mount. 15th century. Pl. LXXXII, No. 4. From Temple Avenue.

A 3935. Small bronze figure of a king hawking, perhaps a chessman, cf. the pipeclay figurines A 3885 and A 14694 (Pl. XCII, Nos. 2–3). Height 2·2 in. Pl. XCII, No. 1. From London.

A 6652. Bronze pin, the head in the form of a crowned head ; cf. A 2929, above. Pl. LXXXIII, right, No. 2. From Grays Inn Road.

A 7395. Wrought-iron alms-box, bearing the arms of England. 15th century. Height 5·7 in. Pl. LXXXIV. From London.

A 8874. Hilt of a miniature bronze sword, presumably a toy. The pommel-form belongs to the 13th century (see p. 24). Fig. 89, No. 2. From the Thames, London.

288

PLATE LXXXVI.

Wooden cradle, falsely supposed by tradition to have been that of King Henry V.
Late 15th century. (See p. 291.)

PLATE LXXXVII. [To face p. 289.

1, A 24742. Carved oak figure of a bishop from Westminster Abbey (¾).
2, A 11805. Carved oak figure, with traces of gilding from Matthew Parker
Street (¼).

(See p. 291.)

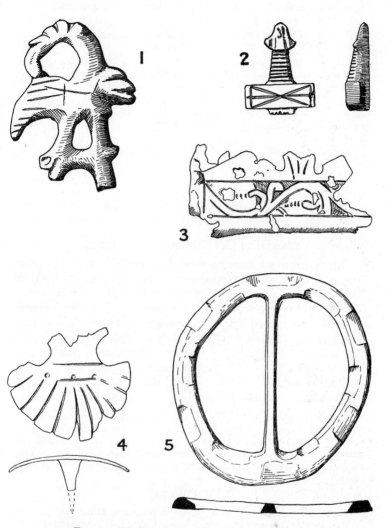

FIG. 89.—Medieval bronze objects from London (¼).
1, 30.46 ; 2, A 8874 ; 3, 36.146/5 ; 4, A 25357 ; 5, 36.146/10.

A 8875. Bronze black-letter A, presumably from a grave-slab. 14th–15th century. From London.

A 17773. Circular bronze plaque, perhaps inscribed IHC. 14th–15th century. Pl. LXXXII, No. 2. From London.

A 21084. Bronze medallion : in relief, the Agnus Dei depicted as a ram. Early medieval. Pl. LXXXII, No. 1. From the site of Gresham House, Broad Street.

A 25357. Bronze stud in the form of rough scallop-shell, presumably a badge of St. James of Compostella (see p. 260). A similar stud was found in association with a pottery-kiln at Rye (*c.* 1280–1380). Fig. 89, No. 4. From St. Mary Axe.

A 25366. Bronze door-knocker, ring missing, in the form of a monkey's head. Diam. 4·2 in. 15th century. Pl. LXXXIII, *left*. From Thames Street.

30.46. Fragmentary bronze object in the form of a conventionalized bird. Fig. 89, No. 1. From London.

36.146/5. Strip of bronze bearing incised 14th-century scroll-ornament. Fig. 89, No. 3. From Fetter Lane. Given by H. S. Gordon, Esq.

LEADEN MORTUARY CROSSES

The custom of burying a small, roughly cut leaden cross with the dead appears sporadically throughout the Middle Ages. It was, however, apparently confined to the monastic orders, and even so was far from universal. A certain number of crudely inscribed specimens belong to the 11th and 12th centuries, *e.g. Proceedings of the Society of Antiquaries,* 1st series, 212–3, dated 1136, from Angers ; *Antiquaries Journal,* IV (1924), 422 ff., 11th century, from Canterbury. Later specimens appear to have been uninscribed, *e.g.* a large series from the monastic burial-ground at Bury St. Edmunds.

A 3336–7, 3339–45, 3347, 3349–55, 3357–62, 3364–7. Twenty-seven small, plain, leaden mortuary crosses, found with interments at Christ's Hospital, Newgate Street, on the site of the Grey Friars' burial-ground. A number of specimens were found, of which five are in the Guildhall Museum, and the whole series appears to have been contemporary, perhaps the result of the Black Death.

WOODWORK

35.51. Carved oak door-frame, removed in 1934 from the west porch of the church of St. Ethelburga the Virgin within Bishopsgate. Late 15th century. Pl. LXXXV. The spandrels of the reverse face contain figures of a man and a lion, symbolizing St. Matthew and St. Mark (see *Twenty-five Years of the London Museum,* Pl. 28). There may have been a second door, the frame of which depicted the other two Evangelists. Lent by the Rector and Churchwardens of St. Ethelburga the Virgin within Bishopsgate.

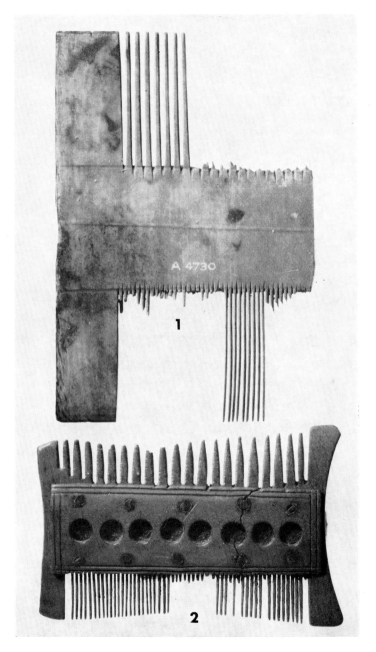

Medieval bone combs from London.
1, A 4730; 2, A 1598 ($\frac{1}{1}$).
(See p. 291.)

PLATE LXXXIX. [*To face p.* 291.

Carvings in bone and ivory from London ($\frac{1}{1}$).
1, A 4725; 2, C 972; 3, A 11804; 4, A 9644.
(See p. 292.)

D 48. Carved oak cradle from Chepstow Castle, traditionally supposed to have been that of King Henry V. The style of its decoration can, however, hardly be earlier than the late 15th century. Pl. LXXXVI. (See E. E. Barnett, "Cradles of the Past" in *The Connoisseur*, XXXII, 1912, No. 129, p. 93; *Twenty-five Years of the London Museum*, Pl. CXXI.) Lent by Her Majesty the Queen.

A 11805. Crowned figure, carved in oak. Possibly one of the Magi from a Madonna Shrine. It retains traces of gilding. Height 6·0 in. 13th century. Pl. LXXXVII, No. 2. (See A. Andersson, *English Influence in Norwegian and Swedish Figure-Sculpture in Wood, 1220–70*, 1949, p. 153, n. 2.) From Matthew Parker Street.

A 24742. Carved oak figure of a bishop. Height 8·0 in. Late 15th century. Pl. LXXXVII, No. 1. Found in the Sanctuary, Westminster Abbey.

BONE AND IVORY
(i) *Combs*

Numbers of decorated medieval ivory, and occasionally wooden, combs have survived (*cf.* R. Koechlin, *Les Ivoires Gothiques Francais*, Vol. I, p. 423 ; A. Goldschmidt, *Elfenbein-skulpturen*). These are always double, and the decoration is concentrated on the central portion between the two rows of teeth. The occasional contemporary representations (*e.g.* Luttrell Psalter, f. 70) seem also to show double combs. On the other hand, single combs were in common use both before and during the medieval period in Scandinavia (F. Winter, *Die Kämme aller Zeiten ;* S. Grieg, *Middelalderske Byfund fra Bergen og Oslo*). They offered less scope for decoration (*cf.*, however, Winter, *op. cit.*, p. 32, a single comb bearing Gothic ornament), but they probably had a certain restricted everyday use. In the later medieval double combs the H-shaped body is regularly broader than it is tall. This shape is also found earlier, but a practically square form (*e.g. Proceedings of the Society of Antiquaries*, 2, XXVIII, 169 f.) is equally common.

A 1598. Comb consisting of three plates of bone and two of bronze placed alternately and fastened in position by ten bone pegs. The teeth were cut in the central plate after assembly. For the slightly curved outline, *cf.* Luttrell Psalter, *c.* 1435–40, f. 70. Pl. LXXXVIII, No. 2. From Walbrook.

A 4730. Portion of a bone comb. Pl. LXXXVIII, No. 1. From Westminster.

(ii) *Game-pieces, Skates, Spoons, Pins*

Several other types of bone object were in common use

during the medieval period. Chessmen and circular game-pieces are both discussed in *London and the Vikings* (*London Museum Catalogue*), pp. 46–9, Fig. 26, and several of the pieces there illustrated are of early medieval date. William fitz-Stephen, author of a 12th-century life of St. Thomas of Canterbury, speaks of skaters on Moorfields who " fit to their feet the shin-bones of beasts, lashing them beneath their ankles " (F. M. Stenton, *Norman London, Historical Association Pamphlet*, No. 93). Bone skates of this type remained in use for many centuries and are well represented in the Museum collections ; and on at least one Scandinavian site, at Lund, examples have been found in a dated medieval context. Bone spoons are discussed above (p. 128). Among other less determinate objects, it may be conjectured that pre-medieval types of bone pin (*e.g. London and the Vikings*, Fig. 28, Nos. 1–4) also remained in use (*cf.* S. Grieg, *Middelalderske Byfund fra Bergen og Oslo*, Fig. 209).

(iii) *Other Objects*

A 1644. Bone stamp. On the front are eleven fleurs-de-lis in relief, on the back a wide longitudinal groove as if for the insertion of a handle. Length 6·3 in. Pl. XC. From London.

A 4725. Leaf of an ivory dyptich. The panel, which represents the Nativity and still retains traces of red paint on the background, belongs to a common school of 14th-century French ivories (*cf. Catalogue of Ivory Carvings of the Christian Era in the British Museum*, Nos. 292 and 294). Pl. LXXXIX, No. 1. From Farringdon Street.

A 9644. Fragment of carved bone, apparently a draped figure. 14th–15th century. Pl. LXXXIX, No. 4. From the Thames, Mortlake.

A 11804. Carved bone mount, a head in a quatrefoil surround. 14th century. Pl. LXXXIX, No. 3. From the Thames, Hammersmith.

C 972. Carved bone handle representing St. George as a soldier in plate armour spearing a dragon. 15th century. Pl. LXXXIX, No. 2. From Lambeth.

HORN INKWELLS

A 292. Horn ink-well bearing incised, compass-drawn ornament. The rim is pierced with two holes for suspension. Pl. XC, *right*. From Finsbury.

A 13339. Horn ink-well bearing incised, compass-drawn ornament. Pl. XC, *left*. From Fresh Wharf, Thames Street.

For an elaborately decorated leather ink-well, see p. 198, Pl. XLV.

A 1644. Bone stamp from London ($\frac{1}{1}$). (See p. 292.)

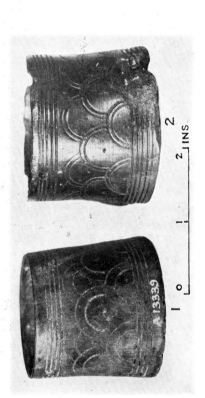

Horn ink-wells from London. *Left*: A 13339; *Right*: A 292 ($\frac{3}{4}$). (See p. 292.)

PLATE XCI. [*To face p.* 293.

15th-century pipeclay figurines.
1, A 3884; 2, A 3883 (¼).
(See p. 293.)

GLASS

B 211. Two fragments of a Syrian glass vessel. The Cufic inscription is treated in gold, outlined with manganese, against a ground of blue enamel. The glass itself is of a slightly opaque yellow colour. The vessel is identified by Mr. Basil Gray as belonging to the so-called Aleppo-group and dates from about 1240–50 (C. J. Lamm, *Mittelalterliche Gläser aus dem Nahen Osten*). The fragments were found in the Pyx Chapel, Westminster. Pl. LXXXIV.

PIPECLAY FIGURES AND TERRA-COTTA CAKE-MOULD

A 3883. Figure of St. Barbara, now headless, carrying tower and palm-branch. Height 3·5 in. 15th century. Pl. XCI, No. 2. From Tooley Street.

A 3884. Male figure in late 15th-century costume. Height 3·2 in. Pl. XCI, No. 1. From London Wall.

A 3885. Horseman in late 15th-century costume, perhaps a chess-piece. The legs of the horse are broken and the two halves of the mould very ill-fitting. Height 2·2 in. Pl. XCII, No. 3. From London Wall.

A 14694. Horseman in late 15th-century costume, perhaps a chess-piece. The two halves of the mould are very ill-fitting. Height 2·5 in. Pl. XCII, No. 2. From Hill Street, Finsbury.

39.190. Cake-mould of terra cotta, depicting St. Catherine with her wheel. 15th or early 16th century. Pl. XCIII. Found in the Old Bailey.

Moulds for the stamping of sweet cakes were known in Gallo-Roman times. They reappear in the 15th and 16th centuries, when they were very common in parts of Europe, and their use has lasted down to modern times. The cakes were commonly sold at fairs, and this example is perhaps to be connected with the Smithfield Fair. (See X. Aubert, *Moules à empreintes pour patisserie*, Dijon, 1930.)

WHETSTONES

Throughout the medieval period whetstones were in use for sharpening iron knives, etc. Usually they are perforated near one end for a thong to suspend the hone from the belt. Whetstones of various kinds of stone are not infrequently found in London, but can seldom be accurately dated. In the Museum are a number of hones of micaceous schist that are almost certainly early medieval (12th century). Hones of this material are absent from prehistoric and Roman deposits in this country, but have been found at a number of sites of the Norman period, but not later, in south-eastern England.

The stone is foreign to the south of England, but extensive deposits are found in Brittany, and hones of the local schist have been found at a few early medieval sites in France. See G. C. Dunning in *Proceedings of the Isle of Wight Natural History and Archæological Society*, II (1937), p. 682.

A 3873. Large hone of grey schist. Pl. XCIV, No. 4. Found in Farringdon Street.

A 4771. Small hone of blue-grey schist. Pl. XCIV, No. 2. Found on the site of the Aquarium, Tothill Street, Westminster.

A 4774. Small well-made hone of grey schist. Pl. XCIV, No. 3. From the site of Christ's Hospital, Newgate Street.

A 7888. Large hone of fine-grained grey schist. Pl. XCIV, No. 1. From the Long Ditch, Westminster.

SEALS

The Museum possesses a few medieval seal-matrices, the usual name for the dies from which the impressions were made. These were usually round or vesica-shaped (pointed oval), though other shapes are known, such as lozenges or shields. The material of which they were made was generally silver or a form of bronze known as latten, but gold, lead, ivory, stone, and even wooden matrices are known. In size they generally range from 4½ in. to 5 in. in diameter for the Great Seals of the sovereign, down to less than 1 in. for the seals of private persons. Most had handles, either a conical shaped projection on the back with a loop, generally trefoil-shaped, for suspension, or a flange usually pierced, running along the major axis in the case of a vesica-shaped matrix. The matrices of double seals, that is seals for impressing both sides at the same time, were provided with two, three, or generally four lugs fitted with pins on one half and with a similar number of holes on the other, through which the pins were passed, so ensuring correct adjustment.

Attempts have been made to date matrices by the shape of the handle or by the lettering. So far as handles are concerned the earlier are generally those with either a loop at one end or with a pierced flange ; but this type persisted throughout and the two illustrated (A 11102 and A 1497) are both of the

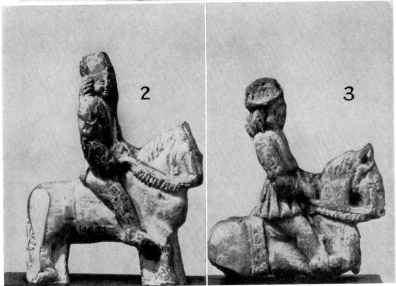

1, Bronze figurine (A 3935); 2, Pipeclay figurine (A 14694); 3, Pipeclay
figurine (A 3885) ($\frac{1}{1}$).

(See pp. 288 and 293.)

PLATE XCIII. [*To face p.* 295.

39.190. Terra-cotta cake-mould: St. Catherine. On the left is a plaster
impression from the mould.
(See p. 293.)

15th or 16th century. The conical handle with pierced loob is far the most common type and is found with increasing elaboration from the 13th century onwards. Of those here illustrated (Fig. 90), however, No. 3 (A 11711) is earlier than the more simple form shown in No. 2 (A 377). It therefore seems clear that it is not possible to date matrices with any exactness by the style of their handles. The same is true of the lettering. The sequence ran from Roman capitals through

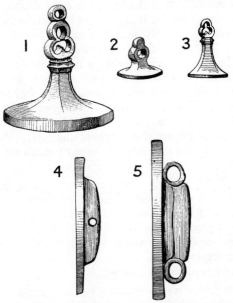

FIG. 90.—Medieval seal-matrices, showing forms of handle.

Lombardic capitals to black letter and back to Roman capitals, but beyond the fact that black letter does not start until about 1345 precision is impossible.

The Museum's collection is small, and the specimens were either found in, or are connected with, London. They vary in date from the 13th to the middle of the 16th century. The finest is the silver matrix of the Brewers' Company of London (A 11013, Pl. XCV, No. 2), representing the Assumption of the Virgin. The date is mid-15th century.

Other seals connected with London are those of a religious house, so far unidentified but probably a hospital, at Mile End, dedicated to God and St. Mary Magdalene (A 11102, Pl. XCVI, No. 1), and the bronze vesica-shaped matrix of St. James's, Cripplegate (A 11010, Pl. XCVI, No. 2) with a standing figure of St. James the Greater.

A matrix of unknown use is a circular bronze one (A 8018, Pl. XCVI, No. 3), with a standing figure of a crowned king holding a sceptre, with a shield of the arms of England (three leopards) in front of his body. The legend reads " Ricardus dei Gracia rex angl." To which, if any, of the three Richards this should be referred is doubtful. The arms point to Richard I, but the lettering makes it impossible for the seal to be earlier than the end of the 14th century, and it is more likely by its style to be 15th. It would therefore appear to be more probably a seal of Richard III, but even then the arms of England make it unlikely, as Richard III would certainly have used the arms of France and England quarterly. What therefore it was made for it is difficult to say ; it may not be a seal at all.

A very fine matrix of renaissance style (A 1497, Pl. XCV, No. 1) is that of a conventual house dedicated to St. Mary, the name of which is abbreviated in the legend to Bei or Bel. It is of gilt bronze and was found in Newgate. The engraver, although an expert craftsman, was quite illiterate and has bungled the legend sadly. Where the house was is doubtful, but the matrix is probably foreign.

Another unknown ecclesiastical seal (27.96) is a small vesica-shaped one with a representation of the Annunciation, with a figure praying in a niche below and a rhyming couplet as a legend. It is probably the privy seal of some bishop or other ecclesiastical dignitary whose Christian name, to judge from the legend, was possibly Thomas. Such privy seals were frequently used by bishops as a counter-seal to their seals of dignity.

The other matrices are of no great interest. There is a crude one of lead (A 11248), of which material many small private seals were made in the 13th and early 14th centuries, and there is an armorial seal (C 2312), which is probably Italian.

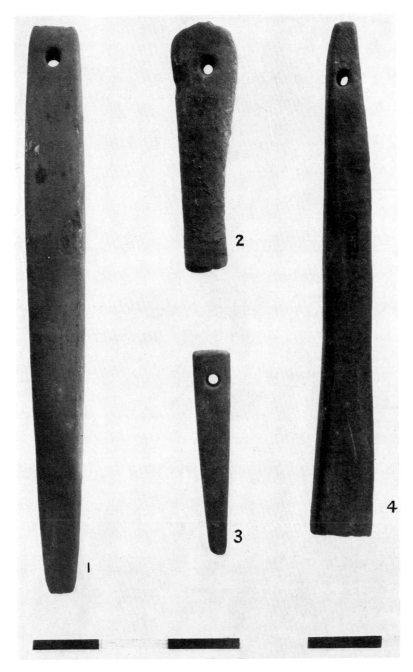

Medieval schist hones from London.

PLATE XCV.   [*To face p.* 297.

2

1

Medieval Seal Matrices.
1, A 1497; 2, A 1013 (½).

The others are small private seals with simple devices and mostly with a motto or other such impersonal legend.

The Museum also possesses two original impressions detached from their documents. The earlier is of the first Great Seal of Edward III, who at the beginning of his reign used the seal of his grandfather Edward I, to which his father Edward II had added a castle on each side of the figure in honour of his mother Eleanor of Castile, and to which Edward III himself added a fleur-de-lis for his mother Isabel of France. The other is an impression of the seal of the Court of Common Pleas. Without its document it is difficult to date this, as the same matrix for these judicial seals appears to have served, with alterations in the sovereign's name, for something like 150 years down to the reign of Henry VIII.

A 11102. Religious House of St. Mary Magdalene, Mile End (Pl. XCVI, No. 1). Vesica 2¾ in. by ¹¹⁄₁₆ in. Bronze matrix, with flange handle pierced for suspension. Under a canopy, the appearance of Our Lord to St. Mary Magdalene. On left our Lord holding the Resurrection banner in his left hand and a spade in his right, on right the Magdalene kneeling, with long hair, and holding the alabaster box of ointment. The figures stand on a bridge of three arches. Legend in black letter : Sigillū ⫶ domus ⫶ dei ⫶ et ⫶ scē ⫶ marie magdelene ⫶ iuxta ⫶ myle ⫶ ende. Late 15th or early 16th century.

A 3441. Vesica 1⅞ in. by 1⅜ in. Bronze matrix, with plain pierced handle. Device and legend indecipherable. 15th century.

A 1497. Conventual House of St. Mary, Bel (?) (Pl. XCV, No. 1). Vesica 3¼ in. by 2 in. Bronze matrix (? gilt) ; plain flange handle, with two rings, which has been broken and a piece soldered on. Under a renaissance canopy, the Virgin standing, crowned, a sceptre in her left hand and the Child on her right arm. In exergue a floriated pattern. Legend in roman caps. : VERO ⫶ : ⫶ : HOT (sic) ⫶ EST ⫶ SIGILLVM ⫶ CŌNENTVALI ⫶ DO'VS ⫶ ЬA'T ⫶ MA̅ ⫶ DE ⫶ ЬEL (?). (Vero . hoc . est sigillum conventualis domus Beate Marie de (?) Bel.) First half 16th century.

A 8018. Of unknown use (Pl. XCVI, No. 3). Circular, 1⅝ in. Bronze, with small pierced handle. Within a traceried opening, a king standing, crowned, a sceptre on his right shoulder and a shield of the arms of England in front of his body. A fleur-de-lis above his left shoulder and between his legs. Legend in black letter : Ricardus ⫶ dei ⫶ gracia ⫶ rex ⫶ angl ⫶. 15th century.

A 11298. Thomas Seouder. Circular, 1¼ in. Lead, with remains of handle on back. An eight-pointed star. Legend in Lombardic caps. : S' TOIME SⱯOVDⱯR. 13th century.

A 11013. London, Brewers' Company (Pl. XCV, No. 2). Circular, 2⅜ in. Silver, with conical six-sided handle, with elaborate trefoil top. Within a circular opening with a border of quatrefoils on the rim, the Assumption of the Virgin. The Virgin stands crowned in prayer, in a rayed aureole upheld by seven demi-angels; above her head God the Father issuing from clouds. Legend in black letter: Sigillum ‡ communitatis misteri ‡ braciatorum ‡ londini ‡ (scroll of four ears of barley). Mid-15th century.

A 11010. London, St. James's, Cripplegate (Pl. XCVI, No. 2). Vesica, 2⅛ in. by 1⅜ in. Bronze matrix, with pierced flanged handle; cut on the back is a × at the top and the number 1377 in arabics on the side. Under a canopy with side shafts, St. James the Greater, standing, wearing a pilgrim's hat and holding a book and a cockle-shell. In base, under an arch, a full-face figure in habit praying. Legend, black letter: : S · scē · (sic) jacobi : apostoli · infra , crepulgat. 15th century.

A 15306. ? Odo. Vesica, 1¾ in. by 1⁷⁄₁₆ in. Bronze, trefoil loop handle at top end on back, with long spine. A church or shrine with two spires. Legend in Lombardic caps.: S'FRIS ODONIS Dᕦ . . . . . ᕦLLOS Dᕦ VALLᕦ (?). 14th century, first half.

A 11711. Anon. Circular, ⅞ in. Bronze, six-sided conical handle with trefoil loop. The trunk of a tree on which is perched a bird, between a man and a woman's head facing each other. Legend in Lombardic caps. : ✱ LOVᕦ Mᕦ . . . . Late 13th or early 14th century.

A 1373. Anon. Circular, ¹¹⁄₁₆ in. Bronze, six-sided conical handle, with single pierced loop. A double-headed eagle displayed. Legend in Lombardic caps. : ✱ AQVᕦLA (sic) IOh'IS. Late 13th or early 14th century.

27.96. Unknown. Vesica, 1½ in. by 1 in. Bronze, with loop and long spine handle on back. The Annunciation: Gabriel on left, the Virgin on right; between them a fleur-de-lis on a long stem. In base under an arch, a figure in his habit kneeling in prayer to right. Legend in Lombardic caps.: OᕫIB' : hᕦᕦ · P · ᕫᕦ · ᕦOᕫSTᕦT · SIGNᕦᕦIO · ThOᕫᕦ · Early 14th century. Probably the private seal of some ecclesiastical dignitary named Thomas.

C 2312. Pautonerius de Podio. Circular, 1⁷⁄₁₆ in. Bronze, with loop handle at the top of back. A pip-shaped shield of arms, a bend between 8 crosses formy 3 and 5. Legend in Lombardic caps. : + S · PAVTONERII : DE : PODIO : . ? Italian. ? 14th century, or might be much later, say, 15th–16th.

A 1361. Unknown secret. Lozenge shaped, ⅕ in. by ⅝ in. Bronze, with loop handle and spine. A fleur-de-lis. Legend in Lombardic caps. : ✱ SIG[IL]LVM SᕦᕦRᕦTI. 14th century, first half.

A 377. Unknown (Fig. 90, No. 2). Circular, 1 in. Bronze, with trefoil handle on back. Much corroded, but the design apparently consists of a cusped inverted triangle, enclosing an indecipherable shield of arms. Legend indecipherable. Date, probably 15th century.

Medieval Seal Matrices.
1, A 11102; 2, A 11010; 3, A 8018 ($\frac{1}{1}$).

INDEX

299

Bankside, S.E.1 : axe from, 63 ; strap-end buckle from, 272
Barbican, E.C.1, key from, 140
Barnett, E. E., 291
Barnham Street, S.E.1, key from, 139
Barrel padlock-keys, see Padlock-keys.
Baselards, 48–50, Fig. 10 Nos. 2, 4, 6, Pl. X.
Basinghall Street, E.C.2, purse-frame from, 119
Battersea, S.W.11, bronze bowl from an old house in, 201
Battersea, Thames at, arrow-head from, 71
Battle axes, 63–65, Figs. 11 (V and VI), 15 Nos. 1–4
Bavaria, Duke Albert of, portraits of, 169
Bayeux tapestry, 58, 73, 79, 94, 123, 125, 138, 202
Bear Garden, Southwark, S.E.1, casket key from, 144
Beard, C. R., 38
Bearded axes, 59, 61, 63, Figs. 11 (IVA and B), 13 Nos. 1–6, 14 Nos. 2, 3
Becket, St. Thomas à, see St. Thomas of Canterbury
Beckton, Thames at, socketed spear-head from, 74
Bell Alley : leather sheath from, 191 ; pottery from, 228
Bellows, smith's, 127
Belvoir Priory, metal stamp for leatherwork from, 185
Belt-chapes, 264–69, Figs. 84, 85 Nos. 1, 3, 4, 6, 7, 8, Pl. LXXV Nos. 9–14
Belt mounts for scabbards, 269–71, Fig. 85 No. 2
Belts, leather, 185, 195–98, Figs. 60, 63
Benevento Cathedral, Italy, bronze doors at, 76
Berenson, B., 127
Berri, *Book of Hours of the Duc de*, 47
Bermondsey, S.E.1, axe from, 59
Bestiary, a late 12th-century English, 205, 207
Beyrouth, Syria, sword from, 25
Biagio, Vincenzo di, painting of " St. Jerome in His Study " by, 181
Bible Picture Book, an English 13th-century, 189
Bible Picture Book, an early 14th-century, 124, 207

Bible of St. Etienne Harding, 56, 76, 124
Bills, 76
Bishopsgate, E.C.2 : socketed spear-head from, 74 ; pottery jug from, 214
Bits, horses', 77–85, Figs. 18–21 ; curb-bits, 77–79, Fig. 18 ; snaffle-bits, 79–85, Figs. 19 (A and B), 20, 21
Bjelovodsk, Siberian stirrup from, 87
Black Death, the, 290
Blackfriars Road, E.C.4, purse frame from, 166
Blackfriars, Thames at : swords from, 33, 37 ; axe from, 65
Blacksmith's tools, 127
Blomfield Street, London Wall, E.C.2, rondel dagger from, 46
Blomqvist, R., 187–190
Blossoms Inn, jug from, 214
Blundevil, T., 116
Bodiam Castle, Sussex, pottery from, 224, 226
Bologna, Italy, tomb of Giovanni d'Antonio Maria Sala at, 75
Book-binding, 185, 187, 198, Fig. 64
Book of Hours of the Duc de Berri, 47
Book of Hours of the use of Sarum, 69
Bordeaux, Gironde, France, poly-chrome pottery jugs from, 217
Borenius, Professor Tancred, 256
Borough High Street, S.E.1, purse frame from, 166
Bosworth Field, battle of, 17 ; quillon dagger from site of, 41, 42
Boulogne, Pas-de-Calais, France, Shrine of Our Lady of, 255–58
Boutell, C., 150, 155
Bowls, metal, 201, 202, Figs. 65, 66, 67
Boxley, Kent, Shrine of the Rood of Grace at, 254
Boyton Manor, Wilts, pottery jug from, 223.
Bramber Castle, Sussex, buckle from, 277
BRASSES, MONUMENTAL :
Abernon, Sir John D', at Stoke d'Abernon, Surrey, 28, 33, 74, 265, 267, Figs. 84 No. 1, 86 No. 3
Abernon, Sir John D', junior, at Stoke d'Abernon, Surrey, 25, 30, 103, Figs. 3 No. 12, 30 No. 1, 84 No. 6, 86 No. 5

301

Chamberlain's Wharf, Thames Street, E.C.4: sword from, 42 ; key from, 137 ; shears from, 157 ; pottery jug from, 228 ; sword-chape from, 286

Chantre, E., 114, 117, 157

Chapes, see Belt-chapes, Dagger-chapes, and Sword-chapes

Charles III of Anjou, King of Sicily, 201

Charters granted to London, 15

Chartres Cathedral, Eure-et-Loir, France, window in, 174

Chatwin, P. B., 190, 236, 242, 243, 250

Chaucer, Geoffrey, 16, 160, 254, 255, 257, 258, 274

Cheam, Surrey, kilns at, 211, 212, 226

Cheapside, E.C.2, key from, 141

Cheek-pieces of snaffle-bits, 80, 81, Fig. 19A

Chelsea, S.W.3, keys from, 143, 144

Chepstow Castle, carved oak cradle from, 291, Pl. LXXXVI

Chessmen: metal, 288, Pl. XCII No. 1 ; pipeclay, 293, Pl. XCII Nos. 2, 3 ; bone, 291, 292

Cherwell Hoard, the, 96, 97

Chest-keys, see Door-keys

Chester, arms of the earldom of, on a disc, 122

Chisels, 126

Christchurch, Hants, carvings on a late 15th-century miserere at, 59

Christ Church, Oxford, wall painting at, 30

Christ's Hospital, Newgate Street, E.C.1, the site of: arrow-head from, 71 ; prick-spur from, 101 ; pottery jug from, 228 ; whetstone from, 294

Christus, Petrus, paintings by, 167

Chronycle of Englonde, printed by Wynkyn de Worde, view of London from, Pl. I

Circular brooches, see Brooches, circular

City, the, bone spoon from, 128 ; leather book-cover from, 198

City Road, E.C.1: key from, 144; purse-frame from, 169

Clapton Common, E.5, key from, 134

Clare, Margaret de, arms of, 172

Cleavers, butcher's, 127

Cloth-dressers' Guild, the, 16

Cloth Fair, E.C.1 : pottery jug from, 215 ; pewter badge from, 263

Cochet L'Abbé, 177

Cockerell, Sir Sidney, see *Maciejowski Bible*

Coins, medieval, 3 (Prefatory note), 138 ,139, 200

Colchester, Essex : horseshoes from, 114 ; belt-mount from, 271

Coleman Street, E.C.1, pottery from, 224

Colleoni, Bartolomeo, statue of, by Verrochio at Venice, 77, 90, Fig. 18 No. 7

Colman Street, prick-spur from, 101

Combs, bone, 291, Pl. LXXXVIII

Commines, Philip de, 255

Compostella, Galicia, Spain, shrine of St. James at, see St. James of Compostella

Compton, Lord Alwyn, 236

Connoisseur, The : XXIX, 1911,pp. 11–16, 133, ff. ; XXXII, 1912, p. 93, 291 ; XCI, 1933, pp. 104–6, 38

Conques, France : carvings in the church of St. Foy at, 137, 174 ; treasure of, 208

Conyers falchion, the, 33

Conway, N. Wales, sword-pommel from, 24

Cooking vessels, metal, 202–207, Fig. 68, Pls. LIV–LVI ; pottery, 220–22, Figs. 71 and 72

Cooper, H. Swainson, 177

Copthall Court, E.C.2, knife from, 53

Coronation spoon and related types, 127, 128

Cornhill, E.C.3, sword-chape from, 286

Costrels, leather, 189, 190, 195, Pl. XLIX

Cottrill, F., 114

Coventry, Warwickshire, leatherwork from, 187, 190

Cox, J. C., 182

Cradle, carved oak, from Chepstow Castle, 291, Pl. LXXXVI

Craven Street, Strand, W.C.2 : kidney-dagger from, 48 ; purse-frame from, 165

Crècy, site of the battle of, 115

Creeny, W. F., 79, 82, 103, 139, 140, 273

Cresset-lamps, 174, 175, Fig. 54

Crevelli, Carlo, painting of the Annunciation by, 180

Crosby Hall, site of, E.C.3, key from, 136

Five Wounds of Christ, pilgrim-signs of the, 262, 263
Flails, metal-jointed, 126
Flesh-hooks, 125, Pl. XXIV
Flødstrop, Denmark, brooches from, 275
Floor-tiles, see Tiles
Foreign settlers in London, 14
Forrer, R., 230, 253 ; and see Zschille, R., and Forrer, R.
Fortrose, Scotland, three-legged metal ewer, containing coin hoard, from, 200
Fouquet, Jean, painting of " the Penitence of David " by, 125
Fourgeais, A., 256
Francke, Master, painting by, 70
Freshfield, C., 210
Fresh Wharf, Thames Street, E.C.3 : kidney-dagger from, 48 ; knife-dagger from, 54 ; keys from, 139, 140, 142, 144 ; pilgrim-badge from, 257 ; horn inkwell from, 292
Friday Street, E.C.4, pottery jug from, 214
Friedländer, J., 159, 167, 171
Froissart, Jean, 18
Full-bladed late-medieval knives, 51, 53, Pls. XI Nos. 8–12, XIII Nos. 8 and 9

Game-pieces, 291, 292
Gask, Norman, 131
Gate Street, W.C.2, strap-end buckle from, 273
Gaunt, the Psalter of John of, see Psalter of John of Gaunt, the
Gay, V., 186
General Post Office, stone cresset lamp from the site of the, 175
Ghirlandaio, Fresco of " St. Jerome in his Study " by, 181
Gipcieres or Gypciere, see Purses
Giraldus Cambrensis, 256
Gisze, Georg, portrait of, by Holbein, 151
Glaives, 75
Glaser, C., 70, 205
Glass : stained, 19, 46, 142 ; Syrian glass vessel, 293, Pl. LXXXIV
Globe Theatre, Bankside, S.E.1, axe from the site of the, 63
Gloucester, horseshoes from, 114, 116
Göksbo, Sweden, cheek-piece from, 81

Goldschmidt, A., 291
Goldsmiths' Guild, the, 16
Gordon, H. S., 120, 143, 264, 276, 279, 286, 290
Gospels, the Stonyhurst, 186
Goswell Road, E.C.1 : arrow-head from, 71 ; shears from, 158
Graham, Dr. Rose, 260
Gray, Basil, 3, 293
Grays Inn Road, W.C.1, bronze pin from, 288
Great Chesterford, Essex, sword from, 25
Great Smith Street, S.W.1, leather sheath from, 192
Gresham House, Broad Street, bronze medallion from the site of, 290
Gresham, Sir Thomas, portrait of, 169
Gresham Street, E.C.2, pottery jug from, 228
Grey Friars' burial ground, mortuary-crosses from the site of, 290
Greyfriars Monastery, Smithfield, E.C.1, jug from site of, 214
Grieg, S., 12, 128, 146, 175, 177, 182, 200, 205, 280, 291, 292
Grosjean, 254
Grosmont Castle, Mon, 13th-century pottery from, 229
Guildford, Surrey, pottery cooking vessels from, 211
Guildhall, the, E.C.2, brooch from, 276
Guilds, the, 16

Haberly, Loyd, 230, 235–239, 242, 246, 247
Hafted weapons, 75, 76
Haithabu, Holland, pottery lamps from, 175
Halberds, 76
Hallwil, Schloss, Switzerland, horse-shoes from, 115
Hammers, 126
Hammersmith, Thames at : axe from, 56 ; arrow-head from, 71 ; sword-chape from, 269 ; buckle from, 279 ; carved bone mount from, 292
Hand-drills, 126
Handle, a carved bone, representing St. George, 292
Hanseatic League, merchant of the, 173
Harris, E., 207

307

318

Vordingborg Castle, Denmark, key from, 148

Waddington, Q., 3
Walbrook, the, E.C.4 : socketed spear-head from, 74 ; bone comb from, 291
Wallem, F. B., 182
Wall-paintings, 19, 30, 40, 59, 76
Walls of London, 14
Walsingham, Norfolk, Shrine of Our Lady of, 254, 255, 259
Walthamstow, Essex : rondel-dagger from, 47 ; pottery from, 221, 222
Wandle, River, at Wandsworth : quillon-dagger from, 41 ; snaffle-bit from, 85 ; dagger-chape from, 286
Wandsworth, Thames at : sword from, 33 ; kidney-dagger from, 48 ; knife from, 52 ; sword-chape from, 286
Ward, Dr. G. R., 3, 116
Watts, W. W., 209
Weavers Guild, 16
Weights, see Steelyard Weights
Wells Cathedral, sculptures at, 274
Westfold, Norway, stirrup from, 86
Westminster, S.W.1 : daggers from, 40, 46, 48 ; knives from, 52, 53 ; axes from, 61, 62 ; spear-head from, 74 ; bit from, 81 ; stirrup from, 94 ; spurs from, 101, 108, 112 ; bronze disc from, 121 ; pewter spoon from, 132 ; keys from, 136, 137, 142, 148 ; shears from, 157, 158 ; leather sheaths from, 190, 191 ; bronze bowl from, 202 ; badge from, 263 ; brooch from, 275 ; buckle from, 277 ; portion of a bone comb from, 291 ; hone from the Long Ditch at, 294
Westminster, the Thames at : sword from, 38 ; kidney-dagger from, 48 ; knife-daggers from, 53, 54 ; rowel spur from, 108
Westminster Abbey : late medieval sword in Undercroft at, 37 ; frescoes in Painted Chamber at, 76 ; tiles from the Chapter-House, St. Faith's Chapel and St. Edward's shrine, see Tiles ; shrine of St. Edward the Confessor from, 261 ; carved oak figure of a bishop from the Sanctuary at, 291

Whetstones, 293, 294, Pl. XCIV
White Castle, Mons, 13th-century pottery from, 229
Whitecross Street, E.C.1, knives from, 53
Whitefriars Street, E.C.4, pottery jug from, 228
Whitelackington Church, Somerset, sword at, 37
White's Ground, Bermondsey, S.E.1, pewter spoons from, 131, 132
William the Conqueror, 13, 15, 17
Williams-Hunt, P. D. R., 236
Wilson Street, Finsbury, E.C.2, spoons from, 131, 132
Winchester Cathedral, Hants : roof-bosses at, 141, 183 ; pilgrimages to, 254
Winter, F., 291
Wooden vessels, 207
Woodmen's axes, 55-56, Figs. 11 No. 1, 12 Nos. 1, 2, 4, 14 No. 4
Wood Street, E.C.2 : bronze pendant from, 120 ; stone cresset-lamp from, 175
Woodwork, 19, 290, 291, Pls. LXXXV, LXXXVI, LXXXVII
Woodwose spoons, 129 ff.
Woody Bay, Isle of Wight, horse-shoes from, 115, 117
Worcester Cathedral, Chantry of Prince Arthur in, 146
Worde, Wynkyn de, view of London from the *Chronycle of Englonde*, printed by, Pl. I
Works, H.M. Office of, 3
Wormwood Street, E.C.2, strap-end buckle from, 273
Worship Street, E.C.2 : quillon-dagger from, 41 ; knife from, 53 ; arrow-head from, 71 ; spear-head from, 74 ; pewter spoons from, 132, 133 ; keys from, 142, 143 ; purse-frame from, 165 ; leather straps from, 195, 197 ; belt-chape from, 269
Writhen-knop spoons, 129 ff, Fig. 41, Pl. XXVII No. 2

York Minster : St. William's window at, 46 ; pilgrimages to, 254
York, window in church of St. Michael-le-Belfrey at, 142

Zschille, R., and Forrer, R., 79, 81, 82, 85, 86, 87, 97

Printed in England for Her Majesty's Stationery Office
at the Alden Press, Oxford

Dd. 505911 K16